Strategies to Engage the Mind of the Learner

Building Strategic Learners

by
Rachel Billmeyer

Second Edition
December, 2006
Printco Graphics Printing
Omaha, Nebraska

Strategies to Engage the Mind of the Learner
Building Strategic Learners

Compiled and written
by Dr. Rachel Billmeyer

Foreword
by Dr. Robert J. Garmston

Credit
Every effort has been made to contact copyright holders for permission to reproduce borrowed material where necessary. We apologize for any oversights and would be happy to rectify them in future printings.

Published by Rachel Billmeyer, Rachel & Associates, Inc.
17445 Riviera Drive, Omaha, NE 68136

Printed by Printco Graphics, 14112 Industrial Road, Omaha, Nebraska, 68144-3332
Desktop published by Donna Flood
Cover by Tom Wise
Edited by Marilyn Kelly

First Printing March, 2003
Printed in the United States of America
Second Edition, December 2006

ISBN   978-0-9711292-5-2   Softcover
Library of Congress Control Number: 2007938911

Strategies to Engage the Mind of the Learner

Building Strategic Learners

Table of Contents

Acknowledgments v
Dedication vi
Foreword vii
About this Book viii
Chapter 1 Introduction 1
Chapter 2 Principles of Learning 5
Chapter 3 Strategies Overview 13

Section 1 - Opening Strategies 14
• Facts and Fibs 15
• Group Activator 16
• MVP - Most Valuable Point 17
• People Search 18
• Strength Bombardment 20
• Team Interview 21
• Team Resume 22
• That's Me 23

Section 2 - Literacy Strategies for Vocabulary Development . 25
• Act the Word 26
• Concept Definition 28
• Forecast 33
• Frayer Model 34
• Mind Sketching 39
• Prevoke/Vocabogram 40
• Semantic Feature Analysis 42
• Stephens Vocabulary Elaboration . . . 46
• SAW - Student Action Words . . . 50
• Super Word Web 54
• Vocabulary Concept Chain 55
• Word Sorts 57

Section 3 - Literacy Strategies for Narrative and Informative Text . . 59
- Anticipation Guide/Opinion Guide/Prediction Guide . . 61
- Character Map 64
- Cloze Method 65
- Cooperative Retelling 67
- DRTA - Directed Reading/Thinking Activity . . 69
- Group Summarizing 71
- K-W-L - What I Know, Want to Know, Learned . . 73
- Learning Log Format 76
- Look for the Signals 80
- Pairs Read 81
- PREP - Preview, Read, Examine, Prompt . . . 83
- Probable Passages 86
- Problem Solving Plan 88
- Proposition/Support Outlines 91
- RAFT - Role, Audience, Format, Topic . . . 95
- Reciprocal Teaching 97
- Save the Last Word for Me 103
- Story Mapping Through Circular Pictures . . 106
- SQ3R - Survey, Question, Read, Recite, Review . . 108
- Summary Wheel 111
- Text Previewing 115
- Text Tagging 118
- Think-Aloud 120
- Thinking from Different Perspectives . . . 122
- Window Pane Summary 126
- Write to Learn 129

Section 4 - Questioning Strategies 131
- Chat and Go Questions 133
- Concept Question Chain 136
- Enlighten Your Thinking Questions . . . 138
- Question-Answer Relationships (QAR) . . . 141
- Unwrap Your Thinking Questions . . . 145
- Questioning the Author 147

Section 5 - Graphic Organizers 149
- Semantic Mapping 151
- Story Mapping for Narrative Text . . . 153
- Thinking/Writing Patterns and Organizational Patterns
  for Informative Text 159

Section 6 - Information-Building Strategies . . . 173
- Carousel Brainstorming 174
- FIRST-MIDDLE-LAST Word 175
- Four Corner Challenge 176

    • Give 1 to Get 1 177
    • Idea Exchange 180
    • L.E.T.S. Connect 181
    • Numbered Heads Together 183
    • Paired Verbal Fluency 184
    • Stir-the-Class 185
    • Synectics Search 186
    • Teammates Consult 187
    • Walk About Survey 188

Section 7 - Discussion Strategies 191
    • Community Circle 193
    • Read and Reflect 194
    • Creative Debate 195
    • Discussion Web 197
    • Scored Discussion 200

Section 8 - Grouping and Energizing Activities . . . 203
    • Grouping Activities 204
    • Songs for Groups 204
    • "Boastful" Adjective Groups 205
    • Line-up Ideas for Groups 205
    • Songs to Energize 210
    • Quick Group Energizers 210

Section 9 - Reflection Strategies 211
    • Back-to-Back Thinking, Face-to-Face Conversing . 212
    • F.I.R.E. 214
    • One Minute Assessment 216
    • Partner Roundup 218
    • Pinwheel Discovery 221
    • Think, Ink, Pair, Share 224
    • Three Minute Pause 226

Section 10 - Closing Activities 229
    • 3-2-1 Send Off 230
    • Four Square Summary 231
    • Head, Heart, Sole 232
    • Personal Action Plan 233
    • Shaping Up a Review 234
    • START-STOP -SAVE 235
    • Three-Point Thinking 236

Chapter 4   Strategy Instruction 237
Chapter 5   Reflecting on Strategy Use 241
Chapter 6   References 247
    Appendix - Strategies Chart for Three Phases of Thinking . . 252
    Appendix - Crosswalk Between Strategies & *Classroom Instruction That Works* 255
    Appendix - About the Author 258

Acknowledgments

I am grateful to many people for allowing me to be a continuing learner and benefiting from their expertise. Among these are Madeline Hunter and Ernie Stachowski who taught me the meaning of effective instruction; Bob Garmston, a skillful presenter, who always shares his expertise for using strategies; and Art Costa, who thoughtfully models the link between using strategies and developing a thinking mind.

Many teachers and colleagues have shared their inspiration, time, support, and knowledge about strategies. I extend a special thanks to all of the teachers who have used strategies with their students and willingly provided me with examples for this book. I would like to acknowledge the hard work of two teachers in particular, Marlys Frohwein and Connie Simons. Thanks to them I have a variety of graphic organizers and thoughtful questions for the strategies in the questioning section.

When it comes to the ongoing support needed when writing a book, there are several close friends I wish to acknowledge and extend my sincerest thanks. To my dear friend and colleague, Sue Presler, I am forever indebted for her continual support in developing and critiquing instructional ideas. Special thanks goes to my friend and business assistant, Carolyn Law, who cheerfully and skillfully worked with me rereading, critiquing, and rewriting each page of the book. Without her earnest attention this book would not have been possible. To Marilyn Kelly for sharing her proofreading expertise. No matter where she was vacationing, she took time to read and reread each chapter of the book. For her notes of inspiration attached to each proofread chapter I am most grateful, they kept me moving forward. To my loyal friend, Donna Flood, who once again shared her creative talents organizing the draft into a masterful script. Her unfailing sense of humor, support, and positive comments kept me on track.

I also offer my sincere appreciation to my proofreaders for sharing their talents and time reading and critiquing the final draft of the book. Thanks to Ellen Billmeyer, my daughter and outstanding sixth grade teacher for Westside Community Schools in Omaha; to Cheryl Dobbertin, a colleague and English teacher at heart, an educational consultant from Rochester, NY; to Sharon Graves, my dear friend and mentoring specialist, a Consultant from Zanesville, OH; to Sally Kelley, a terrific teacher and reading specialist from Washoe County School District in Reno, NV; and to Sandy Zander, my creative thinker, a Staff Developer for Genesee Valley BOCES in Rochester, NY. A special thanks to each of them for sharing their ideas, and challenging my thinking.

Loving thanks to my three capable and talented children, Brian, Ellen, and Peter, who provide me with endless support. They are my source of pride and pillars of strength.

Dedication

This book is dedicated to all of my mentors who taught me the importance of strategy instruction and how to use strategies effectively.

Foreword

New developments in the science of learning emphasize the importance of students taking control of their learning. Rachel Billmeyer, an independent consultant and Cognitive Coaching SM Training Associate has assembled an impressive collection of teaching strategies that serve this goal. Above all, Rachel is a master teacher, and her practical experience, familiarity with learning theory, and research skills have combined to create a readable and highly useful resource for teachers wishing to help students become strategic learners.

When working with teachers, Jay McTighe, co-author of the ASCD publication, "Understanding for Design," poses three questions that are congruent with this work. What do we want students to understand, what is understanding, and how will we know students understand? A strategic teacher is one who is clear that knowing is different from understanding and seeks learning processes in which students apply, explain, analyze or in other ways develop and demonstrate understanding of curriculum content. A strategic learner, writes Rachel, is one who has learned strategies for learning and knows when to apply them. Rachel's goal in this book is to provide teachers with the resources with which their charges can become strategic learners.

Readers will appreciate the eight principles of learning that serve as a foundation for the strategies in the book, in part, to understand the design principles for each class of strategies, and in part, to inform their own inventiveness as they develop additional strategies appropriate for their students and content.

The book is organized into four major areas: a rationale for developing strategic learners, principles of learning, descriptions of classroom strategies for teacher use and blackline masters for selected strategies. One nice feature of the book is that busy teachers can turn to specific areas of interest within ten categories of strategies without having to read through the entire book. Some of the categories are questioning strategies, opening activities, literacy strategies, graphic organizers, information building, and grouping strategies. For each strategy, Rachel provides a statement of purpose, explains how to use the strategy and offers options for alternative uses.

This is a valuable resource in which Rachel not only presents new teaching strategies drawn from her own experience and that of others, but draws forth those good ideas from the past that are congruent with our current understanding of student learning. It is an essential work because students spend only 14% of their time in school, and teachers must make the most of this classroom time to influence student success in school, while also enabling them to be self-directed learners outside the school environment.

Robert Garmston, Ed.D.
Professor Emeritus, Calif State University, Sacramento
Co-Developer of Cognitive Coaching and Adaptive Schools

337 Guadalupe Drive
El Dorado Hills, CA
96762 USA

Phone 916.933.2727
Fax   916.933.2756

About This Book

Strategies to Engage the Mind of the Learner is organized into seven chapters. While Chapter 3 explains with examples ninety-two strategies, it is my hope that you will take time to read and reflect upon information in the other chapters. Chapter 1 explains the rationale for using strategies to engage the mind of the learner and the importance of differentiation. Chapter 2 outlines eight principles of learning and the role strategies play in a learning-focused classroom. Chapter 4 emphasizes the importance of strategy instruction, how to use strategies to differentiate instruction, and the nuts and bolts for teaching a strategy. Chapter 5 focuses on the importance of students reflecting on the benefits of using strategies. If we want students to view strategies as helpful learning tools versus "one more worksheet" it is important students analyze how the strategy enhancs their learning and when they will use it again. Reflection causes students to transfer the skills acquired through strategy use into other learning situations.

You will notice in your reading that I have used a variety of formats to showcase various strategies. My goal was to be thorough and explicit but not to state the obvious or become redundant. The Appendix includes a listing of the ninety two strategies organized into the three phases of thinking (before, during, and after). The Appendix also provides a crosswalk between the nine strategies outlined in the book, *Classroom Instruction That Works* (Marzano, 2001) and the strategies highlighted in this book. To assist your reflection process as you use strategies, a Strategy Reflection Form is included on page IX.

Strategies to Engage the Mind of the Learner is Volume 2 of the Literacy and Learning Trilogy by the author. Volume 1, *Strategic Reading in the Content Areas* (2004) is the foundation for strategic reading in all content areas through the use of strategies. Volume 3, *Capturing ALL of the Reader Through the Reading Assessment System* (2006) demonstrates the use of strategies as assessment tools.

Icons are provided to focus your attention on various portions of the text.

 The most frequently observed icon is the text icon. The icon alerts you to prepare yourself for reading.

∿∿ Another frequently used icon is the "notes" icon. It directs you to spaces where notes might be written.

☯ At various junctures in your learning you will be challenged to reflect on your reading either alone or with a colleague. The yin-yang icon denotes an opportunity for reflection.

📖 The open text icon provides you with a brief overview of the section. This overview provides a type of anticipatory set, prompting you to connect with your prior knowledge.

⌘ Strategies and Process activities are found throughout the text. The synergy icon depicts an opportunity to process information—usually with one or more colleagues.

◻ As stated earlier in the book, the purchaser of the text has permission to reproduce specific pages for classroom use. Those pages are denoted by the blackline master icon.

I hope this information is complementary to your style of learning. RB

Strategy Reflection Form
Transfer and Application Ideas

Strategy Name	How the Strategy Was Used	Ways I Can Use Strategy	Notes & Details

Chapter 1 Introduction
The Challenges of Engaging the Mind of the Learner

"The greatest sign of success for a teacher . . . is to be able to say,
'The children are now working as if I did not exist.'"
- Maria Montessori

"Why did you call on me? I didn't raise my hand." We have all seen the look of surprise from students who prefer not to participate. As a matter of fact,when teaching adults, I notice even they will scoot down in their chairs or sheepishly look at the floor when I pose a question to the group. Perhaps it is just human nature operating under the law of least effort or a fear of being wrong.

Yet years of research indicate that getting all students actively involved in learning increases student achievement. Renowned educator John Goodlad (1983) once stated: "Being a spectator not only deprives one of participation, but also leaves one's mind free for unrelated activity. If academic learning does not engage students, something else will."

Thirty years ago, Anderson & Faust (1973) suggested that teachers seek to incorporate three levels of active response from students:
• The first level requires listening, watching, or reading.
• The second level requires a particular covert (mental) response.
• The third level requires a particular overt (visible) response.

One of the hallmarks of successful teaching appears to be keeping all students mentally engaged in productive activities throughout the entire lesson, rather than waiting for something to happen. There is truth in the old adage: "When I hear, I forget; When I see, I remember; When I do, I learn."

When students become active participants in learning processes they become empowered learners. Social relationships, critical thinking, curiosity, and self-discipline are developed when teachers maximize student participation (Shor, 1992).

More recently with the focus on brain-based learning, researchers such as Patricia Wolfe, Robert Sylwester, and Eric Jensen state that effective instruction involves the use of a variety of strategies to engage all learners. Current research on differentiated instruction emphasizes a variety of classroom practices to allow for differences in students' learning styles, interests, and prior experiences. A differentiated classroom requires that teachers have a vast storehouse of strategies to enable all students to learn curricular concepts and ideas. When teachers use strategies to create engaging, meaningful, and relevant lessons student motivation and achievement soar. The end product is a strategic learner.

What is a Strategic Learner?

*"Education is what happens to the other person,
not what comes out of the mouth of the educator."*

- Miles Horton

A strategic learner is one who has learned strategies and knows when to apply them. Strategic learners have a repertoire of strategies they selectively use to successfully complete tasks in all content areas. They are not passive observers. Rather, they are active learners who reflect on their own thinking while learning, analyze their use of strategies, and make revisions as necessary. A strategic learner is heavy on understanding of topics being studied and light on memorization of facts.

Strategies are used to construct meaning before, during, and after learning. For example, strategic learners devise a plan to focus their efforts, asking questions while learning such as: "How can I make sense of this?" or "What does this mean?" "How does this connect to other things I know?" or "What can I do to better understand what this says?" Strategic learners know the importance of summarizing their learnings as well as reflecting on themselves as learners. In some circles this is referred to as metacognition.

In summary, strategic learners are independent learners who actively engage themselves in learning processes. Their goal is to make sense of and fully understand what they are learning. They know that strategy implementation offers them the opportunity to be lifelong learners.

What is Strategic Learning?

"If we succeed in giving the love of learning, the learning itself is sure to follow."

- John Lubbock

A strategy is a plan or action undertaken to achieve a specific aim. Strategic learners know and apply plans or actions to achieve learning. Strategic learning implies that students possess and independently apply effective strategies.
A learning strategy, unlike study skills or activities, is a focused activity with a specific outcome in mind. For example, the Team Interview strategy (p. 21) is used to focus the learner's mind at the beginning of a training. The purpose of the strategy is to activate prior knowledge by having participants interview each other using a questioning process. Occasionally strategies are referred to as study skills. Study skills tend to be more limited because they focus on general skills, such as notetaking. Study skill instruction often does not involve teaching students about the thinking behind the learning. As a result, the skill may not transfer to other

learning situations (Cook, 1989). Activities, of and by themselves, can be merely time fillers or busy work with no specific outcome congruent to the intended learning. The focus of this book is on strategies that will engage the mind of the learner toward achieving a specific outcome. Researchers have acknowledged the importance of strategies. The emphasis today is not only on teaching students the strategies they need, but more specifically on what a strategy is, how to use it, why it works, and in what situations it can be used. Madeline Hunter identifies this as "conditional learning." This is a clear indication of mastery.

Strategic learning not only emphasizes the importance of learning strategies but focuses on student effort. A strategic learning climate encourages students to gain a greater sense of control over their own learning. Teachers promote independent and interdependent learning by developing a risk-taking environment that supports learning and experimentation. When students are in control of their learning, they assess progress and can attribute success to their efforts in using learning strategies (Halloway, 2000).

Strategic learning is a direct result of strategic teaching. Strategic teaching prepares students for learning, involves the presentation of content in a relevant, meaningful way, and finally, helps students apply and integrate the content for future use. Strategies are an integral part of strategic teaching. Teachers create learning opportunities for students to pursue. The point of learning anything in school is to be able to do well in life (Eisner, 2002).

The goal of strategic learning is to develop strategic learners who assume responsibility for their own learning. Elliot Eisner (2002) states, "We want students eventually to become the architects of their own education. The long-term aim of teaching is to make itself unnecessary." (p. 582)

Much education today is monumentally ineffective. All too often we are giving young people cut flowers when we should be teaching them to grow their own plants.

- John W. Gardner

Benefits of Incorporating Strategies:
- Increases student achievement
- Creates motivated learners
- Creates critical thinkers
- Engages the learner's mind throughout the lesson
- Develops independent and interdependent learners
- Increases retention, understanding, and ability to apply concepts learned
- Provides opportunities for students to engage in self-assessment activities

Teacher Goals for Strategy Instruction:
- Facilitate higher level thinking about the concept being studied
- Create independent and interdependent learners
- Cause reflective practice
- Support an effectively planned curriculum
- Provide all students with a tool kit of fix-it strategies to apply when learning

Criteria for Strategy Selection:
- Determine the learning objective and select strategies congruent to the objective.
- Determine the appropriate reading attributes/skills necessary to comprehend the passage (p.76).
- Determine the levels of thinking needed to understand the concept and select a strategy appropriate for the level.
- Analyze the level of difficulty of the concept being studied and select strategies which match the level of difficulty and students' levels of learning (differentiated instruction, p. 237).
- Decide if a specific phase of thinking should be emphasized (before, during, or after reading).
- Decide if the students will benefit by working independently and/or interdependently.
- Select strategies appropriate for the time available for learning the concept.
- Determine how much time and effort the strategies will require and decide if the concept is worth the additional time and effort. As Madeline Hunter once said, "It is not necessary to bring in an elephant to teach the color gray."

Chapter 2
Principles of Learning

"The question is not, 'Is it possible to educate all children well?' but rather, Do we want to do it badly enough?"
- Deborah Meier

Creating "Student-Centered" Classrooms

Knowing how students learn is the basis for effective decision making in the classroom. Renowned educator Madeline Hunter defined teaching as a decision-making process in which teachers make decisions before, during, and after teaching. She stated that learning is situational because students bring their own unique perspectives and needs to each learning experience.

In recent years, the classroom focus has shifted from "teacher-centered" to "student-centered" with the emphasis on the learning process. Instead of simply "covering the material" or presenting content, teachers must determine how students can interact with the content in order to learn effectively.

One goal of education is to create strategic learners who self-select effective learning strategies and assess their own progress. Research suggests that a learning-focused classroom embodies the eight principles of learning (listed below). These principles provide a framework for decision making before, during, and after teaching. Included in this book is an overview of each principle; for an indepth understanding see *Capturing ALL of the Reader Through the Reading Assessment System*, Billmeyer, 2006. For connections between the eight principles of learning and the reading process see *Strategic Reading in the Content Areas*, Billmeyer, 2004.

A Strategic Learner

- Relies on cognitive and metacognitive abilities
- Sets goals and reflects on progress
- Works actively to construct meaning
- Links new information to prior knowledge
- Uses organizational patterns
- Considers individual learning style
- Collaborates with others to learn
- Engages in three phases of thinking

• A Strategic Learner relies on cognitive and metacognitive abilities.

Metacognition, often referred to as "thinking about one's thinking," is to be aware of and to have control over one's cognitive abilities. Productive thinking and learning requires goal setting, frequent monitoring before, during, and after learning, and assessing and reassessing. Strategic learners tend to incorporate these behaviors into their learning process automatically. While it might appear that the students who demonstrate these behaviors are on automatic pilot, what makes them strategic learners is the ability to recognize when there is a problem with the learning and to use strategies to solve the problem.

One of the key differences between the thinking of adults and the thinking of children is in the area of metacognition. Students become effective adult thinkers as they learn to develop their metacognitive abilities.

Modeling, ongoing guidance, and opportunities for practice in applying effective self-monitoring strategies to academic tasks such as writing, reading, and problem solving help to create strategic learners. The "think-aloud" strategy (p. 120) is beneficial in developing an understanding of what happens while reading; the strategy makes a difficult text more accessible and shows students why reading is important (Ivey & Fisher, 2006). Explicit teaching of skills such as summarizing (Summary Wheel, p. 111 or Window Pane Summary, p. 126), questioning (Section 4, p. 131), and mapping (Section 5, p. 151), as well as when to use them, are keys for learning metacognition. Thoughtful application of metacognitive abilities is central to becoming a strategic thinker and a confident learner. Reflection strategies (Section 9, p. 211) are designed for developing metacognitive learners.

• A Strategic Learner sets goals and reflects on progress.

Goal-oriented people tend to be more successful in life. People perform better when:
- They know the goal.
- They know what is expected of them in order to accomplish the goal.
- They are given clear models and examples for goal completion.
- They know how to assess their performance.

                                             - Herman and Winters, 1992

There are many benefits of goal setting. People who set goals increase the likelihood of task completion. The higher the quality of the goal, the higher the quality of the task. Because reflecting and self-assessing are fundamental to goal setting, most people can learn from failures as well as from successes.

Goal setting is motivational and encourages active participation in the learning process. For example, the K-W-L (p. 73) and the DRTA (p. 69) strategies ask students to determine "what they want to learn" during the unit of study. Goals might be global in nature such as "become a better writer," or "be more accurate when using percentages," or they may be more task-specific such as "do more research on molecules before writing my physics paper," or "use percentages to calculate the price of clothing on sale racks." Goal achievement is accomplished when strategic learners continually reflect on their progress and make adjustments when necessary.

• A Strategic Learner works actively to construct meaning.

Meaning is not created by a lecture or the words on the written page. Meaning is created when learners construct it through their interaction with what is heard or read. If the information does not become meaningful it will quickly be forgotten. Imagine circulating at a social gathering and being introduced to many new people. How many names will you remember once you leave the party? Probably very few, unless you have made a meaningful connection with them.

We each have our own mental maps of the world, and when we read we constantly compare our mental maps with what the author says. As we read we can construct meaning if we bring forward the appropriate prior knowledge and use the necessary processing strategies. To illustrate this point, read the following highlighted passage. As you read it, analyze what your brain is doing to understand it, and decide upon a title for the passage.

> *A newspaper is better than a magazine, and on a seashore is a betterplace than a street. At first, it is better to run than walk. Also, you may have to try several times. It takes some skill but it's easy to learn. Even young children can enjoy it. Once successful, complications are minimal. One needs a lot of room. Rain soaks in very fast. Too many people doing the same thing can cause problems. If there are no complications, it can be very peaceful. Something heavy works as an anchor. If it breaks loose you may not get a second chance.*

Reference: Aulls, Mark W. (1982). *Developing readers in today's elementary school*. Toronto: Allyn and Bacon, Inc.

If you had trouble understanding the author's message (and you probably did), why did you find it hard to comprehend? What's missing? What did you do to help yourself construct meaning while reading? When comparing your mental maps to the author's did you notice something was wrong? Did you notice the pronouns in the passage had no referents? This deprived you from using your own prior knowledge to construct meaning. Would it help you construct meaning if you knew the passage was about kite flying? Read the passage again comparing what your brain is doing this time to the first time you read it.

Now consider the classroom implications. It is vital that students construct meaning when learning. Generating questions (Section 4, p. 131) before, during, and after learning and discussion strategies (Section 7, p. 191) are powerful meaning-making tools. As students use strategies to construct meaning it is important that they continually self-assess their own ability to construct meaning.

• A Strategic Learner links new information to prior knowledge.

Strategic learners know how to bring forward their stored knowledge about a topic in order to learn the new information. Marzano (2004) believes that an earnest focus on background knowledge enables all students to succeed. Madeline Hunter spoke of the importance of helping students connect with what they already know about a topic. She talked about providing an anticipatory set at the beginning of a lesson to help students bring forward the correct or appropriate prior knowledge.

Let me illustrate with a simple example. As you read the passage, use your prior knowledge to fill in the missing information.

> "Anyone interested in te_____ is concerned about
> c_____. It's hard to imagine te_____
> sch_____ without them. Although they can sometimes
> be bothersome, we t_____ them. When t_____ go wrong,
> we sometimes blame the p_____, instead of accepting
> responsibility for the consequences ourselves."
>
> - Cummings, 1990

Now check your work to see how well you did.

> "Anyone interested in television is concerned about
> commercials. It's hard to imagine television schedules
> without them. Although they can sometimes be bothersome,
> we tolerate them. When things go wrong, we sometimes
> blame the product, instead of accepting responsibility for
> the consequences ourselves."

How many of you were accurate with this task? I suspect very few! You were probably thinking about children, teachers, and parents. Unless prompted, you brought forward information most familiar to you.

Supplying the missing information is more difficult for some than for others. The degree of difficulty is related to the varying amounts of information and a variety of experiences that the learner brings to the situation. As this exercise shows, it is important to capitalize on the "right" information in order for the learning to occur.

Strategic learners have a repertoire of strategies to help them develop and access their prior knowledge. The DRTA strategy (p. 69) is a familiar, open-ended activity that asks learners to pull forward what they "know." The Anticipation Guide (p. 61), on the other hand, asks the teacher to suggest through sentence completion what prior knowledge the learner should pull forward. Marzano (2004) emphasizes the importance of vocabulary development to build background knowledge. Vocabulary strategies such as Concept Definition Mapping (p. 28) or Frayer Model (p. 34) help students relate new vocabulary words to known concepts. Research is clear that when teachers focus on prior knowledge, students' academic learning increases.

• A Strategic Learner uses organizational patterns.

Strategic learners know that organizing information is critical for thinking and learning. Organizational patterns help students develop the appropriate frame of mind for learning. For example, the Venn diagram, frequently used to compare two or more items, can be constructed mentally or on paper.

Since providing structure for learning enhances retention, the sorting of information following an organizational pattern is helpful. When studying vocabulary words to prepare for the SAT students may try to group words into categories with familiar characteristics. When reading, it is advantageous to discover structure. Two common text structures are narrative and informational. When reading a narrative text, the reader pulls forward information about story elements such as beginning-middle-end and uses that structure as scaffolding (Section 5, p. 149). The scaffold can then support the learning of new vocabulary. Prevoke/Vocabogram (p. 40), an effective vocabulary strategy, asks students to predict which new words might be associated with selected story elements.

Learning theory supports the use of graphic organizers (Section 5, p. 149) to enhance learning and comprehension. Visual organizers such as mind maps, attribute webs, and flow charts provide a framework for thinking. Venn diagrams, story maps, and time lines graphically display patterns and connections. Teaching students to use graphic organizers through ongoing modeling and practice can create successful, independent learners.

• A Strategic Learner considers individual learning style.

Brain research is prevalent today, and researchers believe their findings provide important implications for brain-compatible classrooms. Gardner (1982) emphasizes teaching to eight intelligences (linguistic, logical-mathematical, spatial, bodily-kinesthetic, musical, interpersonal, intrapersonal, naturalistic) but feels that traditional schooling focuses mainly on verbal-linguistic and logical-mathematical.

Most learners have strengths in several intelligences. Classrooms for successful learners provide learning opportunities which focus on all intelligences (Group Activator, p. 16, Act the Word, p. 26, or Mind Sketching, p. 39). To demonstrate concepts learned some students prefer writing a research paper, while some prefer to give an oral presentation or compose and sing a lyric or rap. Others might want to create a video or graphic design.

Tremendous variety also exists in the modes and speeds with which learners acquire knowledge. Some students who are auditory learners need to hear the ideas being learned and tend to process information quickly. Visual learners construct mental pictures or replay "movies" of past experiences to help retrieve prior knowledge. Kinesthetic learners are physically active and often need to move some part of the body in order to learn and tend to need more wait time to process information.

It is not only important that the teacher understands how learning styles and intelligences vary but also how to help students understand their own learning style preferences. A classroom environment that provides choices and opportunities to use differing learning styles encourages strategic learners.

Another aspect of strategy use is to differentiate instruction to accomodate individual learning styles. Effective use of strategies help students to process or "make sense" of content, ideas and/or skills, see possible connections to other topics and increase the potential for application and transfer of knowledge. The appropriate matching of learning strategies to students' styles, needs, and what students are to know and do is the key that unlocks the door to mastery. Therefore, teachers must not only be flexible but sensitive to strategies that invite students to become fully engaged in the learning process.

Teachers using Tomlinson's (2001) concept of tiered instruction (See Chapter 4, p. 238) can meaningfully differentiate any strategy along a continuum of complexity. This ensures that students are working on tasks that are appropriately challenging whether they are struggling learners or advanced learners. "Tiering" an activity means creating several different versions of the same task, thus causing students to learn more about an essential concept, learn essential facts, or practice skills within their individual zones of proximal development.

• A Strategic Learner collaborates with others to learn.

Learning is a socially interactive process and students need to interact with one another in order to learn (Resnick, 1987). Real-life situations often require individuals to work together. Collaboration with other students on learning tasks or in shared problem solving is important. Students who work together learn to listen to each other with respect, build upon each other's ideas, support their own assertions with evidence, and acknowledge different points of view. These abilities enable them to move from egocentric to allocentric thinking.

Research states that the use of cooperative groups has a powerful effect on learning (Marzano, et al, 2001). Many strategies in this book (See Appendix p. 257) incorporate different structures for collaboration. When students assume teaching roles in order to help others learn they become more responsible for their own learning. How often have you heard the comment, "I never really understood this until I had to teach it?" When students discuss new learnings with each other, the discussion enhances understanding of the concept as well as offers students an opportunity to examine and compare the ideas with their own information and beliefs (Perkins, 1993). The Information-Building strategies (Section 6, p. 173) provide a variety of ways for students to work with each other. The benefits are twofold when students teach each other. First, strategic learners must independently form their own understandings and beliefs about the topic, and second, group work develops interdependence among members of a learning community.

• A Strategic Learner engages in three phases of thinking.

Successful learning involves three phases of thinking. The thinking begins with the "planning phase" which prepares the mind for learning. The second phase, referred to as "during learning," occurs throughout the learning process. The third phase is "reflective thinking" which integrates, connects, applies, and values what was learned. Strategic learners use metacognitive skills and strategies in each phase of thinking in order to comprehend text, compose, listen, and generate arguments. A strategic learner understands the importance of thinking about and controlling the learning process during all three phases. First-Middle-Last Word strategy (p. 175) emphasizes the three phases of thinking. Strategies are selected based on which level of thinking needs to be emphasized to increase learning. (See Appendix p. 252).

The planning phase might be the most important phase of the learning process because it sets the stage for learning. The learner is encouraged to analyze the task at hand and to plan an effective approach for learning. Learning begins when the learner sets goals, activates prior knowledge, and makes predictions about the learning. Strategies such as the Learning Log Format (p. 76) and the PREP Plan (p. 83) help the learner assess and prepare for the learning.

The "during learning" phase requires students to use metacognitive strategies to think about and monitor their learning. The students may use graphic organizers or outlines to organize their thinking (Section 5, p. 149). Students are also encouraged to compare what they are learning with what they already know about the subject and with what they predicted while previewing it. The strategic learner knows when the learning process breaks down and the importance of using fix-it strategies to get back on track. Guiding students to ask questions about what they are learning or to stop and clarify concepts helps them regulate their learning process.

During the reflective phase strategic learners integrate new information with existing knowledge and apply what they have learned. Students reflect on their learning and decide whether they have achieved the purpose, accomplished the assigned tasks, and integrated new information with previously learned information. They discover ways to extend what has been learned by applying the new knowledge to unique and/or new situations (Section 9, p. 211). Journal writing can provide students an opportunity to reflect on what they have learned. Chapter 5 (p. 241) discusses journal writing and other ways to develop self-assessing learners.

Conclusion

As you use strategies in this book you will be able to make connections with the eight principles of learning, using them when making decisions before, during, and after teaching. When all eight principles of learning are consciously incorporated to guide the learning process, students will benefit; they will become strategic learners.

Do not follow where
the path may lead.
Go instead
where there is no path
and leave a trail.

Chapter 3
Strategies Introduction

Notes:

"Children are living messages we send into the future, a future that we will not see. In effect we are building the house of tomorrow day by day, not out of bricks or steel, but out of the stuff of children's bodies, hearts, and minds."

- Melvin Konner

This chapter describes strategies I have used or have observed teachers using during more than 25 years in education. The strategies are appropriate and adaptable for all grade levels and subject areas. Each strategy includes an explanation for how to use it and how the strategy assists learning. The rationale for why these strategies are beneficial comes from research, from teacher testimonials, and from my own teaching experience. With a deeper understanding of how students learn we can select strategies that fit the needs of learners in particular learning situations and to achieve specific outcomes. All strategies are linked to the principles of learning explained in Chapter 2.

Educators participating in training sessions frequently ask where they can locate the strategies being used. As I thought about the question, I realized that the strategies I use come from a variety of sources, so I decided to create a compendium of these strategies. Access to a compendium of strategies from which teachers can choose will not only enhance learning for students, but will make the teacher's job easier. Blackline masters are included for teacher and student use as overheads, charts, or student copies.

The strategies are organized into ten sections:
- Section 1: Opening Activities activate prior knowledge and set the stage for learning (p. 14)
- Sections 2 and 3: Literacy Strategies enhance reading and writing processes in all content areas (p. 25 and p.59)
- Sections 4: Questioning Strategies cause creative, interpretive, and metacognitive thinking when interacting with a task, the author, the content, or the situation (p.131)
- Section 5: Graphic Organizers create visual representations of content (p. 149)
- Section 6: Information-Building Strategies extend thinking by interacting with content in new and different ways (p. 173)
- Section 7: Discussion Strategies enhance thinking and understanding by moving classroom talk beyond recitation into forms of discussion (p. 191)
- Section 8: Grouping and Energizing Activities incorporate humor and movement into learning (p. 203)
- Section 9: Reflection Strategies support the idea that we do not learn from our experiences but by reflecting on experiences (p. 211)
- Section 10: Closing Activities organize and summarize thinking (p. 229)

Section 1 - Opening Strategies

"The art of teaching is the art of assisting discovery."

- Mark Van Doren

Rationale

How the class begins is often how it ends. The first few minutes of class are critical; norms are set for the rest of the class session. There are many ways to involve students in learning at the very beginning that establish the norms for a productive environment. My mentor, Bob Garmston, taught me that opening strategies focus the learner's mind, energize the learning community, and establish rapport. An effective opening activity also helps to develop a strong sense of community in which each student feels valued. They feel opinions, cultures, and background experiences are important; everyone becomes a respected and honored stake holder.

National presenters Bob Garmston and Bruce Wellman (2002) express the importance of using an opening strategy to ground the group at the beginning of a learning experience. They believe that a well-chosen grounding is an excellent inclusion activity for the following reasons:
 • Brings every person's voice into the room in a friendly manner
 • Establishes the need for active listening
 • Sets the norm for active participation
 • Causes everyone to focus on the topic and assess prior knowledge
 • Encourages students to connect with one another and establishes or sets the need for a community of learners

Opening activities vary in length. When a teacher is connecting with the group for the first time or at the beginning of a unit of study, the activity may be more involved, requiring more time. Other times, opening activities are quick with the intention of activating and engaging the learner's mind.

Opening strategies included in this section.

	Page
• Facts and Fibs	15
• Group Activator	16
• MVP - Most Valuable Point	17
• People Search	18
• Strength Bombardment	20
• Team Interview	21
• Team Resume	22
• That's Me	23

Facts and Fibs

Facts and Fibs is a quick ice-breaker in which students learn information about each other. It engages and energizes the group immediately. The strategy helps to develop a risk-taking environment in which students are more willing to share. The strategy can be used when working with a group for the first time or at the beginning of a unit of study.

How to Use the Strategy
1) Explain the purpose of strategy.
2) Model the strategy for the students by sharing three statements about yourself. Ask the students to determine which statement is the fib and why it is a fib. Example statements:
   • I have been teaching for thirty years.
   • I have ten grandchildren.
   • I incorporate a lot of group work when I teach.

3) Ask students to create two factual statements and one fib about themselves. Statements can pertain to the students personally, to the course content, or can be a mixture.
4) As a large group or in small groups, students take turns sharing their three statements while others determine which one is a fib.
5) Discuss the decision making processes students used to determine which statements were fibs.
6) Ask the students to share what they learned about each other.

Option
Use Facts and Fibs at the end of a unit of study. Students create two facts and one fib about the topic studied. As statements are shared by each student, the class determines which one is a fib. Students must tell why the statement is a fib and reword it as a true fact about the topic. Facts and Fibs can be used as a written assignment. Students write their facts and fibs about the topic studied and exchange papers with another student who must write a fact or fib, tell why it is a fib, and then turn it into a fact.

The Group Activator strategy sets the whole brain in motion. Students draw from different modalities as they activate what they know about a certain topic. Group Activators energize and focus learners.

How to Use the Strategy

1) Determine the unit of study and specific ways students can assess their prior knowledge about topics within the unit.

Example statements:

- Record strengths you bring to this topic
- Illustrate a politician at work
- Sketch how an electric current works
- Jot down what you know about electricity
- Draw a healthy body
- List ingredients for healthy living
- Create a graphic organizer of civic workers in our area
- Sketch a civic worker on the job
- Create a bumper sticker for . . .
- List non-examples of . . .

2) Record selected statements on chart paper, chalkboard, or overhead.

3) Explain the purpose of the Group Activator and that it is a three part strategy.

4) Part I: <u>Record</u> Students independently record their response to each statement.

5) Part II: <u>Exchange</u> Students take turns exchanging recorded ideas with a self-selected partner. When students are asked to record ideas representing different modalities they feel safer exchanging ideas with a self-selected partner.

6) Part III: <u>Report</u> Students report what they heard their partners say and sort for themes; what is important to the group.

Options

Student information can be recorded on chart paper for future reference.

Make overheads of drawings, sketches, or graphic organizers and refer to them throughout the unit of study.

Progress always involves risk; you can't steal second base and keep your foot on first.
- Frederick Wilcox

MVP - Most Valuable Point

Bob Garmston introduced me to the MVP strategy; a quick way to activate and engage the mind of the learner. Students summarize their learnings about a topic previously discussed by recording what they believe to be the most valuable idea learned.

How to Use the Strategy

1) Determine which topic students will summarize.
2) Write a huge, colorful MVP on chart paper or the chalkboard and explain the purpose of the strategy to the students.
3) Ask the students to analyze their learnings about the topic studied and select what they believe to be the Most Valuable Point. Next instruct them to record their idea and why they think it is an important learning.
4) Organize students into pairs or trios so they can discuss their Most Valuable Points.
5) Conclude with a large group exchange. Ask students to reveal valuable points they heard during the partner share. Listen for themes.

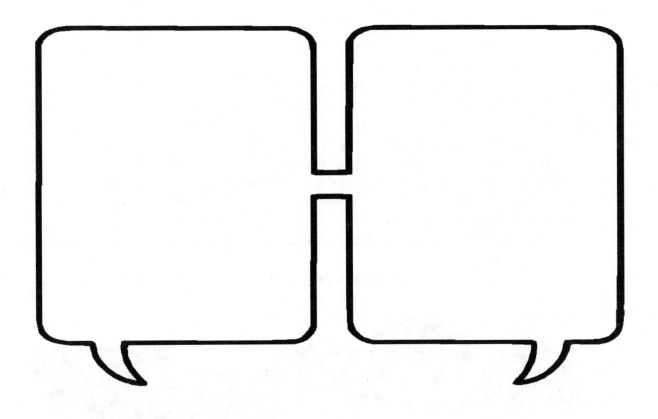

The People Search strategy helps students become familiar with their classmates' interests, activate prior knowledge about the topic they will be studying, and review content previously studied. The strategy energizes through movement because students quickly move about the classroom trying to locate other students who fit specific descriptions.

How to Use the Strategy

1) Determine an appropriate time to use the People Search strategy, for example at the beginning of the semester, the start of a new unit of study, or as a review activity. Develop a student handout stating the descriptors students must locate during the People Search. Descriptors can be displayed in boxes, one statement per box, or each statement can be followed with a signature line. Examples of descriptors:

Health - Find someone who . . .
- has had stitches
- knows his/her blood type
- has taken classes in CPR

Get to Know Each Other - Find someone who . . .
- is a good listener
- likes to work on tasks in a group
- is a new student to the school

Reading - Find someone who . . .
- recently read a good book
- prefers reading magazine articles over books
- likes to read informational text

2) Explain the purpose of the People Search strategy.

3) Instruct students to find at least one person who fits each of the descriptors recorded on the handout. Explain that when students find a classmate who fits a description, the classmate signs the blank line in the box or the line following the statement. Students must find a different person for each item.

4) Allow students time to complete their search and be seated when each descriptor has a signature.

5) Process the strategy by asking students to relate learnings about their classmates.

People Search: Find Someone Who...

...likes the same food as you do.	...has your astrological sign.	...has a grandchild.
...writes with left hand.	...bases decision on intuitive feelings.	...preferred algebra versus geometry.
...likes to be the talker instead of the listener.	IDENTIFY YOURSELF HERE.	...is always on time for meetings.
...likes to work on tasks in a group.	...keeps track of the checking account to the penny.	...prefers social situations planned in advance.
...moves furniture, changes office decor frequently.	...tends to cry easily at movies, weddings, etc.	...problem solves by prioritizing and writing all ideas before choosing.

Strength Bombardment

Strength Bombardment is a strategy I learned from my friend John Dyer. As teachers, we constantly try to develop students who are persistent, build on their strengths, and know they make a difference. This strategy helps create efficacious learners because students reflect on their strengths, as well as develop an awareness of their peers' perceptions of them.

How to Use the Strategy

1) Explain the purpose of strategy.

2) Ask the students to record three of their strengths. Record three strengths of your own and then model the Strength Bombardment strategy for students.

3) Explain they are to guess the three strengths you have recorded about yourself. Examples might include:

- I am a good listener.
- I look at all sides of an issue before making a decision.
- I am an interesting, good writer.
- I try to build on everyone's strengths when I teach.

4) When students guess a strength you wrote, thank them. If they do not guess the strength, use the following response: "That statement is true, thank-you, but that is not what I wrote." The response statement could be written on the board for easy access. Encourage all students to participate. Once students have determined your three strengths ask them if they have any questions about the strategy.

5) Organize students into small groups so all are recognized for their strengths.

6) Conclude with a class discussion on strengths.

Team Interview

The Team Interview (Kagan, 1992) is a lengthy opening strategy that teaches the interview process and can be used as an introductory activity at the beginning of the semester, to conclude the semester, or to help students process concepts they are learning throughout the semester. Team Interviews engage the mind of the learner through questioning.

How to Use the Strategy

1) Determine when to use the Team Interview strategy and develop appropriate interview questions. Example interview questions:
- Who are you as a learner?
- What do you enjoy about (subject)?
- What is a learning goal you have set for yourself this semester?
- What did you find confusing about the reading?
- What are you learning about yourself as a writer?
- What did you learn from the group project?
- If you could be a president from the past, who would you select and why?

2) Explain the purpose of the strategy and that it consists of three parts:
- Individual response
- Partner interview
- Team introductions

3) Instruct students to record their individual response to each interview question. Allow two to three minutes for students to record ideas.

4) Use a grouping strategy (Section 8, p. 203), assign students a classmate to interview. To ensure that students listen carefully when interviewing, tell them to record their partner's response to each interview question. Allow three to four minutes for students to interview each other.

5) Instruct each pair of students to join another pair, forming quartets. Team introductions begin by having each student introduce his partner to the new pair. The student shares his partner's responses recorded during the interview. Students listen for similarities and/or differences as information about each interview question is shared.

6) Conclude the strategy by asking students to report out similarities or differences for each interview question. Information can be charted for future reference. Individual responses to some interview questions, such as "What is a learning goal you have set for yourself this semester?" can be monitored throughout the semester.

Team Resume

The Team Resume strategy is a community-building activity in which team members work together to create a profile of their skills and talents. Team Resumes can be developed as students embark on a major team project or at the beginning of a semester. This comprehensive opening activity can be displayed for future use.

How to Use the Strategy

1) Determine the purpose for the Team Resume and decide topics to be included in the resume. Record resume ideas on chart paper, the chalkboard, or the overhead. Example resume topics:
- Who are you? something personal about yourself (hobby, favorite book)
- What are your learning goals?
- What will you contribute to make this a productive learning experience?
- What do you know about (concept)?

2) Share the purpose of the Team Resume strategy with the students. Organize students into teams.

3) Present the information to be included on the Team Resume. Instruct the teams that they can create their resume using chart paper and markers. Monitor team progress.

4) Have teams determine how they will present their Team Resume to the rest of the class. Inform them that it should be a group presentation.

5) Have each team present their resume to the class. Team presentations can be followed by a group process of the presentation.

6) Periodically revisit the Team Resumes. Check to see if students are accomplishing their learning goals and if they are making the contributions they set out to make. Team members can make changes to their resume as needed. Team Resumes can serve as a self-assessment activity.

That's Me

This strategy is a quick opener! Use it when working with a group for the first time or when beginning a new unit of study. That's Me engages and energizes the group immediately. It provides students an opportunity to learn interesting yet relevant information about their classmates.

How to Use the Strategy

1) Select statements appropriate for the age group and the subject area. Select statements so all students are involved several times.
Examples of statements are:
   • I went on a family trip this summer.
   • I am a morning person.
   • I am a night owl.
   • I enjoy reading.
   • I am musical (play an instrument, sing in a choir).
   • I have a pet.
   • I like to know the rationale behind why we learn things.
   • I appreciate having an agenda or schedule for each class.
   • I enjoy working with classmates.
   • I prefer working alone.
   • I like projects, performance tasks.
   • I enjoy writing papers, essays.
   • I enjoy working out (run, walk, bike, lift weights).
2) Explain the purpose of the strategy to the students.
3) Explain the strategy to the students. Students listen carefully as statements are shared and each time a statement pertains to them, they jump up, throw their arms in the air and say "That's Me." Encourage students to mentally connect with students in order to remember specific facts about each one for future learning opportunities. For example, when students are asked to find a learning partner during a unit of study, they could refer back to the That's Me strategy and select accordingly.
4) Begin with a practice statement which applies to everyone, such as "I got up this morning." To add a little humor, I usually follow that statement with, "Notice, I did not say I wanted to get up this morning." This breaks the ice right away and students love it.
5) Conclude with an energizing statement! An example is, "Please join me in acknowledging all of the awesome students here about to embark on an exciting learning journey." (Everyone applauds.)

Option

That's Me can be used at a unit of study to determine student's prior knowledge about the topic. For example, sample statements in health could be:
- I have taken a first aid class.
- I have had an operation.
- I know my blood type.
- I have never been inside a hospital.

Option

That's Me can be used as an opening activity for Parent's Night. My daughter used the following statements with her sixth grade parents:
- I read with my child.
- I talk with my child about what he/she is learning in school.
- This is my only child in school.
- I have some fun memories from elementary school.
- I like to help my child with homework (if I can!!!).

Section 2 - Literacy Strategies for Vocabulary Development

"If I were to do one thing to raise test scores, even on standardized tests, it would be to build vocabulary. In chemistry, for example, students would write 'Dilute the solution with three milliliters of water' rather than simply, 'Add more water.'"

- Heide Hayes Jacobs, 1998

Rationale

Vocabulary knowledge is a key predictor of how well a student understands a selection. Each content area has a unique vocabulary. In order for students to learn the subject matter, they must understand the vocabulary words that represent the concepts they are learning. Meaningful understanding of vocabulary words involves more than looking the word up in the dictionary. A seventh grade student was assigned to look up the words in the dictionary and then use each word in a sentence. So, the student looked up the word frugal in the dictionary and it said "to save." The student wrote, "I was drowning in the swimming pool and yelled, 'Frugal me, frugal me.' My friend jumped in and frugaled me."

Using only the dictionary often results in unclear, vague understanding, or incorrect interpretation of the word. Not only do students need to elaborate and connect the word to what they already know, but they need to be exposed to a new word numerous times. Research indicates that most children need six to twelve exposures before remembering a new word (Wolfe & Nevills, 2004). Students need opportunities to wrestle with the meaning of the words, to develop personal examples for the meaning, and to differentiate between similar words. Vocabulary strategies offer students that opportunity. Each strategy causes the student to think about the words they are learning in different ways. Selection of the appropriate strategy depends upon how you want the students to think about the words they are learning.

Vocabulary strategies included in this section.

	Page
• Act the Word	26
• Concept Definition Mapping	28
• Forecast	33
• Frayer Model	34
• Mind Sketching	39
• Prevoke/Vocabogram	40
• Semantic Feature Analysis	42
• Stephens Vocabulary Elaboration	46
• SAW - Student Action Words	50
• Super Word Web	54
• Vocabulary Concept Chain	55
• Word Sorts	57

How to Use the Strategy

1) Determine words to be studied
2) Assign students to cooperative groups of three or four.
3) Assign each student a role of actor, director, and coach.
   - Actors - act out the words
   - Director - distributes the words, decides the order for presentation, and directs the presentation
   - Coach - keeps the group on task, encourages each group member, and checks to see that each group member knows the words
4) The director distributes the words to the group members.
5) Members learn the meaning of each word with the coach's assistance as needed.
6) Group members brainstorm different ways to act out each word. They select the best action to teach the word to the class.
7) Group members teach their words to the class. The director instructs the rest of the class to act out the word, tell the meaning, and to pronounce it.
8) The teacher instructs the class to stand in a circle and calls out a word for the students to demonstrate the learned action, saying the meaning, and the word.
9) Older students learn from and enjoy acting out vocabulary words which describe historical events, chemical reactions, math theorems, or musical performances.
10) Instruct the students to explain their performances and how the demonstration increased their understanding of the word.

Benefits of the Strategy

- Supports whole-brain learning
- Involves movement which increases the retention of more vocabulary words
- Develops communication skills among team members
- Increases accountability by having each student responsible for acting out the words
- Creates a positive learning environment because acting out words involves risk-taking
- Increases student motivation for learning vocabulary words
- Brings laughter to the classroom and humor is an essential ingredient for learning

Reference: Chapman, C. (1993). If the shoe fits. Palatine, IL: IRI/Skylight Publishing, Inc.

Act the Word Sample List of Words (to act out)

applause	clapping of the hands
asthenia	loss of bodily strength, weakness
atomize	to reduce or separate into atoms
bawl	to sob or cry loudly
blink	to close and open the eyes rapidly
contort	to twist or bend severely out of shape
cultivate	to prepare land by plowing and fertilizing
desist	to cease doing something
deviate	to turn or move increasingly away from a prescribed behavior
gambol	frolic, to leap around playfully
gemutlich	having a feeling of warmth or congeniality
ichthyology	the study of fishes
inertia	the tendency of a body to resist acceleration
grab	to take or capture suddenly
grist	ground grain
grouchy	tending to complain and grumble
jollify	to be merry
kvetch	to complain or find fault persistently and querulously
mellifluous	flowing with honey or sweetness
mollify	to lessen in intensity; temper, to soften
nimble	quick, light, or agile in movement
oppugn	to oppose, contradict or call into question
palavering	idly chattering, talk intended to charm
querulously	expressing or showing a complaint
rallentando	to slow down, gradual reduction in tempo
soprano	the highest singing voice
tweedle	to produce tunes
yammer	talk persistently, to shout

Why Use the Strategy

Concept Definition Mapping (Schwartz and Raphael, 1985) is a powerful vocabulary strategy, focused on vocabulary development of key concepts within a unit of study. All too often students are told to look up the vocabulary words in the glossary and write the definition. Students copy the textbook definition, spending minimal time actually learning the meaning of the word. The Concept Definition Mapping strategy causes the student to internalize the meaning of words. Concept definition maps are a visual representation of the critical components of the vocabulary words. There are different types of concept definition maps from which to choose. One graphic representation requires the student not only to explain what the word means but what it does not mean. A thorough understanding of what something is, requires knowing what it is not. Another graphic representation requires the student to explain what the word is like. Explaining what something is like causes the student to make associations or connections with other ideas based on personal knowledge. All of the concept definition maps require students to cite personal examples of each word. Giving personal examples of a vocabulary word causes the brain to create pictures based on the reader's own experience. Because the brain also remembers pictures, the use of examples increases retention of vocabulary words.

How to Use the Strategy

1) Determine the critical words that students must know within the unit of study in order to understand the concept being studied. Examples of concepts are: industrialism, liberty, energy, and estimation.

2) Provide an example of a Concept Definition Map.

3) Explain the meaning of the questions on the concept map:
   - What is it?
   - What is it not? (This one can be a difficult question.)
   - What is it like?
   - What are some examples?

4) Select one type of concept definition map and model how to use it with a vocabulary word familiar to the students. This allows the students to focus on the process of using the strategy rather than working hard to understand the word.

5) Using the same type of map, model the process using a vocabulary word from a current unit of study. Seek information for the map from the students. For example, a math teacher might select the concept proportion. If the category is fractions, "What is it like?" responses might include: ratio, a certain amount, a share of something. Examples might include: part of a candy bar, slice of a pie, or part of my allowance.

6) Have students work with a partner to complete a concept map using a word from a current unit of study. They may need to use a dictionary, thesaurus, or glossary, but encourage them to use information from their own experience.

7) After the students complete their concept maps, instruct them to write a definition of the concept using the information on the map. The definition should include ideas from all areas of the concept map.

8) As the unit of study progresses, encourage the students to create more maps using new words. Also, have students revisit previously made concept maps in order to refine them by adding newly learned information.

9) Follow the same process described above using each type of concept definition map. Discuss the differences of each map and when to use the different maps.

When to Use the Strategy

- This strategy enhances learning of vocabulary words in all content areas. Teachers identify critical words students need to know in order to understand a concept. Math, science, social studies, art, music, and business teachers find this strategy very beneficial.

- When students prepare for a vocabulary test, they can categorize the words and create concept maps for each category. For example, in science the categories could be rain forests and deserts. In music, the categories could be harmony and rhythm.

Link to Assessment

The completed Concept Definition Map of a vocabulary word serves as an assessment tool. Students use their prior experiences and knowledge in order to complete the map. Instead of writing a short paragraph about a concept learned, the map can provide a comprehensive assessment.

Concept Definition Mapping Example

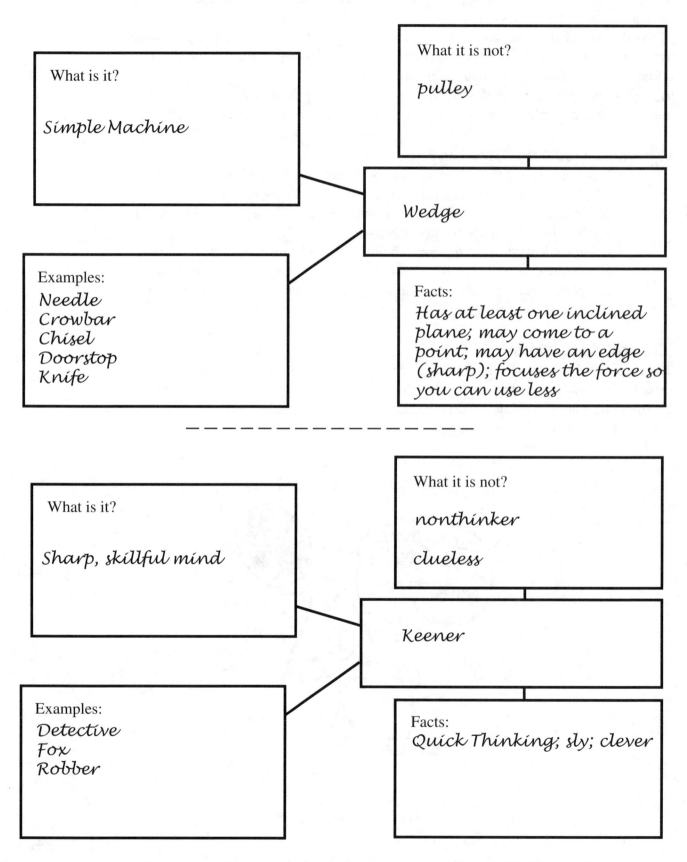

What is it?

Simple Machine

What it is not?

pulley

Wedge

Examples:
Needle
Crowbar
Chisel
Doorstop
Knife

Facts:
Has at least one inclined plane; may come to a point; may have an edge (sharp); focuses the force so you can use less

What is it?

Sharp, skillful mind

What it is not?

nonthinker

clueless

Keener

Examples:
Detective
Fox
Robber

Facts:
Quick Thinking; sly; clever

Concept Definition Mapping

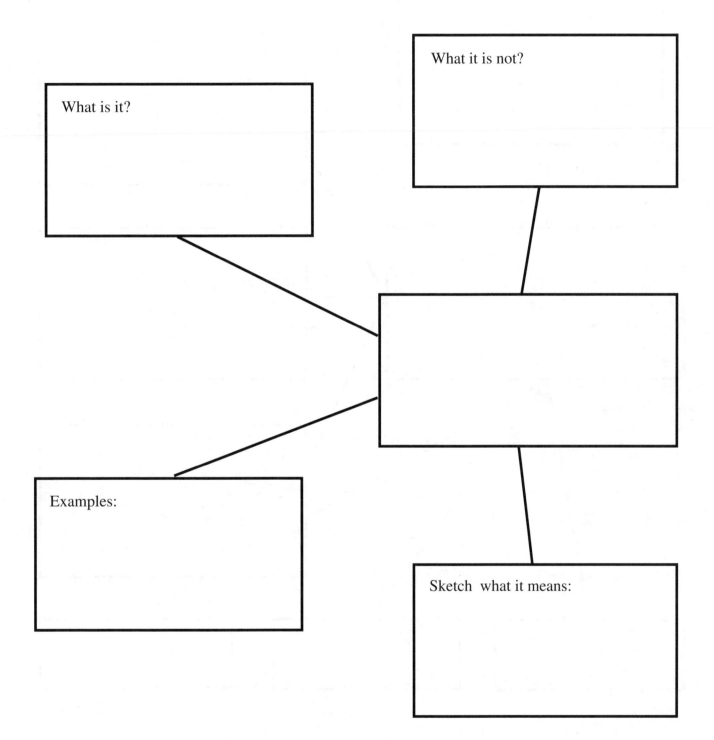

What is it?

What it is not?

Examples:

Sketch what it means:

Schwartz and Raphael, 1985

Concept Definition Mapping

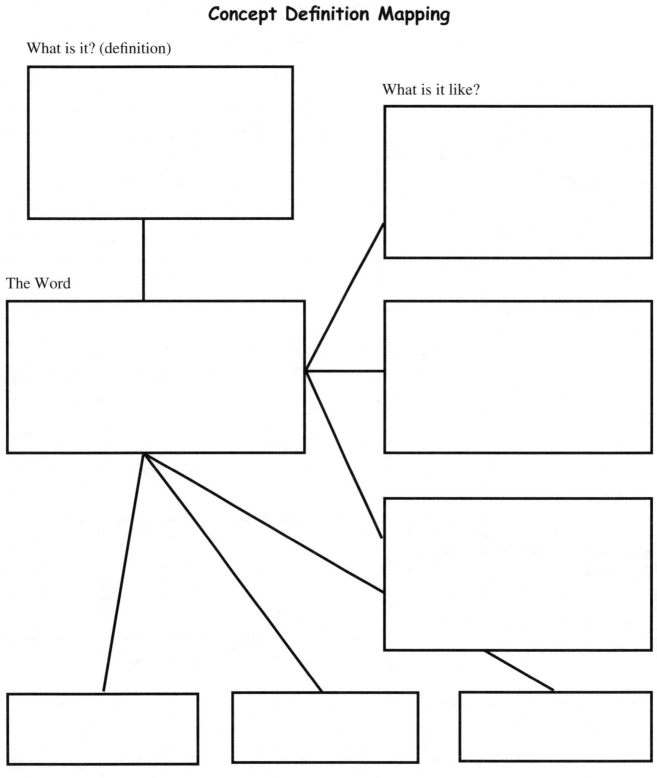

What is it? (definition)

What is it like?

The Word

What are some examples?

Schwartz and Raphael, 1985

Forecast

How to Use the Strategy

1) Select a theme to be studied, for example, friendship.

2) Choose a literature selection or passage about the theme.

3) Select several key vocabulary words from the book related to the theme.

4) Take the first word and make one space per letter on the chalkboard or chart. End with the number of letters in the word.

Example: _ _ _ _ _ _ _ (7)

Represent each word in this manner on the chalkboard.

5) Introduce Forecasting by explaining the topic to the students and they will forecast key words associated with the topic.

6) Begin with the first word by writing the first letter on the first space. Ask, "What word begins with L _ _ _ _ (5) and is associated with friendship?"

Working alone or with a partner, students brainstorm ideas. Ask for their ideas and if no one has the correct word give them another letter. L O _ _ _ (5)

Continue until they forecast the correct word.

L O Y _ _ (5)

7) Move to the next word and write in the first three letters. Explain that this word is also related to the theme of "Friendship." Continue with the same process described in 6 above.

Example: T H O _ _ _ _ _ _ _ (10)

T H O U G H T F U L (10)

8) Continue with the process, until the students Forecast all of the new words listed for the story.

9) Ask students to explain how the words in the Forecast are related to the theme of "friendship."

10) Have students predict what they think the story will be about based on the words from the Forecast.

11) Read the selection and have students focus on the words as they read.

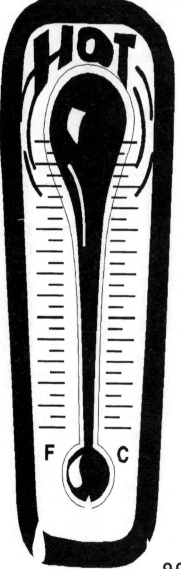

Benefits of the Strategy

• Motivates students to want to learn vocabulary words
• Builds interest for the topic being studied
• Activates prior knowledge
• Causes students to predict
• Assists with correct spelling of words

Why Use the Strategy

The Frayer Model (Frayer, Frederick, and Klausmeier, 1969) was developed to analyze and assess attainment of concepts. The strategy uses a graphic organizer divided into four components for recording information related to the concept. Frayer considers it essential to present concepts in a relational manner so students see the components in the learning process. The "Four Square" graphic organizer might include both essential and nonessential characteristics as well as examples and nonexamples. The Frayer Model works well with all ages of children, even the little ones.

How to Use the Strategy

1) Determine the concept or word being studied.
2) Explain all of the attributes of the Frayer Model to be completed. Provide an example using a word familiar to the students.
3) Use a familiar word (for example, friendship or home) to model the process with the students.
4) Have students alone or with a partner complete a Frayer Model diagram using an assigned word.
5) Once the diagram is complete, have students share their work with other students. Diagrams developed on chart paper with markers can be displayed and shared. Students should be encouraged to revisit their Frayer Model diagram adding newly learned information.

When to Use the Strategy

- This strategy enhances learning of vocabulary words in all content areas. Teachers identify the critical words students need to know in order to understand a concept. Teachers from all content areas find this strategy very beneficial. For example, critical words for the concept of photosynthesis: chlorophyll, cells, chemical energy, and oxygen.
- When students prepare for a vocabulary test, they can organize all of the words into categories and create the Frayer Model diagrams for each category.

Link to Assessment

The completed Frayer Model diagram of a vocabulary word serves as an assessment tool. Students must use their prior experiences and knowledge in order to complete the map. Instead of, for example, writing a short paragraph about a concept learned, the map can provide a comprehensive assessment.

Frayer Model Example

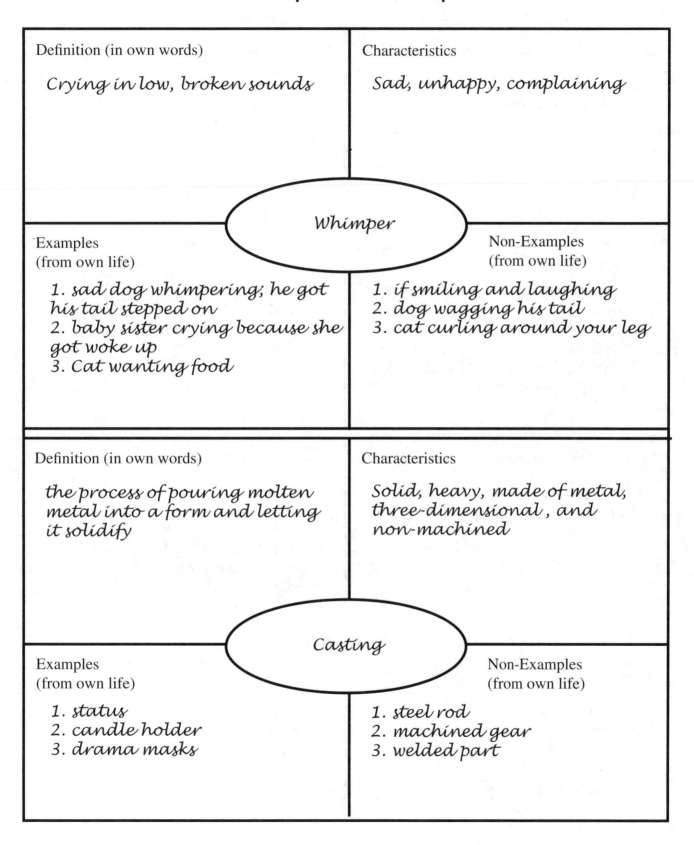

Definition (in own words)	Characteristics
Crying in low, broken sounds	*Sad, unhappy, complaining*

Whimper

Examples (from own life)	Non-Examples (from own life)
1. *sad dog whimpering; he got his tail stepped on* 2. *baby sister crying because she got woke up* 3. *Cat wanting food*	1. *if smiling and laughing* 2. *dog wagging his tail* 3. *cat curling around your leg*

Definition (in own words)	Characteristics
the process of pouring molten metal into a form and letting it solidify	*Solid, heavy, made of metal, three-dimensional, and non-machined*

Casting

Examples (from own life)	Non-Examples (from own life)
1. *status* 2. *candle holder* 3. *drama masks*	1. *steel rod* 2. *machined gear* 3. *welded part*

Frayer Model Example

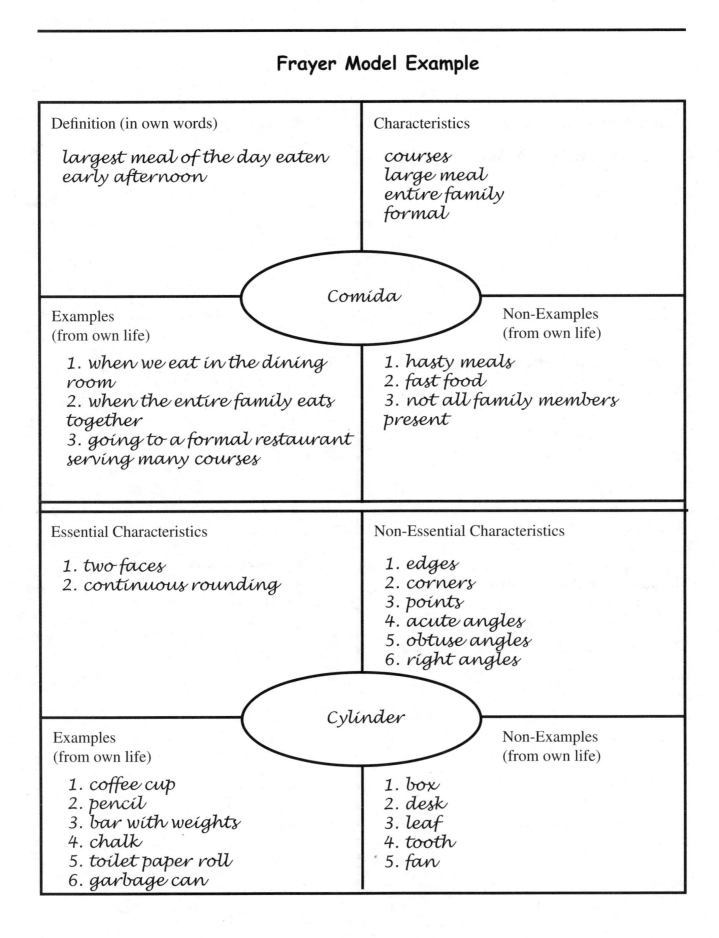

Definition (in own words)

largest meal of the day eaten early afternoon

Characteristics

courses
large meal
entire family
formal

Comida

Examples
(from own life)

1. when we eat in the dining room
2. when the entire family eats together
3. going to a formal restaurant serving many courses

Non-Examples
(from own life)

1. hasty meals
2. fast food
3. not all family members present

Essential Characteristics

1. two faces
2. continuous rounding

Non-Essential Characteristics

1. edges
2. corners
3. points
4. acute angles
5. obtuse angles
6. right angles

Cylinder

Examples
(from own life)

1. coffee cup
2. pencil
3. bar with weights
4. chalk
5. toilet paper roll
6. garbage can

Non-Examples
(from own life)

1. box
2. desk
3. leaf
4. tooth
5. fan

Frayer Model

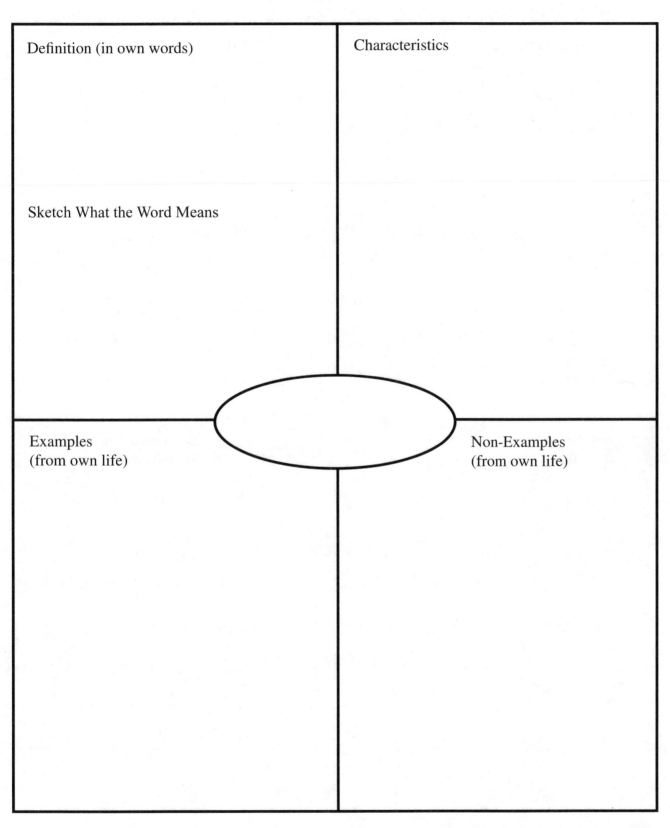

Definition (in own words)

Characteristics

Sketch What the Word Means

Examples
(from own life)

Non-Examples
(from own life)

Frayer, Frederick, Klausmeier, 1969

Frayer Model

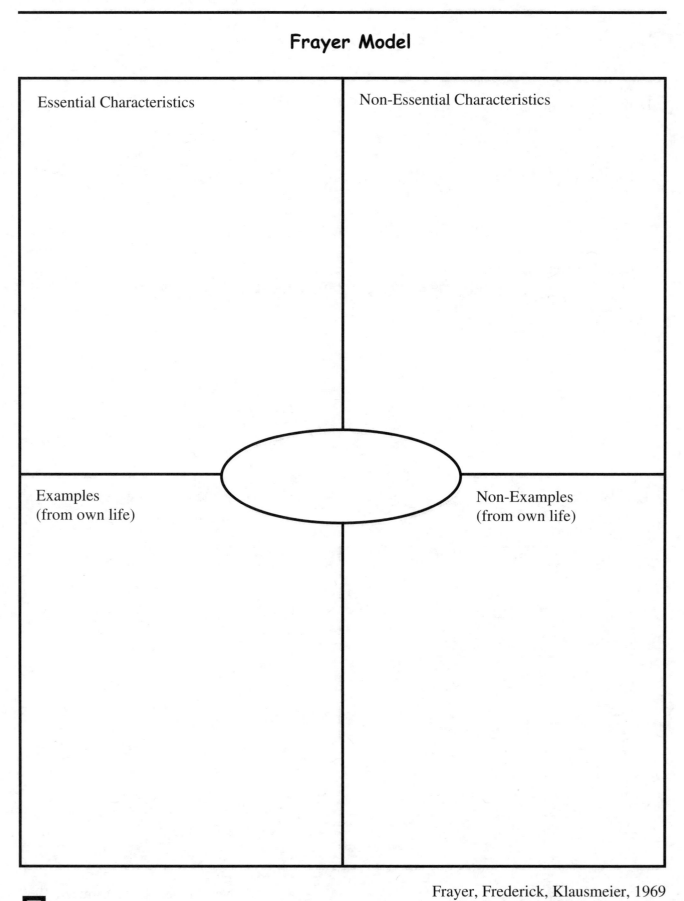

Essential Characteristics

Non-Essential Characteristics

Examples
(from own life)

Non-Examples
(from own life)

Frayer, Frederick, Klausmeier, 1969

Mind-Sketching

Why Use the Strategy

The Mind-Sketching (Juntune, 1983) strategy encourages the reader to picture the meaning of a vocabulary word. The brain thrives on pictures. We have all heard, "a picture is worth a thousand words." When students sketch what a word means, they think analytically and use ideas from their background of experience. Most students dread vocabulary study because they find it boring. The Mind-Sketching strategy motivates students to want to learn new words, helps them develop accurate definitions, and enhances retention of words.

How to Use the Strategy

1) Select the vocabulary words which promote understanding of the topic to be studied.

2) Depending on the number of words to be learned, students can be organized into small groups and assigned some of the words.

3) Students are assigned words and work individually to:
- Write the word and look it up in the dictionary or a glossary.
- Study the definition to gain a clear understanding of the meaning (some words might require students to seek further assistance).
- Sketch what the word means.
- Share the meaning of each sketched word with other students assigned the same word and revise the sketch if necessary.

4) Small Group Activity:
- Share the word, the meaning, and the sketch.
- Study the sketch and discuss what it means.
- Look up the definition of the word and share it with other group members.
- Revise the sketch to clarify or enhance the meaning.
- Write a short descriptive phrase which defines the word.

When to Use the Strategy

- Students who struggle with vocabulary development enjoy this strategy and find it very helpful. It allows visual elaboration and taps into a visual mode of learning.
- Words which look or sound similar but have different meanings are mentally clarified through sketching (i.e. cinnamon and synonym, knight and night).
- Difficult concepts can be made easier to understand, for example by sketching the process of photosynthesis.
- As students prepare for vocabulary sections of standardized tests, this strategy can be a beneficial aid to understanding and memory.

Link to Assessment

If students can sketch the meaning of words and write a definition in their own words, they will communicate their understanding of the words. Frequent use of the vocabulary words in other content areas is a key to long-term retention.

Why Use the Strategy

Prevoke/Vocabogram (Rasinski, 2000) is a prereading strategy which helps the reader develop vocabulary and prediction skills. Readers are challenged to use specific vocabulary words from the designated selection by categorizing them into predetermined categories. The categorized words then serve as the basis for formulating a prediction about the selection to be read.

How to Use the Strategy

1) Select an informational or narrative selection to read.
2) Identify 10-20 key vocabulary words or phrases from the text.
3) Determine categories into which the words should be categorized (for example, story elements, story sequence, emotional connections, fact/fiction).
4) Display the key words on chart paper, chalkboard, or individual handout.
5) Share the words with the students and discuss the general meaning of each one.
6) Explain the categories into which the words are to be placed. Have students, working alone or in groups, categorize the words and then formulate a written prediction. Predictions might result from purposeful questions that will engage students as they read the selection.
7) Share predictions and the rationale for the predictions among the class. List predictions on the chalkboard or chart paper.
8) Read the selection orally or silently. As the selection is read, make key vocabulary words visible so students can refer to them as they listen.
9) After reading the entire selection, ask students to compare their list of categorized words to what actually happened. Students make necessary changes.
10) Ask students to process how using the strategy assisted their reading comprehension. Discuss the benefits of making a prediction before reading.

When to Use the Strategy

- To develop student interest, use as an introduction to a short story, poem, novel, or informational passage.
- When introducing a new unit of study in any content area, provide the key vocabulary words from the unit and have the students categorize the words into sub-topics. Predictions are then made about the learnings.
- To teach the concept of categorizing select a short, interesting story and ask students to develop categories for organizing the words. For example, words could be provided for a fairy tale. Discuss with students what it means to categorize, and then brainstorm possible categories.

Link to Assessment

Student's ability to make logical predictions is assessed. Teachers can observe student understanding of vocabulary words before, during, and after selection is read. The criteria for categorizing words can be used as an assessment topic (for example, story elements are used within the following example).

Prevoke/Vocabogram
Example 1 - Narrative Text

"Pappa's Parrot"
Every Living Thing by Cynthia Rylant

Words/Phrases

candy and nut shop	Rocky
Harry	"Where's Harry?"
friends	"Hello Rocky"
Mr. Tillian	children
caramels	sobbed
embarrassed	visit
ambulance	burger place

Categorize Words According to Story Elements

setting   characters   events/action   problem/goal   resolution   theme

Written Prediction

_ _ _ _ _ _ _ _ _ _ _ _ _ _ _ _ _

Prevoke/Vocabogram
Example 2 - Informational Text

"To Stop a Headache" (author unknown)

Words/Phrases

"roaming the desert, blowing like the wind"	relaxation techniques
migrane headache	nerve disturbances
tension headache	positron emission tomography
magnesium	environmental
vitamin B2	hormonal
homeopathic therapies	dietary
neurologic & chemical abnormalities	massage
excessive pill popping	"rebound" headaches
medications containing caffeine	primary-care doctors

Categorize words according to:

Part of the PROBLEM   **Part of the SOLUTION**

Written Prediction

Why Use the Strategy

Students will not be able to understand what they are reading if they are stumbling over the words in a text. Research tells us that vocabulary knowledge is an indicator of whether or not a student will comprehend what is read. We also know that students will not acquire adequate vocabulary knowledge only through their spelling lessons and using a dictionary. The Semantic Feature Analysis (Johnson and Pearson, 1984) strategy helps students determine what a word means by comparing it to other words from the same category. The students develop a matrix grid which gives a visual representation of key words or terms associated with the category and specific features of each word. The grid provides students a visual reminder as to how the words are alike and different.

How to Use the Strategy

1) Model the Semantic Feature Analysis with your students using a familiar category. Display the matrix grid using an overhead or a large chart. First, students provide examples of the category and they are listed vertically in the left column. For example, if the category is vegetables, words listed could be: carrots, potatoes, lettuce, beets. Next, students provide different features of vegetables, such as: green and leafy, grown in the ground, grown on vines, have roots, and grown from seeds. The features are written horizontally across the top. Model how to mark the correct features for each vegetable.

2) Allow the students, working with a partner, to practice the strategy. Select a category from a unit of study, such as sports, farm animals, geometric shapes, or political parties. Record different terms or words from the category in the left column of the matrix. For example, if the category is land formations, different words might be: island, peninsula, continent, and mountains.

3) Have the students provide several features that the formations share. The features might include: near body of water, shaped by movement of earth, located near the equator, inhabited by humans.

4) Students need to code each feature with a (+) if the word has that feature and a (-) if the word does not have the feature. If the student does not know for sure a (?) is put in the column.

5) Students can add more features to the grid and then mark what is similar or different for the words or terms for each category. The teacher's role is to challenge the students' thinking as they work and facilitate a discussion about the uniqueness of each feature. Students are encouraged to find other features that are related to the category.

6) Once the matrix grid is complete, students have fun comparing their examples with other students.

When to Use the Strategy

The Semantic Feature Analysis is an excellent strategy to introduce new vocabulary and terms as you begin a unit of study. Students can begin with familiar words and add new terms and features of the terms as they progress throughout the unit. The strategy can be used as an organizational tool for writing assignments, a guide to review terms before a test, and a study tool when given assessment tasks. Semantic Feature Analysis is a helpful strategy when terms are very similar. Students can differentiate the critical attributes of each term within the category, and the grid serves as a visual reminder.

Link to Assessment

The completed Semantic Feature Analysis serves as an assessment tool. The matrix provides a visual representation of the vocabulary, terms, and knowledge of specific characteristics or features that the students have learned.

Semantic Feature Analysis Examples

Vegetables / Features	Grow Above Ground	Green	Leafy	Grow below ground	Grow on vines	Have roots	Grow from seeds
Carrots							
Potatoes							
Lettuce							
Beets							
Broccoli							
Onions							
Green Beans							

Features

	Location			Size			Behavior		
Types of Fish	Bottom	Middle	Top	Small	Middle	Large	Peaceful	Aggressive	Violent
Algae Eater									
Angelfish									
Black Molly									
Dwarf Gourami									
Goldfish									
Guppy									
NeonTetra									
Piranha									
Siamese Fighting									
Zebrafish									

Semantic Feature Analysis

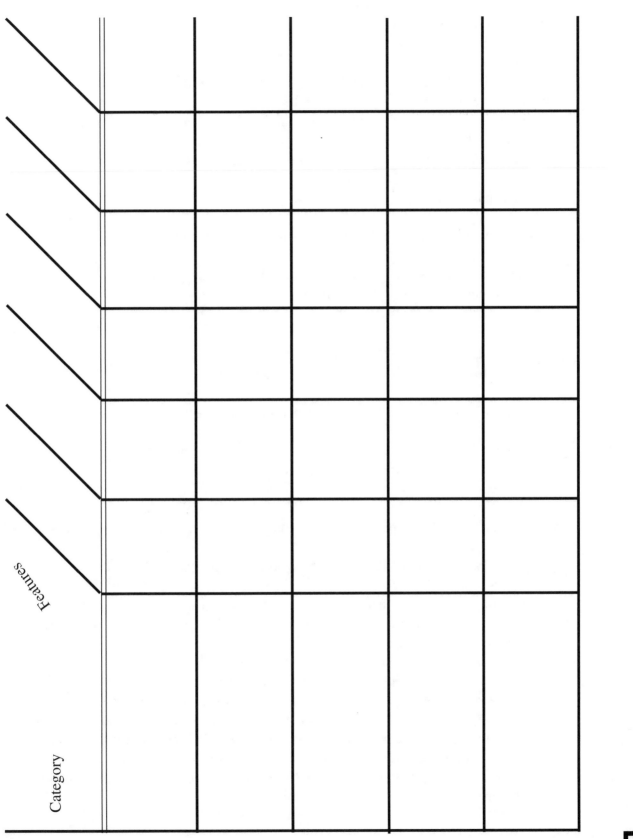

Features

Category

Why Use the Strategy

The Stephens Vocabulary Elaboration (Brown, Phillips, and Stephens, 1993) is a comprehensive thinking strategy which causes the reader to develop an in-depth understanding of a new concept. The strategy is effective because it not only broadens the students knowledge of the topic, but it also helps them differentiate between similar or related words. Students record new words in a vocabulary notebook and analyze them for different meanings, nuances, and emotional implications. For example, the word "plot" was recorded three different times, with the following meanings: conspiracy, piece of land as a cemetery plot, and the rising action or falling action of a story.

Students can also use a graphic organizer format which causes them to analyze the context in which the word is used, relate it to a common category, provide examples and non-examples from their own life, and state the common characteristics of the word. Teachers state that when students are able to complete the graphic organizer for new words or terms learned, they have a thorough understanding of the concept.

How to Use the Strategy

1) Model for the students how to use a vocabulary notebook using the following steps:

- Share a new word you recently discovered and write the new word and the date it was encountered.
- Record the context in which the word was found and how it was used.
- Suggest a definition for the word based on the context.
- List examples and then non-examples based on your own experiences or prior knowledge. Non-examples can help the students see the nuances of words.
- Write a definition of the word using your own words. Compare with a dictionary definition.
- Record situational definitions of the word. This part helps the students understand the different meanings of the same words. For example, elements of the word matter in science are: has weight, takes up space, and changes form. The elements for the word *matter* used in a novel, "It was a business *matter*." could be: circumstance, affair, and occurrence.
- Create the graphic organizer for the new word.
- Add expanded meanings of the same word to the vocabulary notebook and compare the new usage of the word with a previously recorded example. For example, the word *division* from a math unit was recorded as: separation, inverse of multiplication, and break apart. In science *division* means: reproduce (cells) and one or more classes (plant organization), and in social studies, *division* was referred to as: separation of the legislature, one part of the country, and major administrative or tactical unit of the military.

2) With students working in groups, assign each group a new word from a unit of study. Guide them through each step of the process.

3) Each group teaches their new word to the class using the graphic organizer. Copies of the graphic organizer can be given to each group for further study.

When to Use the Strategy

Stephens Vocabulary Elaboration strategy can be used in any subject area at any grade level. For the young child, the graphic organizer can be simplified by eliminating the essential elements or characteristics of the word section. Students can use the vocabulary notebook and graphic organizer as a study device for a test. The strategy reveals how new words are related within a unit of study. For example, when reading *Diary of Anne Frank,* the concept Nuremberg Laws is associated with the following words: degredation, discrimination, bigotry, and prejudice.

Link to Assessment

Use the strategy as an assessment tool by having students complete the graphic organizer for a concept recently studied.

Stephens Vocabulary Elaboration Strategy Example

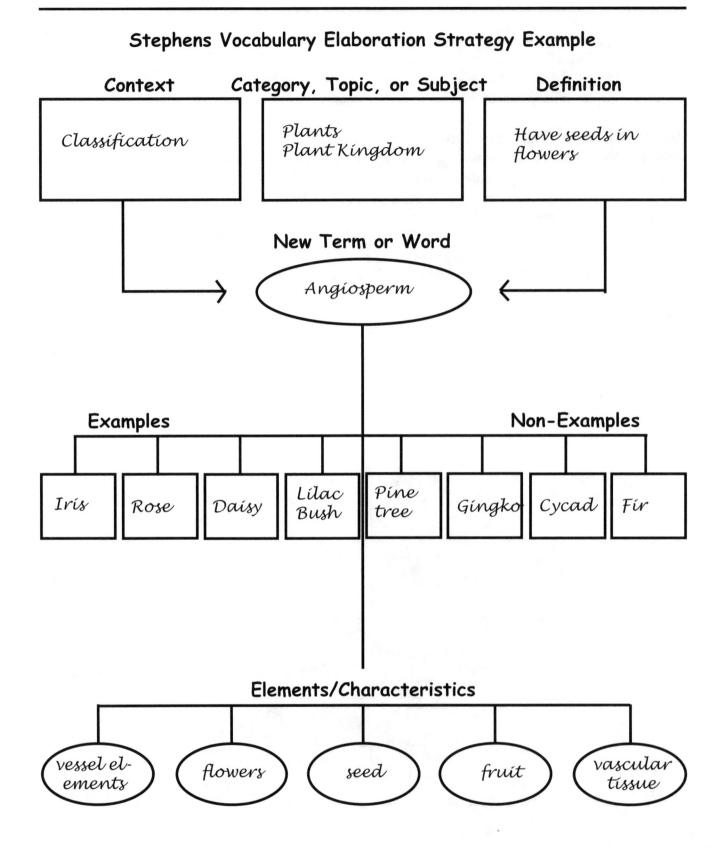

Context
Classification

Category, Topic, or Subject
Plants
Plant Kingdom

Definition
Have seeds in flowers

New Term or Word
Angiosperm

Examples
Iris | Rose | Daisy | Lilac Bush | Pine tree

Non-Examples
Gingko | Cycad | Fir

Elements/Characteristics
vessel elements | flowers | seed | fruit | vascular tissue

Brown, Phillips, and Stephens, 1993

Stephens Vocabulary Elaboration Strategy

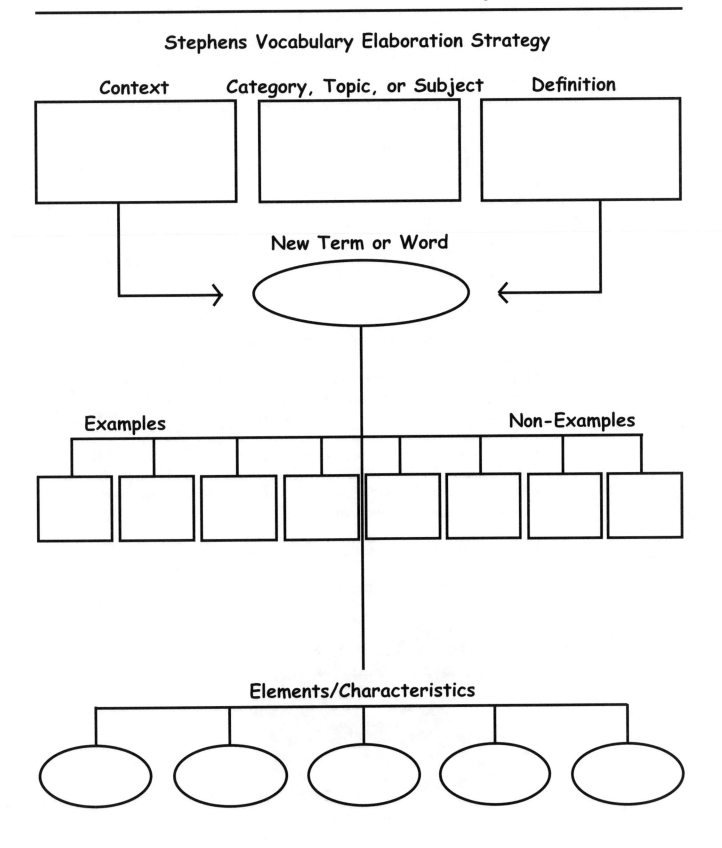

Brown, Phillips, and Stephens, 1993

How to Use the Strategy

1) Quote the actual sentence in which the word or phrase appears. Write the reference and page number.

2) Write the word and the predicted definition.

3) Check the word's meaning in a dictionary or glossary and write its definition in your own words.

4) Use a thesaurus to list antonyms and synonyms.

5) Write one good sentence to show how the word can be used.

6) Draw a symbol, image, or word association to help you remember the word.

7) Share your Student Action Words with a friend. Explain why you choose those particular words and why your friend might want to learn them.

Benefits of the Strategy

- Increases motivation because students self-select the words they find intriguing
- Encourages whole brain learning because students interact with their selected words in visual, aural, symbolic, and experiential ways
- Reinforces the importance of examining the context in which words are used when defining them
- Causes students to remember words because they develop a personal dictionary of words which allows them to use their words multiple times
- Provides an opportunity for students to share words with each other which creates an enthusiasm for word study

Reference: Lynn Thurber, Millard Public Schools, Omaha, NE

SAW - Student Action Words

Name _____

Date _____

Day # _____

SAW

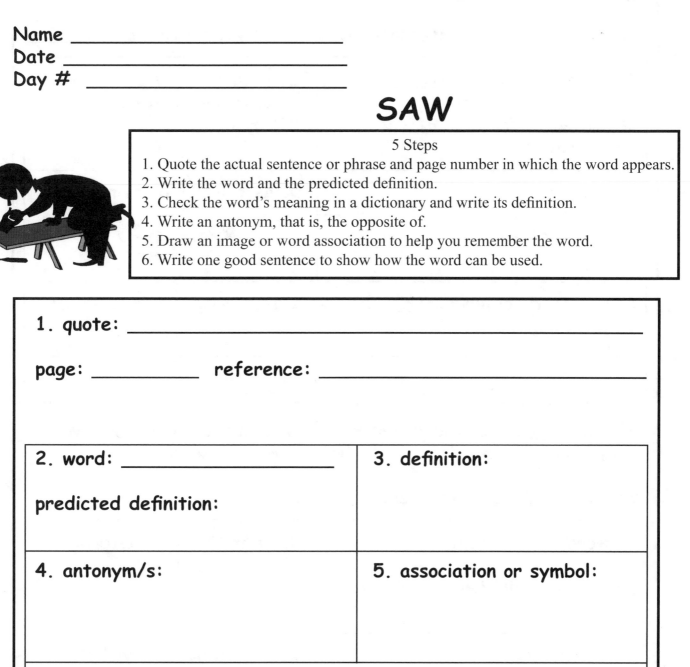

5 Steps
1. Quote the actual sentence or phrase and page number in which the word appears.
2. Write the word and the predicted definition.
3. Check the word's meaning in a dictionary and write its definition.
4. Write an antonym, that is, the opposite of.
5. Draw an image or word association to help you remember the word.
6. Write one good sentence to show how the word can be used.

1. quote: _____

page: _____ reference: _____

2. word: _____	3. definition:
predicted definition:	
4. antonym/s:	5. association or symbol:

6. one good sentence: _____

_____

SAW - Student Action Words Examples

1. quote: *The first time he woke he heard Templeton gnawing a hole in the grain sack.*

page: _32_   **reference:** *Charlotte's Web, Chapters 5 & 6*

2. word: _gnawing_ **predicted definition:** *biting, chewing*	**3. definition:** *chewing or biting; wearing away, bit by bit*
4. antonym/s: *drinking*	**5. association or symbol:**

6. one good sentence: *The beaver is gnawing on a piece of the tree.*

---

1. quote: _"..there were more than a dozen vessels of various kinds, formed roughly into concentric circles."*

page: _5_   **reference:** _sphere_

2. word: _concentric_ **predicted definition:** *round*	**3. definition:** *having a common center*
4. antonym/s: *imbalanced*	**5. association or symbol:**

6. one good sentence: *The two outer rings of the target were concentric circles.*

 www.rachelbillmeyer.com • *Strategies to Engage the Mind of the Learner* • © 2006 Rachel Billmeyer

SAW - Student Action Words Examples

1. quote: _____

page: _____   reference: _____

2. word: _____ predicted definition:	3. definition:
4. antonym/s:	5. association or symbol:

6. one good sentence: _____

_____

---

1. quote: _____

page: _____   reference: _____

2. word: _____ predicted definition:	3. definition:
4. antonym/s:	5. association or symbol:

6. one good sentence: _____

_____

Super Word Web

How to Use the Strategy

1) Select a vocabulary word and share the word as it is used in context.
2) List three to four synonyms or defining phrases for the word.
3) List or draw three or four associations about the word.
4) Select another word and complete the steps asking for student assistance.
5) Organize students into groups and assign several words to each group.
6) Once students have completed the organizer for each assigned word, have them share their words with other students or with the class.

Example of word as it appears in the sentence.

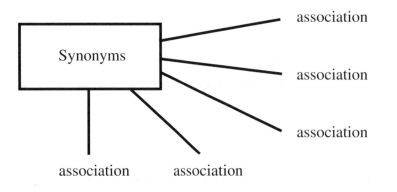

Super Word Web Example

Example: Balsa wood has much buoyancy.

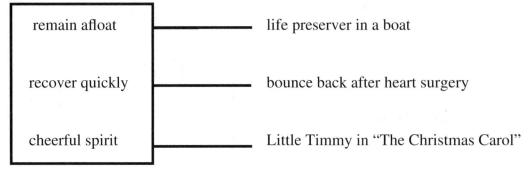

Benefits of the Strategy

- Causes students to relate vocabulary words to their own background of experience
- Increases vocabulary development by expanding the depth and the breadth of word knowledge
- Provides students with an advanced organizer
- Serves as an informational and narrative text pre-reading exercise
- Works as a post-reading activity for narrative and informational text

Reference: Graves, M. (1986). Improving schooling in the 1980's: Toward the non-replication of non-events. *Educational Leadership*, 58 (3), 85-86.

Vocabulary Concept Chain

Why Use the Strategy
The Vocabulary Concept Chain strategy allows students to use prior knowledge when learning new words as well as to connect new learning with the concept being learned. Students are asked to reflect upon a concept learned and the vocabulary words relating to it. The vocabulary words are linked logically or sequentially and circularly forming a Concept Chain. Students are asked to share the organization of the words in the chain. As students share their rationale for organizing the words, their prior knowledge of the words becomes evident. The connection of ideas into a Concept Chain assists students in understanding the concept and aids in retention.

How to Use the Strategy
1) Students study the vocabulary relating to the concept being studied.
2) Students pull forward their prior knowledge about each vocabulary word and determine how the vocabulary words are related.
3) Students organize the words into a Concept Chain by creating a circular set of words.
4) After all of the vocabulary words are placed in the appropriate order, students write a relationship sentence which summarizes how the chain of words expresses the meaning of the concept.

When to Use the Strategy
- Can be used to increase understanding of the relationship between ideas when learning a new concept.
- When students read about a concept from narrative and informational text, the strategy can help them organize related information.

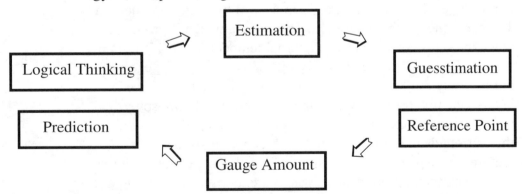

Relationship Sentence: When estimating anything, one must think logically, making a guesstimation using predictions based on realistic reference points.

Link to Assessment
The graphic representation of the concept map with key vocabulary linked in sequential fashion would reveal student understanding of the concept.

Vocabulary Concept Chain Example

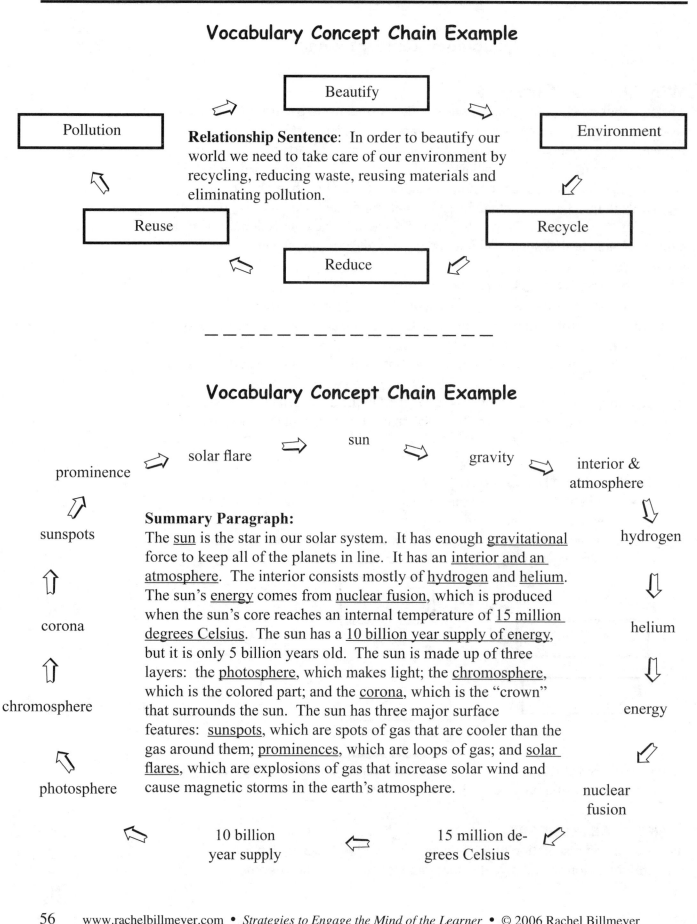

Beautify

Pollution

Environment

Relationship Sentence: In order to beautify our world we need to take care of our environment by recycling, reducing waste, reusing materials and eliminating pollution.

Reuse

Recycle

Reduce

- -

Vocabulary Concept Chain Example

prominence   solar flare   sun   gravity   interior & atmosphere

sunspots

hydrogen

Summary Paragraph:

The sun is the star in our solar system. It has enough gravitational force to keep all of the planets in line. It has an interior and an atmosphere. The interior consists mostly of hydrogen and helium. The sun's energy comes from nuclear fusion, which is produced when the sun's core reaches an internal temperature of 15 million degrees Celsius. The sun has a 10 billion year supply of energy, but it is only 5 billion years old. The sun is made up of three layers: the photosphere, which makes light; the chromosphere, which is the colored part; and the corona, which is the "crown" that surrounds the sun. The sun has three major surface features: sunspots, which are spots of gas that are cooler than the gas around them; prominences, which are loops of gas; and solar flares, which are explosions of gas that increase solar wind and cause magnetic storms in the earth's atmosphere.

corona

helium

chromosphere

energy

photosphere

nuclear fusion

10 billion year supply   15 million degrees Celsius

Word Sorts

Why Use the Strategy

Word Sorts are an effective prereading strategy for activating and sharing prior knowledge. The strategy introduces students to important vocabulary words or phrases in a meaningful way. Word Sorts help students understand the relationship between concepts because they are sorting vocabulary words into similar categories.

There are two kinds of word sorts: open sorts and closed sorts. With an open sort the teacher presents words to the students and asks them, either working alone or in a small group, to categorize the words into meaningful groups. Students select the categories based upon prior knowledge. Open sorts encourage divergent thinking by having the students search for meanings and discover relationships among words. For example, students studying different musical instruments are asked to decide upon meaningful categories and then to classify the word cards accordingly.

With a closed sort the teacher provides the student with the categories. The closed sort reinforces classification skills. A teacher may provide words for different animals and ask the students to classify them into vertebrates and nonvertebrates. Both types of word sorts encourage students to discover similarities in words, set a purpose for reading, and build curiosity.

For younger children Picture Sorts can be used. Students classify the pictures representing key vocabulary words into similar categories.

How to Use the Strategy

1) Select the concept students will study and the critical vocabulary words or phrases students need to know.
2) Prepare sets of word cards and distribute them to pairs of students. Students can create their own set by writing one word or phrase on a 3"x5" card using all of the assigned words.
3) Model the "Open Sort" process by presenting key vocabulary words to the students, asking them to brainstorm possible categories into which the words can be organized. Help the students create meaningful categories and then sort the words accordingly. If a "Closed Sort" is used, present the words and the selected categories to the students and work with them to sort the words.
4) Have students create a set of word cards. If necessary have them work with a partner or in a small group. Direct them to group the word cards into categories that make sense.
5) Organize students with new partners and have them explain their categorized words, as well as the rationale behind their classification system.
6) To increase prior knowledge and to encourage further exploration of concepts being studied, finish the lesson with the entire class sharing.

7) If a Picture Sort is used, some students might be able to copy the vocabulary word on a post-it note and place it on the correct picture. Students can also use the pictures for the Cooperative Retelling strategy (p. 67).

8) Another word sort option is using the following categories:

<u>I know</u>   <u>I sort of know</u>   <u>I don't have a clue</u>

Students categorize their set of words into one of the three categories. Explain to the students that they are responsible for knowing the meaning of each vocabulary word. Next, organize the students into small groups and have them share how they categorized the words. Have the students assign unknown words to each group member. Their task is to learn the words so they can teach the unknown words to other group members. Using an "Open Sort" students classify the known words into meaningful categories. For adept language learners, a list they build for themselves could be more beneficial and useful.

When to Use the Strategy
- When introducing a unit of study, the Word Sort strategy serves as a pre-reading activity.
- The strategy can be used at the end of a unit of study, such as reviewing vocabulary words for a test.
- Word Sorts assist in extending the knowledge base of a concept previously taught.
- The strategy can be used to teach thinking skills, such as classification and deduction.

Link to Assessment
Students can create a set of word cards for several units of study. To test their understanding of the relationship between concepts learned, students can be asked to organize their words into meaningful categories. Students can share their thinking either verbally or in writing.

To make headway, improve your head.

- B. C. Forbes

Section 3 - Literacy Strategies for Narrative and Informative Text: Reading and Writing to Learn

"Adults entering the adult world in the 21st century will read and write more than at any other time in human history. They will need advanced levels of literacy to perform their jobs, run their households, act as citizens, and conduct their personal lives."
- Richard Vacca

Rationale

Generous amounts of purposeful reading, rereading, writing, and talking are the foundation for a trained, powerful mind. A strategic reader is a thinker capable of weighing the meaning of words and articulating ideas with clarity (Schmoker, 2006). How often have you grabbed a pencil to write notes in the margin or discussed the meaning of a selection with a friend? Strategic readers use a variety of reading and writing skills to help them process what they read. When students are encouraged to talk about or write a response to a selection, they express their inner thoughts, interpretations, and connections with prior knowledge and make the knowledge their own. In addition, when students write, teachers can see evidence of thinking and learning as it occurs. Through talking and writing, students integrate content knowledge with personal knowledge.

Heidi Hayes Jacob (2006) insists that each teacher at any grade level in any subject area is a language teacher. This means all teachers must be skilled in helping students listen, speak, read, and write in the subjects they teach. Teachers know that reading and writing must be an integral part of all content area teaching. Why then is it not a more frequent practice in the classroom? Pressured to cover material, teachers have a tendency to assign chapters for students to read but then lecture on the same content and expect students to write verbatim what has been lectured. Teachers are frequently unaware of the multitude of strategies available to improve reading and writing skills in all content areas.

The use of strategies creates strategic readers and writers; students who know how to use the necessary cognitive skills for comprehension. These cognitive skills, often called attributes, include such strategies as predicting, summarizing, or questioning. Attributes guide students' thinking when interacting with text. A variety of strategies incorporate reading and writing attributes. For example, the Learning Log Format (p. 76) facilitates the conscious use of reading attributes, causing students to be active thinkers. In math, students can write out steps for solving an equation or create their own story problem (Problem Solving Plan, p. 88).

Strategies can also serve as assessment tools. If a student successfully completes a Proposition-Support Outline, (p. 91), further testing may not be necessary. Reading and writing are essential modes of communication and part of daily life and work. Students need many opportunities to develop and strengthen their reading and writing talents.

	Page
• Anticipation Guide/Opinion Guide/Prediction Guide . .	61
• Character Map	64
• Cloze Method	65
• Cooperative Retelling	67
• DRTA - Directed Reading/Thinking Activity . .	69
• Group Summarizing	71
• K-W-L - What I Know, Want to Know, Learned . .	73
• Learning Log Format	76
• Look for the Signals	80
• Pairs Read	81
• PREP - Preview, Read, Examine, Prompt . . .	83
• Probable Passages	86
• Problem Solving Plan	88
• Proposition/Support Outlines	91
• RAFT - Role, Audience, Format, Topic . . .	95
• Reciprocal Teaching	97
• Save the Last Word for Me	103
• Story Mapping Through Circular Pictures . .	106
• SQ3R - Survey, Question, Read, Recite, Review . .	108
• Summary Wheel	111
• Text Previewing	115
• Text Tagging	118
• Think-Aloud	120
• Thinking from Different Perspectives . . .	122
• Window Pane Summary	126
• Write to Learn	129

Anticipation/Opinion Guide Strategy

Why Use the Strategy

The Anticipation/Opinion Guide (Herber, 1978) activates prior knowledge and promotes purposeful reading. The guide asks students to formulate thoughts and opinions about the concept to be studied before (and often after) they read. An Anticipation/Opinion Guide allows the teacher to detect misconceptions students have about the concept to be learned. This strategy promotes active reading and critical thinking during reading. Students read to gather support for their opinions. After reading, a discussion can focus on those areas where students may have changed their minds or have discovered additional information. The postreading discussion allows students to share what they learned and encourages further exploration (Rasinski, 2000).

How to Use the Strategy

1) Select the content students will study and decide how the concepts within the unit of study might support or challenge their thinking.

2) Create three to eight statements that might support or challenge the students about the topic. Statements may focus on main ideas, supporting details, possible misconceptions or controversial ideas. Avoid simple questions like, "What color is the horse?" to avoid skimming for answers rather than reading for meaning.

3) Create a worksheet listing the statements in the order in which evidence or possible answers emerge in the reading.

4) Present the Anticipation/Opinion Guide to students and ask them, working individually or with a partner, to think about each statement, to formulate a written response, and to be prepared to give support for their opinions.

5) After students have formulated responses for each statement, lead a discussion so that students can share their ideas and knowledge with each other.

6) Students read the selection looking for information to support or refute their stated opinions.

7) After reading, students complete the After Reading Column (if included). Students are asked to confirm their original opinions, revise them, or decide what additional information is needed. Some guides ask students to record the correct page number on which the statement is found or to write a written response showing understanding of the concept addressed within the statement. Students may be encouraged to rewrite each statement that was not true in a way that makes it true.

8) Finally, the teacher conducts a class discussion about each statement.

When to Use the Strategy

Use the strategy to:
- Enhance comprehension in any content area. Presenting major concepts as questions focuses students' learning and assists their understanding of the concepts.
- Help students with learning disabilities. It assures them that they know

something about what they will be reading. Talking about specific concepts being studied helps students focus and develop a purpose for reading.

• Prepare students for testing situations in which they must read and answer questions about the selection. The use of the Anticipation/Opinion Guide strategy helps students develop the "looking back" strategy needed in testing.

• Increase awareness and practice modes of thinking which may be prompted by various types of questions. Questions created may be literal (Right There), inferential (Think and Search), or speculative (On My Own) in nature. Each type of question asks the reader to interact with the selection differently.

Link to Assessment

Students are able to confirm or revise their initial opinions with written support. This strategy helps students to examine the text closely while reading and to demonstrate a thorough understanding of the concept studied. When students provide written support for each essential statement using their own words, learning is pushed to a higher level of understanding.

– – – – – – – – – – – – – – – – –

Anticipation Guide Example

Directions: Read each statement about spiders. In the "Before" column, check the ones you agree with. Be ready to explain your thinking.

Before		*After*	*Page/s*
_____	1) Spiders are insects.	_____	_____
_____	2) Spiders can move in any direction.	_____	_____
_____	3) Spiders have eight eyes and eight legs.	_____	_____
_____	4) Spiders are helpful.	_____	_____
_____	5) Some spiders can float through the air.	_____	_____
_____	6) Spiders use the same webs over and over.	_____	_____
_____	7) The silk in spider webs is stronger than iron.	_____	_____
_____	8) The silk in spider webs has been used in microscopes and telescopes.	_____	_____
_____	9) Spiders won't bite unless they are disturbed.	_____	_____

Directions: Now that you've read about spiders, read the statements again. This time check the statements you agree with in the "After" column. Then in the "Pages" column, write down the page or pages in the book that helped you decide. Again, be ready to explain your thinking.

Anticipation Guide Example

American History

Directions: Before you read Chapter 3, read the statements and mark the following statements as True or False. After you read the chapter, reread the statements. Using your new knowledge, mark the statements again as True or False. Write the page number where you found the answer and a summary statement on the lines below to support your answer.

Before you read   *After you read*

   True   False   *True   False*

_____ _____   1) The Navigation Acts were made by England   _____ _____
                          to control the colonies' trade with other countries.

_____ _____   2) The colonies wanted to be dependent on their   _____ _____
                          mother country, England.

_____ _____   3) Colonial settlers moved westward to the Ohio   _____ _____
                          Valley because it was good for farming.

_____ _____   4) France and England fought against the colonies   _____ _____
                          in the French and Indian War.

_____ _____   5) England won the war because they had more   _____ _____
                          people and were helped by the Native Americans.

Evidence #1: p.48 *The Navigation Acts were passed in 1660-1665 to control colonial trade with France.*

Evidence #2: p. 47 *Colonies wanted to be independent of England.*

Evidence #3: p. 49 *Americans went to the Ohio Valley because of fertile lands.*

Evidence #4: p. 50 *France and England fought against each other.*

Evidence #5: p. 52 *England won the war because they were more prepared and had better weapons.*

Why Use the Strategy

Character Maps help students develop a thorough understanding of the characters in a story and the actions they take. A character map instructs the student to identify major character traits and to construct a summary statement about the traits. Students of all ages need opportunities to summarize information read. The strategy helps students read between the lines and reinforces the reading attribute "summarizes information read" (Billmeyer, 2006). Character maps can be used in any subject area where characters are presented, and students of all ages find them beneficial and fun. The map can be created during reading or after reading the selection. The visual image of the character fosters better retention.

How to Use the Strategy

1) Determine the selection for students to read.
2) Decide if students are to create the character map while they read the selection or after the selection has been read. Students can draw their own characters, have their own body traced for the character map, or use a pre-drawn map.
3) Decide if students will read the selection independently, with a friend, or listen while it is read to them.
4) Instruct students to write the character's name at the top of the map. On the descriptor lines students record facts, traits, properties, or qualities about the character.
6) To summarize learnings about the character, students create a comprehensive sentence and write it at the bottom of the character map. To expand thinking, students can construct a descriptive paragraph about the character.
7) If the story has more than one central character, students can complete a character map for each one. The data from both maps can be used in a comparison activity or as a summary writing activity.
8) Provide time for students to share and compare their Character Maps.

When to Use the Strategy

Character Maps can be used in any content area. For example, in history character maps can be created of the presidents, in science of famous inventors, in art they can be used to describe artists, or in music, famous composers. The most frequent use of Character Maps is in Language Arts/English while reading fiction or biography. Students can use them instead of the typical book report or story summary.

Link to Assessment

The completion of a Character Map which includes a descriptive paragraph can provide valuable assessment information. Students can create a "reference log" of important people studied throughout the entire school year. A synopsis report could be used as a cumulative assessment task.

Cloze Method

Why Use the Strategy

Cloze Method is a strategy which assesses understanding of a passage read. The reader uses context clues to identify words they need to know for comprehension and tries to figure out unfamiliar words they have heard but may not have seen in print. The reader uses meaning within the passage and sentence along with their own knowledge to predict the unknown word. For example, consider the following sentence:

> "I am out of bread and milk so I need to go to the s_____."
> Readers can identify the unknown word by combining the information in the sentence with what they know about buying food. Given this information the reader makes the prediction that the unknown word is probably store.

Once students fill in the blanks for the missing words, they share their answers and the various strategies used to predict the correct word. By verbalizing their thinking, the teacher and students learn different ways to figure out new words.

The title "cloze" comes from a psychological understanding that humans need to provide closure or completeness to an incomplete idea or illustration. In the cloze procedure the reader attempts to bring closure to an unfamiliar word or words by using the context clues within the passage. The Cloze Method is a powerful strategy because it helps students use meaningful context and phonics clues for word recognition.

How to Use the Strategy

1) The teacher selects a passage to read. The selection can come from a literature book, poem, basal reader, student created stories, or subject-matter texts. It is important to begin with a passage relatively easy to read and progress to more difficult selections. Teachers can gear the passage to the needs of the students.
2) Next, determine how many deletions are appropriate for the reader. Cloze activities can contain as few as one deletion and up to twenty or more missing words. A determining criteria is level of difficulty for the reader, the more deletions the more difficult the task. It is a good idea to leave the first sentence intact so that readers can establish a mental framework for the passage. To make the task easier for the student, place possible answers next to each blank or list all of the deleted words at the end of the passage.
3) The Cloze Method has different variations; determine the type of deletion system appropriate for the situation. Cloze variations are:
   • Multiple-choice: possible answers are placed next to each blank or there is a listing of all the deleted words at the end of the passage.

He walked toward the_____ (well, sink, refrigerator)
intending to pump himself _____(water, coke, milk) to quench his thirst.
- Partial word deletion: every selected word is partially deleted. Such as only initial consonants, blends, digraphs, or initial vowels are deleted.

"I do love to sit and __ook out the window. Why do I __eed TV
when I have forty-eight apartment windows to watch across
the vacant __ot, and a sliver of Lake Erie?"

or only consonants are given and all vowels are deleted.

"I do love to sit and l____k out the window. Why do I n____d TV
when I have forty-eight apartment windows to watch across
the vacant l__t, and a sliver of Lake Erie?"

Reference: From Fleischman, P. (1997). *Seedfolks.* New York: Harper Collins.
- Systematic word deletion: every nth word is deleted in the passage (every fifth, eighth, or twentieth word is deleted).

"Wayne is my older brother by two _____ and so he thinks
he knows more _____ I can ever know. Miss Halverson,
who _____ eighth grade, told him spring was a _____ of
awakening, but I think she's wrong."

Reference: Paulsen, G. (1989). *The winter room.* New York: Bantam
Doubleday Dell.

4) Introduce the strategy to the students. Begin by modeling the process to them. Once students understand the Cloze Method, they can complete the cloze passage individually or in small groups.

5) After completing the passage, students share their words and discuss the clues they used to make their predictions. Students can share as a large group, small group, or in pairs. The teacher may provide the actual words used by the author.

When to Use the Strategy
The Cloze Method can be used to help students:
- Analyze their use of strategies to determine unknown vocabulary word.
- Learn to use context clues when figuring out unknown words and not rely only on phonetic clues.
- Become familiar with different types of reading selections.
- Determine how important an unknown word is and if they need to know it in order to understand the passage.

Link to Assessment
The Cloze Method is a helpful assessment tool because it helps teachers understand how students approach unknown words. When students verbalize their thinking the teacher and student develop a deeper understanding of the strategies they are using. The Cloze Method helps the reader decide what is hard for them and what comes easily. This strategy relies on self-assessment and develops independent readers.

Cooperative Retelling

Why Use the Strategy

One easy, powerful way to assess whether students are able to understand and reconstruct meaning of a selection they read is to have them retell the story. Retelling provides opportunities for students to synthesize, interpret, and personally recast the texts and stories they read. The instructional value of retellings has been well documented with students of various ages and abilities. Practice with retellings results in greater oral language complexity, improved comprehension, and increased awareness of different text structures (Anthony, Johnson, Mickelson, and Preece, 1991).

A cooperative retelling requires students to predict the content of a passage, read the passage, and then retell it in their own words. Students can compare their individual predictions in a cooperative context. When students share in a cooperative context they can check their understanding with that of their group members.

How to Use the Strategy

Prepare
1) Immerse students in the genre which you want them to be able to retell or paraphrase.
2) Select a text which suits the purpose of the retelling. If the focus is on text structure, determine if narrative or informational text is appropriate.
3) Prepare a copy of the text for each student and fold the copy so that only the title is visible.
4) Place students in groups of four to six and have them:
   • Read the title
   • Each write or draw a prediction of what the text might be about
   • List words and phrases they would expect to find in the text
   • Share perceptions

Listen and Read
1) Tell students to unfold their copies and follow along as the teacher reads aloud.
2) Encourage students to reread the text silently as many times as they like.
3) Specify the audience and intent of the retelling.
4) Have students put text away and work on their own to retell the text in writing without looking back.
5) Remind the students to write quickly.

Share and Compare in Pairs
1) Have the students compare and contrast their retellings, looking for similarities, differences, paraphrases, and confusions.

2) Provide prompt questions which support rather than criticize one another such as:
- What did I leave out that is different from what you did not include?
- Why did you not include this part?
- Does leaving something out change the meaning?

Write a Collaborative Retelling
1) Have students return to their groups and write the best possible group product drawing upon the strengths of each other's original work.
2) If students are not proficient writers have them present their retellings orally through a dramatization or with pictures.

When to Use the Strategy

Cooperative retelling should be used with students who have a grasp of the reading and writing processes. The strategy can be used with all genres and is effective whenever it is appropriate for students to paraphrase their understandings of a text. It works well with informational text and can be used to highlight specific vocabulary, structures, and features of texts found in particular content area. It assists readers in identifying authors' organizational patterns such as time-lapse, near to far, cause-effect, or step-by-step process.

Link to Assessment

When used as an assessment technique, retellings can be richly informative. However, the students should become familiar with what is expected of them during a retelling, and have practiced to gain experience with the procedure before retellings are used for assessment purposes.

Teachers can use both the process and the product of a cooperative retelling as tools for evaluation. It is important that teachers collect data on retellings over a period of time and not make judgments about readers based on one telling.

DRTA - Directed Reading/Thinking Activity

Why Use the Strategy

The Directed Reading/Thinking Activity (Moore, Readence, and Rickelman, 1982) helps the reader prepare for reading by activating prior knowledge about the topic to be read and assisting in making predictions. This prethinking is a meaningful investment in reading because it establishes a purpose for reading. When a reader reads for an established purpose, it is natural to revise predictions while reading. The Directed Reading/Thinking Activity creates an active mind which then leads to increased comprehension. The reader continually revises, rejects, or confirms predictions about the topic. The learner then completes the DRTA process by recording what has been learned.

How to Use the Strategy

1) Students are given a passage to read. Before reading they are asked to preview the article and pull forward any prior knowledge about the topic. Students record what they know about the topic as they think from two perspectives: what they "Know They Know" and what they "Think They Know."

2) The next step is to make a prediction; record what you "Think You'll Learn." This type of thinking results in meaningful reading because the reader seeks to prove or disprove his or her prediction.

3) Next, students read and reread as necessary to confirm or reject their predictions. Hypotheses are refined as new information is gathered from further reading or from sharing ideas with other students.

4) The last step of the DRTA asks the learner to reflect on learnings and evidence of learning. The reader records ideas in the "Know You Learned" box, citing evidence from the passage. Students might form an opinion about the passage's topic and record it in the box with a rationale from the passage which supports their opinion.

When to Use the Strategy

The strategy can be used:

- With any narrative or informational selection.
- Instead of the What I Know; Want to Know; Learned strategy for variety.
- When teaching students about "predicting" or "establishing purpose" for reading.
- When students are asked to work in small groups to complete a reading task. DRTA helps them pool their prior knowledge about a topic to be studied and to establish a purpose for their work. The culmination is a collaboration of what they learned about the topic.

Link to Assessment

The DRTA strategy helps students to mentally engage with the new topic and emphasizes key reading attributes of prior knowledge, predicting, questioning, and assessing learning.

DRTA - Directed Reading/Thinking Activity

What I know I know:

What I think I know:

What I think I'll learn:

What I know I learned:

Moore, Readence, and Rickelman, 1982

www.rachelbillmeyer.com • *Strategies to Engage the Mind of the Learner* • © 2006 Rachel Billmeyer

Group Summarizing

Why Use the Strategy
Group Summarizing (Brown, Day, and Jones, 1983) is a strategy that requires students to understand and condense information read. The strategy helps students remember the important ideas of a selection, as well as practice the reading attribute "summarizes information read" (Billmeyer, 2006). Summarizing can be a difficult skill for students because it requires them to look beyond the individual trees to see the forest. Students benefit from teacher support and modeling in the use of this strategy.

How to Use the Strategy
1) Before reading, determine the important ideas presented in the selection. For example, if reading about colonization, students can read for descriptions of the colony, problems encountered, people, and reasons for colonization.
2) List the important ideas on a class chart divided into four sections ("Descriptions of Colony," "Problems," "People," and "Reasons for Colonization"). The charted ideas will remind students of their purposes for reading.
3) After reading the selection alone or with a partner, have students write ideas on the class chart. Class discussion is essential during this process in order to attain complete and accurate summaries.
4) Write summaries and share them with the class.

When to Use the Strategy
- Teachers from all content areas find this strategy beneficial when teaching students how to summarize information.
- The strategy can build cooperation among students. They need to work together in order to develop an accurate and complete summary.
- In social studies often more information is shared than needed. This strategy helps students focus on the main topic and critical components of the main topic as they read.

Link to Assessment
Using this strategy, students should be able to write or tell the summary of the selection read which includes all important information.

Description of Colony

By James River
On Peninsula
Named for King James I

The colonists settled along the James River on a peninsula. They named their settlement Jamestown after their King, James I.

People

Captain John Smith
Pocahontas

John Smith went to the Indians to trade for food. The Chief's daughter, Pocahontas, saved him from death and brought food to the colonists. Smith then took charge of Jamestown and ordered all men to work for their food.

Problems

Swampy land
Mosquitoes
Lack of food
Relations with Indians
Lack of work

Jamestown was built on low, swampy ground and the settlers caught many diseases from the mosquitoes. Their main concern was looking for gold. They did not know how to find their own food or plant crops.

Reasons for Settlement

London merchants sold stock
Share cost of colony
Company paid for travel
Colonists would repay in gold

London merchants wanted to make money by establishing colony in America. They sold shares of stock in their company in order to share the cost of starting a colony. They promised to pay the way to America in return for shares of any gold the colonists found.

K-W-L - What I Know; Want to Know; Learned

Why Use the Strategy

K-W-L is a strategy used to increase reading comprehension by asking students to identify what they already know about a topic and what they want to know prior to reading. This strategy helps the reader make predictions and connect new information with prior knowledge (Ogle, 1989). From the "What I Know" column the teacher can detect gaps or misconceptions students may have about the topic to be learned. When readers determine what they "Want to Know" about the selection, they are setting goals which help them focus while reading. Writing what they want to know in the form of a question creates a questioning mind. The "What I Learned" column provides an opportunity for reflection after reading and assists students in assessing the accuracy of their knowledge.

How to Use the Strategy

1) As an individual or small group, students receive a prepared handout with three columns labeled K-W-L. As a large group activity three chart papers are prepared with three columns labeled K-W-L. Large chart paper examples may be displayed throughout the unit of study.

2) The strategy begins with the students identifying everything they "Know" (or think they know) about the topic selected for reading. For example, before beginning a unit of study on endangered animals, students would record in the "K" column what they already know about that topic. As information is recorded, ideas can be categorized. Helping readers learn how to categorize information assists in retention.

3) The second step asks the reader to set a goal. The students are directed to write what they "Want to Learn" about the topic. Students could write their statement as a question. Sample questions might include: "What are recent discoveries about endangered animals?" or "What is causing the dolphin and bald eagle to be on an endangered animals list?"

4) Have students read the selection trying to answer the questions recorded in the "W" column. Upon completion of the reading task, students should identify all of the new information they learned about the topic and record it in the "L" (What I Learned) column. If the selection is long, students are encouraged to return to their K-W-L form periodically while reading to record new learning and/or answers to their questions. Intentional thinking and recording during reading assists in comprehension. During this phase of the learning process, students may realize that what they thought they knew about the topic was incorrect. Corrected learning is recorded in the "L" column.

When to Use the Strategy

- When introducing students to the idea of using reading strategies to help with understanding of content, the K-W-L strategy is an easy one to use. Several reading attributes (predicting, questioning, and assessing learning) are highlighted in the strategy, making it a powerful one.
- When students are unfamiliar with a topic to be studied, the K-W-L strategy used in a large group allows prior knowledge from all the learners to be pooled and used by all. Determining as a class what topics might be learned can lower anxiety and help learners to work together to find answers to their questions.
- Because learning is cumulative in nature, the K-W-L is also a useful learning strategy for students who are involved in interdisciplinary classes or units of study. For example, K-W-L generated learnings about the concept of population density in social studies might also be used in the study of that concept in science class.

Link to Assessment

Comparing the "What I Know" section used at the beginning of study with the "What I Learned" section at the end of study provides a visual representation of how much students have learned.

K-W-L Example
Mystery Photo

Know	Think	What	Learned
Describe what you know about the mystery photo.	Record what you think the mystery photo may be linked to.	Identify what you need to do to make an educated guess. Tell what topics and references you used to develop your guess.	Identify what you learned is important about the mystery photo.

K-W-L CHART

What I Know	What I Want to Know	What I Learned

Ogle, 1989

Learning Log Format

Why Use the Strategy

Strategic Readers work actively to monitor reading before, during, and after reading. They know that focusing on specific reading attributes/skills during the reading process strengthens understanding. For example, the attribute "establishing purpose for reading" (Billmeyer, 2006) forces readers to be clear about why they are reading the passage as well as the outcome after reading. Reading attributes frequently used on standardized tests are: distinguishes story elements, attributes meaning to symbols, distinguishes main idea, makes predictions, builds on prior knowledge, draws conclusions, makes inferences, summarizes information read, judges the effectiveness of word choice, and detects bias. The Learning Log Format facilitates the conscious use of reading skills which causes students to be active thinkers and to use the necessary process skills in order to comprehend the passage.

How to Use the Strategy

1) Select a reading passage and read it to determine the types of thinking needed to assist comprehension.

2) Determine the expected outcome. You might ask yourself, "Why do students need to read this passage?" and "How do I want students to think as they read the selection?" Based on those decisions, determine the appropriate reading attributes/skills for each box on the Learning Log Format and type them in or have the students write them. Create the format on chart paper or an overhead transparency to model the process.

3) Explain each reading skill chosen. If a reading attribute is "making a prediction before reading," discuss predictions and give the students twenty seconds to look through the pages they will be reading to examine subtopics, pictures, or bold print. After previewing, ask students to share example prediction statements. Record their ideas in the box on the chart.

4) If students are using individual forms, have them formulate their own prediction statement. If they cannot create their own, invite them to use an example from the chart.

5) Explain the next attribute on the Learning Log. If students are asked to mentally develop questions while reading, the attribute "questions asked while reading" would be recorded in the next box. Ask the students to share an example of a question they have asked themselves while reading a different selection. Record sample questions in the box. Students record their questions during reading.

6) Explain the third attribute selected. For example, "to cause thinking after reading," students might be asked to summarize the information read. They are expected to create a summary statement using their own words, writing in complete sentences. A higher level of processing occurs when students summarize in complete sentences using their own words. If students are not familiar with summary statements, provide practice by summarizing popular movies or songs.

7) The fourth box on the Learning Log Format might require students to react to the passage read. If the selection allows for a personal interpretation, the reading attribute "formulate an opinion with supportive evidence from the passage" (Billmeyer, 2006) is used.

8) Once the attributes chosen for the Learning Log Format are explained, have the students read the selection and complete the remaining boxes. Remind them to revisit their prediction statement to check for accuracy.

When to Use the Strategy

The Learning Log Format supports a thorough understanding of any difficult reading selection. The strategy can promote active thinking before, during, and after reading. The format can replace the "fill-in the blanks" worksheets that students often complete when assigned a chapter in the text. Fill-in-the-blanks worksheets do not encourage students to be readers. Instead, students tend to only look for the correct word or idea to go in the blank. In order to complete the Learning Log Format the student must read and think about the selection.

The strategy is a meaningful way to incorporate writing. The 1998 National Association of Educational Progress (NAEP) results indicated that students who had more opportunity to write demonstrated higher reading performance. The strategy causes intense thinking, processing, and reflecting.

Link to Assessment

The traits and attributes of a strategic reader are effectively assessed with the Learning Log Format. The teacher decides which attributes need to be assessed. Students can complete the log independently and submit it to the teacher as an assessment tool.

The future is not some place
we are going to, but one we are creating.
The paths are not to be found, but made,
and the activity of making them
changes both the maker
and the destination.

- John Schaar

Learning Log Format Example

Subject *Spanish I&II*   **Article** *Ferdinando*
Name   **Pages** *249 - 250*

My prediction for the reading is:	**Questions I am asking myself while reading are:**
It is bull fighting.	*Why was he named Ferdinando?* *Why doesn't the bull want to fight?*
Which reading strategy/strategies did you use to make this prediction? *preview the text*	In the parade procession, what was the order? *Banderilleros, picadores, matador Ferdinando*
A summary statement is: *Ferdinando is a very kind bull who gets put in the bullring and he doesn't want to fight.*	**I am more like** *Matador* **because:** *I am kind and like to get along with people.*

- - - - - - - - - - - - - - - - - -

Learning Log Format Example

Concept - Reading
Name   **Pages -** Chapter 16-19

(Before Reading) My prediction is:	**(During Reading) Questions I am asking myself:**
That Matt's father, mom, and sisters will come home. I think Matt and his his mother will read stories out of the Bible to Attean. I also think Attean will understand the alphabet better.	*How did Matt kill the bear? Why did Attean's grandmother not like the white man? Why did Matt read stories to Attean?*
(After Reading) A summary statement is: *In chapters 16-19 Matt got invited to go to the Indian celebration for Attean's killing the bear. The main part was when Matt noticed Attean's dog in a trap so he ran to the Indians for help and they saved Attean's dog.*	**(After Reading) If I could change one thing......** *I would change the part where the dog was in the trap. I would change that part because the dog got hurt and also because Attean wasn't there to save his own dog.*

Learning Log Format
(add appropriate reading attributes/skills)

Subject_____ **Article**_____

Name _____ **Pages** _____

Why Use the Strategy

Look for the Signals (Opitz and Rasinski,1998) strategy helps students pay attention to text features that support comprehension. Metacognitive research tells us that readers perform better when they are conscious of the purpose and use of the conventions of print. Readers also make use of those features more consistently in the context of reading passages as opposed to learning the conventions of print out of context.

How to Use the Strategy

Typographical signals help readers better understand an author's intended message. Question marks, for example, signal the need to raise intonation at the end of the sentence to create the intended meaning. To demonstrate the procedure, the teacher selects specific sentences within a text and shows students how typographic signals, such as punctuation marks, large and bold print, underlining, and italics convey meaning.

When to Use the Strategy

This strategy fits well with both Shared Reading and Guided Reading sessions. Students encounter the "signals" during shared reading and gain an awareness of their presence and purpose. Mini-lessons for instruction and practice enhance this understanding in the Guided Reading sessions, and finally, students internalize the use of the signals in their independent reading.

Link to Assessment

Look for the Signals, as an assessment strategy, serves the purpose of diagnosis and development more than for the purpose of a summative assessment or grading. Students can show what they know about the signals over time. The students can record their knowledge and comfort level on a self-assessment recording form, or the teacher can periodically check for understanding.

Pairs Read

Why Use the Strategy
Students are able to support each other's learning with the Pairs Read strategy. Working in pairs, students read the text aloud to each other. By working together they increase their understanding of the selection read. While one student reads a section aloud, the other student listens carefully in order to summarize the main idea of what was heard. Students find the Pairs Read strategy especially helpful when a selection is hard to understand.

How to Use the Strategy
Choice 1 - Read to Understand
1) The teacher determines the selection to be read with a partner.
2) Students work in pairs with one student as the reader and the other assuming the role of the listener. Depending upon learning style, the listener may or may not read along silently with the text in front of him. Auditory processors have a tendency to listen while kinesthetic learners read along and highlight main points.
3) The reader reads the first section aloud to the listener. The length of each section to be read aloud is determined by the difficulty of the selection. The more difficult the selection, the greater the need to divide the reading into shorter sections so that students can stop to summarize their understandings more often.
4) The listener summarizes the main idea of the section read. For better understanding the listener and the reader paraphrase and discuss ideas learned. Encouraging students to develop examples relating to the topic increases comprehension.
5) Students then reverse roles and the new reader reads the next section aloud and the listener summarizes the main idea. Students continue to alternate the reading and listening until the entire selection is read.
6) After the selection is read, each pair cooperatively summarizes in writing the main idea of the entire selection. Students are encouraged to create their written summary in any format, for example, graphic organizer or paragraph.

Choice 2 - Read to Analyze
1) Determine the selection to be read with a partner.
2) Students work in pairs with one student as the reader and the other assuming the role of coaching partner.
3) Each student in the pair reads the first paragraph silently. The length of each section to be read silently is determined by the difficulty of the selection. Students might stop in the middle of the paragraph to discuss the hard to understand ideas.
4) The reader summarizes the main idea of the section read aloud. To push for analytical thinking, the coaching partner asks clarifying, probing, and inferential questions.
5) Students reverse roles and both read the next section silently. The reader summarizes for the coaching partner with the coaching partner asking questions.

6) Continue reading, summarizing, and asking analytical questions for the entire selection. For example:

"As you see Joe's behavior, what do you believe he is feeling?"
  • Reader must identify various actions and/or behaviors.
  • Reader must see a pattern.
  • Reader must connect evidence to identify mood.

OR

"Considering the essayist's comments on nuclear power, do you think she is a proponent or opponent of building more nuclear power plants?"

7) After the selection is read, students cooperatively summarize in writing the main idea of the entire selection. Students are encouraged to create their written summary in any format, for example, graphic organizer or paragraph. To extend thinking, students can develop analytical questions for class discussion.

When to Use the Strategy
  • The Pairs Read strategy is beneficial when reading technical material.
  • Science teachers find the strategy helpful for students when learning difficult science concepts.
  • Students with disabilities enjoy and learn from reading aloud with a student more knowledgeable in the subject area.
  • When reading plays or poetry, students may grasp the meaning of the selection easier if it is read aloud. They also enjoy working with a partner to increase their understanding.
  • Assists students' comprehension when reading narrative selections.

Link to Assessment
The written summary statements display clear understanding of the concepts that have been learned. Summary statements of each section could also be written and turned in with the final summary statement.

PREP- Preview, Read, Examine, Prompt

How to Use the Strategy

1) <u>Preview</u>

The PREP (Langer, 1981) strategy begins by having the students preview the selection to be read. Create a road map of the selection by having the students examine the title, pictures, charts and graphs, and headings or subheadings. Have the students read the first and last paragraphs to strengthen their purpose for reading. Students complete a Pre-Reading Plan or a Learning Guide. The Learning Guide instructs the students to construct questions before reading. The questions keep the learner mentally engaged and also focuses their thinking while reading. Creating questions before reading is not an easy task for students. Questioning is made easier with prompt words like who, what, how, why, when, and where. Teacher modeling and eliciting examples of questions from the entire class help students get started.

2) <u>Read</u>

The second step involves reading the selection and completing the Pre-Reading Plan. The Pre-Reading Plan or Learning Guide facilitates meaningful note taking while reading.

3) <u>Examine</u>

This step causes the students to examine the work for clarity and understanding. They revisit their questions and answers recorded while reading and elaborate on their answers. Teachers find that students who write questions before reading are more engaged in the class discussion after reading and ask more questions about what they read.

4) <u>Prompt</u>

The final step is designed to help the students remember what they read. They used the completed Pre-Reading Plan or a Learning Guide as a memory prompt. Students can use their completed Reading Plans to facilitate discussion in small groups.

Benefits of the Strategy

- Helps students organize and retain information through note taking
- Causes students to use before, during, and after reading skills
- Activates and extends prior knowledge
- Incorporates meaningful class discussion

Pre-Reading Plan

Name Subject

Title of selection:

Type of text:

What I know about myself when I read this type of text:

Topic of study:

What I know about this topic:

My purpose for reading:

What I expect to learn about the topic:

A summary of my learnings about this topic:

Learning Guide

Name
Name of Selection
Topic

Pages _____

Before Reading

What I already know . . . .

During Reading

Questions I have to focus my learning . . .

After Reading

What I have learned . .

Probable Passages

How to Use the Strategy

1) Select a story for the class to read and determine the important vocabulary words students must know.

2) Review the story elements: setting, characters, problems, solution, and ending. To enhance retention attach pictures to each element. (See sample)

3) Teach the vocabulary words to the students and then have them categorize the words according to the story elements.

Probable Passages

Story Elements

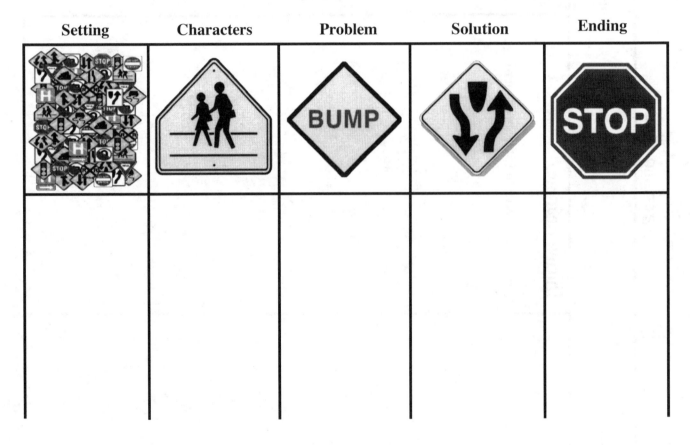

Setting	Characters	Problem	Solution	Ending

4) Next have the students write a Probable Passage (Wood, 1988) by using the words from each category in a story frame.

Story Frame Example

The story takes place _____

The characters are _____

A problem occurs when _____

_____ solves the problem by _____

The story ends _____

5) Have the students read the story or read it aloud to them. As the story is read, have them compare it to their Probable Passage. Instruct students to modify their predicted story by writing a new summary paragraph including all the story elements.

Benefits of the Strategy
- Teaches pre-reading and pre-writing skills
- Incorporates important vocabulary in a meaningful way before reading
- Reinforces the story frame concept of before, during, and after reading
- Reviews the story elements with meaningful symbols
- Develops independent readers and writers

Story Frame Example

The story takes place *in the tree houses in the backyard. Chrissy* is a character

who *has a tree house and put a Keep Out sign on the door*. A problem occurs

when *hurt feelings started.* The story ends when *they are friends again and*

then they make a bridge.

The Story

The Tree House

The story takes place in the backyards of Chrissy and Leah's house. Chrissy is a character who gets in a fight with Leah because Chrissy told Leah she couldn't come in her tree house. Chrissy said, "My house is better than your house" and then they said, "I hate you!" to each other. A problem occurs when hurt feelings started. "I don't like what you said, Chrissy." "I don't like you either, good-bye!" The story ends when they are friends again and then they make a bridge to each other's houses.

Why Use the Strategy

When students read a math problem as if it were a short story, the problem becomes a meaningful passage (Braselton and Decker, 1994). The Problem Solving Plan makes problem solving easier for students because they use prior knowledge to construct meaning. The plan consists of a five-step process and is represented as a graphic organizer in the shape of a diamond. The brain loves pictures, and the visual representation for problem solving is a powerful learning and memory device.

How to Use the Strategy

1) Explain the five-step problem-solving process.
   - Restate the problem as if it were a story.
   - Determine what information is critical for solving the problem.
   - Draft a plan to solve the problem.
   - Follow the steps to reach the answer.
   - Check the answer to be sure it makes sense.

2) Use an overhead copy of the problem-solving graphic organizer to explain the importance of the diamond shape to the students. Say that all problems begin with information (top of the diamond) and end with solution to the problem (bottom of the diamond). The middle of the diamond shape is expansive to correlate with thinking. Students use different steps based on their experiences and reasoning skills to solve the problem, and in the process their thinking expands.

3) Review the five steps as stated on the graphic organizer.

4) Use the four-steps of modeling to teach the problem solving process.

        Step 1: I will do it!
        Step 2: You help me!
        Step 3: I will help you!
        Step 4: You do it!

Step 1: I will do it! Display the first word problem on an overhead and read it aloud to the students. Thinking aloud, model the process for solving the problem using the five steps. Begin by translating the problem into a "story" relating it to prior knowledge. If necessary, restate the problem several different ways. Next, underline the information in the problem that is critical for finding the solution. Referring to the underlined information, explain the steps in the problem solving process. It is important to model different ways to solve a problem so students realize there is not only one correct set of steps. Emphasize that students can think in different ways and still get the correct answer. Once the problem is solved and the answer is recorded, state why the answer makes sense.

5) Using an overhead of the diamond-shaped graphic organizer, record thinking for the five steps. Have the students talk through each step of the process with a partner.

6) **Step 2: You help me!** Ask the students for their assistance in solving the next word problem. Record productive ideas on the overhead of the diamond-shaped graphic organizer. Again, have the students talk through each step of the process with a partner.

7) **Step 3: I will help you!** Have the students, working with their partner, complete another problem. Give each pair a copy of the diamond-shaped graphic organizer. Monitor student progress as they solve the problem, providing assistance when necessary.

8) To reinforce the idea that students think differently when solving problems, provide them an opportunity to explain their problem solving steps to another pair.

9) **Step 4: You do it!** Assign several more problems for the students to complete.

10) Throughout the week, review the Five-Step Problem Solving strategy. Remind the students that the purpose of the graphic organizer is to guide their thinking. The goal is to be able to solve word problems without a guide.

When to Use the Strategy

The Problem Solving Plan strategy can be used with any math problem at any grade level. In science use it when completing experiments, in physical education when figuring out a game, or use it when solving a discipline problem.

Link to Assessment

Students need to know how to think when solving problems. Each student's thinking can be analyzed and assessed with this strategy. The graphic organizer can serve as an assessment tool.

Problem Solving Plan Example

Problem: Ellen works 3 hours a day 7 days a week.
             How many hours does she work in a half year (26 weeks)?

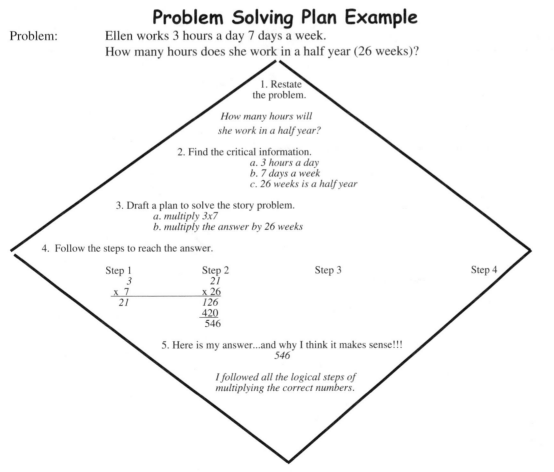

1. Restate the problem.

How many hours will she work in a half year?

2. Find the critical information.
   a. 3 hours a day
   b. 7 days a week
   c. 26 weeks is a half year

3. Draft a plan to solve the story problem.
   a. multiply 3x7
   b. multiply the answer by 26 weeks

4. Follow the steps to reach the answer.

Step 1	Step 2	Step 3	Step 4
3	*21*		
x 7	*x 26*		
21	*126*		
	420		
	546		

5. Here is my answer...and why I think it makes sense!!!
   546

I followed all the logical steps of multiplying the correct numbers.

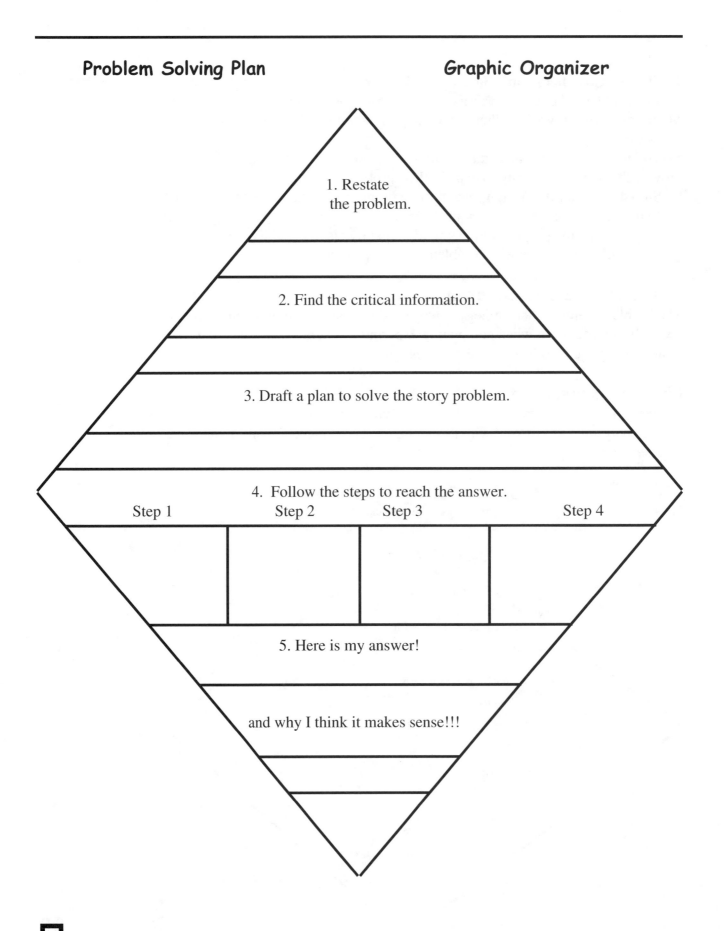

1. Restate
the problem.

2. Find the critical information.

3. Draft a plan to solve the story problem.

4. Follow the steps to reach the answer.

Step 1   Step 2   Step 3   Step 4

5. Here is my answer!

and why I think it makes sense!!!

Proposition/Support Outlines

Why Use the Strategy

Proposition/Support Outlines (Santa, 1988 & Buehl, 2001) teach students how to support a proposition with evidence. When reading the editorial section in the newspaper you find authors offering various propositions with convincing or not so convincing support. This strategy provides students with a framework so they can analyze the types of justifications (facts, examples, scenarios....) authors use to support their proposition. As a result, students develop critical reading skills.

Proposition/Support Outlines used before, during, or after reading help students organize their thinking, writing, and ideas for a discussion. The outline offers students an organizational framework when working on an independent research project. Students are encouraged to collect evidence in five different areas: facts, statistics, examples, expert authority, and logic/reasoning.

How to Use the Strategy

1) Begin the lesson with a discussion about the difference between facts and opinions. Brainstorm a list of examples stating why it is a fact or an opinion. "George W. Bush is the 43rd President of the United States," is a factual statement. "President Bush is a great leader," is an opinion. Reinforce that facts can be proven to be true or not true.

2) Explain the term proposition as "an idea claimed to be true." Model the process of developing proposition or opinion statements. Examples include:
- *Rain forests in the world need to be preserved.*
- *Schools need more financial support for technology-based curriculum.*
- *The bald eagle should be removed from the threatened species list.*
- *Dogs make the best pets.*
- *Student fees should not be charged for participation in school initiated activities.*

Model how to create an argument supporting one of the listed propositions. Have students generate defensible arguments supporting a proposition.

3) Explain the five areas of support represented in the Proposition/Support Outline using an overhead transparency. Have students organize the proposition statements into the correct areas.

4) Assign students an article with the proposition/support framework. As a group determine the proposition statement. Working with a partner, have them read the article and complete the outline.

5) Pair students with a new partner and instruct them to share their completed outlines. Encourage them to discuss their rationale for the recorded support statements.

6) Once the outlines are shared, model how to construct a summary paragraph based on the proposition statement and supporting evidence. Students work with their partner to complete the summary paragraph.

7) Show students how to analyze their summary paragraph using the following checklist:
- Is my proposition clear?
- Did I include evidence for all of the assigned areas?
- Is my strongest argument written in a convincing manner?
- Is my convincing argument at the beginning of the paragraph?
- Did I include the necessary facts in an order that is easy for the reader to understand?

8) Provide opportunities for students to develop their own proposition statements. Once they feel comfortable formulating propositions, they are ready to use the Proposition/Support Outline independently.

9) Brainstorm with the students situations in which they might be able to use the strategy.

When to Use the Strategy

Proposition/Support Outlines are useful in a variety of subject areas, especially with issue-related content. Language arts, science, and social studies teachers find this strategy extremely helpful. The outline can be simplified for elementary students by eliminating the statistics and logic/reasoning sections. Teachers use the outline as a prewriting activity to prepare students for the Constructed Response sections on state assessments.

Link to Assessment

The outline can be used to assess students' analytical-thinking abilities. After reading the assigned selections about a topic, they can record justifiable evidence for the areas listed. Students can use the outline format when writing their response to a test question that asks for their opinion about the topic.

Proposition/Support Outline Example

Topic: Reintroduction of wolves to Yellowstone National Park

Proposition: Ranchers should not worry about threats from the wolves in YNP

Support:	**1) Facts** • *Presence of wolves could shut down mining, grazing, timber operation* • *Ranchers let sheep and cattle graze with federal permit* • *No cases on record of healthy wolves attacking and killing humans* **2) Examples** • *Suzanne Laverty (program director in Boise for the Wolf Education and Research Center) said they are not trying to shut down forest use.* **3) Expert Authority** • *"We don't fear a few wolves back in our wilderness area," said W.C.Greg Nelson, director of public affairs for the Idaho Farm Bureau.* **4) Statistics** • *100 wolves to Idaho, Wyoming, Minnesota* • *66% of land owned by government (destroying forest)* • *Between 1600 - 1950, 2 million wolves killed* • *Almost killing off all wolves in 48 states* **5) Logic/Reasoning** • *After sixty years, Colorado heard the call of the wild from the wolves being reintroduced. Later, an article from Julie Anderson said that a wolf which was not a part of the program was poisoned.*

Proposition/Support Outline

Topic:

Proposition:

Support: **1) Facts**

2) Examples

3) Expert Authority

4) Statistics

5) Logic/Reasoning

RAFT - Role, Audience, Format, Topic

Why Use the Strategy

The RAFT (Santa, 1988) strategy offers a meaningful way to incorporate writing in all content areas. While using this strategy, students are required to read and write from a perspective other than their own to an audience other than the teacher. They do this using a creative format. RAFT, an acronym, means:

R - Role of Writer - Who are you as the writer? *gardener, chef, plant, lawyer*

A - Audience - To whom are you writing? *tourists, public, sun, editor*

F - Format - What format will you use? *poem, recipe, letter, editorial*

T - Topic - What topic have you chosen? *support botanical gardens, persuade owners to try a new menu, beg for relief, demand payment*

Students who use the RAFT strategy learn more content because they actively interact with the information at a higher level of cognitive processing. In turn, the RAFT strategy develops motivated writers by allowing them to be creative and react on a personal level. It provides students with a structured organizational pattern for writing. When students use the RAFT strategy, they examine information from different perspectives which causes them to think about the content in new and different ways.

How to Use the Strategy

1) Select a unit of study and determine the important information students need to know. Analyze the information for possible writing assignments and consider how writing would increase learning. For example, writing from the perspective of different characters in *The Settling of the West* may cause students to be more empathic, or writing about the circulatory system may increase understanding.

2) Share with students the unit of study. Preview with them the information they will read. Discuss with students their prior knowledge about the topic.

3) Explain the purpose of the RAFT strategy to the students. Write what the acronym RAFT represents on chart paper or a chalk board and share examples for each of the four components. Writing is easier if the fourth component, Topic, includes descriptive verbs to help explain the purpose for writing about the topic. Descriptive verbs include: beg, convince, demand, persuade, plead, refute, support, and warn.

4) Brainstorm possible roles students could assume when writing about the topic. List ideas on the chalkboard or chart paper. Roles related to *The Settling of the West* could include problems the Indians and the pioneers faced. Continue to brainstorm ideas for audience, format of writing, and topic to be addressed when writing. Remember to emphasize the use of descriptive verbs with the topic.

5) After discussing the topic and/or students have completed the reading assignment about the topic, have them select one of the examples to write about.

6) Provide time for students to share how the RAFT strategy increased their learning by sharing their written selections with each other.

When to Use the Strategy

The RAFT strategy is appropriate for all content areas, including science, math, and social studies. The strategy can be used at the beginning of a lesson to activate prior knowledge (Cook, 1989). Students can use this strategy to create a written summary of their learnings about any topic. This strategy also works with young children. They are capable of thinking from different perspectives and their ideas can be recorded by the teacher or an older student.

Link to Assessment

The strategy provides meaningful ways to incorporate writing when assessing students' knowledge about a particular topic.

RAFT Writing Activities Examples

Role	Audience	Format	Topic
measuring cup	chefs or cooks	recipe	express importance of measurement
son	dad	poem	persuade people of pitfalls of alcoholism
puppy	caretaker	song	recommendations for a happy existence
banana	fruit	travel guide	explain travels through digestive system
lungs	smokers	TV commercial	convince people to stop smoking
criminal	jury	brief	explain why innocent
scientist	public	news release	warn about hazards of forest fires
columnist	senators	news column	demand gun control

 www.rachelbillmeyer.com • *Strategies to Engage the Mind of the Learner* • © 2006 Rachel Billmeyer

Reciprocal Teaching

Why Use the Strategy

Reciprocal Teaching (Palinscar, A. & Brown, A., 1984) strategy promotes self-directed, content area learning. The strategy teaches students how to study and learn from challenging text. Students who use the reciprocal teaching strategy demonstrate greater ability to independently answer comprehension questions and to summarize the main idea of the selection.

Reciprocal Teaching is an interactive dialogue between the teacher and the students or among students in small groups as they read a selected text. Four strategic reading attributes are extensively taught when using this strategy:

- **predicting** what the segment is about,
- **generating questions** about the selection,
- **clarifying** difficult concepts, vocabulary words, and
- **summarizing** the main points.

The strategy is a series of steps first used by the teacher to model the process and later by students to follow the teacher's example in serving as a discussion leader with the large group or in small groups. It is a teacher-intensive procedure, and the success of a reciprocal teaching lesson depends on the teacher's ability to model how a strategic reader uses the four reading attributes to comprehend text. The four skills do not flow in any special order. They are incorporated as necessary to comprehend the passage.

Reciprocal teaching is a powerful strategy because it uses the four reading attributes as a foundation for conversation about the passage. Just because students can explain reading skills does not mean that they can use them effectively to comprehend text. In reciprocal teaching, students have an interactive conversation about their predictions, ideas they need clarified, their summaries of the main points, or questions to enhance thinking.

How to Use the Strategy

1) Anticipate any problems that may exist in learning the new information, for example, difficult vocabulary, unexpected concepts, or misconceptions. Share the text difficulties with students and the rationale for using the strategy.

2) Give an overall description of the Reciprocal Teaching strategy and an explanation of the four comprehension skills:

    • **Predicting -** the readers use background information to forecast where the text is going next. Reading to prove or disprove a prediction provides a purpose for reading. Examining the text clues, such as headings, subheadings, and questions embedded in the text helps the reader formulate a prediction.

    • **Clarifying -** is necessary when the reader has a difficult time understanding or interpreting the text. Thus, clarifying emphasizes that the goal of reading is to make sense of what is being read. Difficult concepts, new vocabulary, or unfamiliar reference words may make a text very hard to understand. The reader may clarify the unknown word or concept for himself or herself or may ask for clarification.

  • **Questioning** - pushes for deeper understanding of the selection. The reader thinks about what he or she doesn't know, needs to know, or would like to know. Raising questions before, during, and after reading promotes purposeful reading by helping the reader focus. Raising questions also pushes the reader to infer and apply new information from the text.

  • **Summarizing** - encourages reflection and increases understanding of the passage. The information read is synthesized into the reader's own words. If an accurate synopsis is not articulated, the strategic reader uses a fix-it strategy such as rereading or clarifying. The reader begins by summarizing sentences and, over time, progresses to summarizing paragraphs and longer passages.

3) Introduce the reciprocal teaching strategy by teaching and modeling the four comprehension skills. For maximum student understanding, teach and practice each skill individually. Once students understand and can successfully use a specific skill, teach another skill. Teach each skill using familiar content. For example, students may practice summarization by summarizing a scene from a favorite movie or television show.

4) After students have mastered the four comprehension skills, the teacher models the reciprocal teaching strategy. First, students and the teacher read the selection individually. Next, the teacher leads the discussion, centering around the four comprehension skills. Eventually the teacher and the students take turns leading a discussion about the selection.

5) As students become more familiar with the procedure student discussion leaders are chosen. Each leader is assigned a specific segment of the selection from which they are asked to generate questions, to determine a prediction statement, to locate difficult vocabulary or concepts needing clarification, and to create a summary.

6) When students are ready to assume full responsibility for reciprocal teaching, small groups are formed with a discussion leader assigned to each group. The teacher then assigns a passage of approximately 1,500 words in length to be read.

7) The teacher assumes the role of a coach, providing guidance to group leaders when necessary. Coaching-style prompts might include:

  • Prompting - "What question do you think the teacher might ask?"
  • Instructing - "Remember, a summary is a shortened version; it doesn't
   include a lot of detail."
  • Modifying - "If you're having a hard time thinking of a question,
   why don't you summarize first?"
  • Soliciting Help from Other Students - "Who can help us out with this one?"

8) Other group members are invited to comment on or assist with understanding of the passage being discussed. They may make predictions, ask for further clarification of other vocabulary, summarize, or answer questions.

When to Use the Strategy

Reciprocal Teaching is a very complex, yet worthwhile, strategy for all ages. Students who struggle with comprehension benefit greatly from the use of this strategy. When the text selection is a very difficult one to understand, this strategy pushes for clarity. Reciprocal Teaching may be used in any content area with any type of reading.

Example: The following example of Reciprocal Teaching is taken from a seventh grade physical education/health class. The selection read was *"The Immune System and Disease."* The student leader had previously read the passage and was prepared to lead the discussion.

Student Leader: The selection is about your body's immune system and how it deals with disease. (a summary statement)

Student Leader: What do you predict it will tell us about immune systems and disease?

Student A: It probably will talk about how our bodies fight germs that could hurt us.

Student Leader: What happens within the body to let the body know it's a bad germ? (question raising)

Student B: What are some bad diseases and how does our body fight them? (question raising)

Student Leader: There are some tough words in the reading we probably need to look at first. One word used a lot is microbes. I think microbes are different germs. (providing clarification and maybe asking for help with clarification)

Student C: There are a lot of different kinds of microbes like bacteria and fungi.

Student Leader: Another word we'll run into is antibodies. They are the good guys and fight the microbes.

Student Leader: I'll read the first section aloud so we can find out if it tells us how our bodies do fight germs. (students could read section silently)

Student Leader: Let's talk about this. What are microbes? How about those antibodies? (question raising) Student discussion.

Student C: All in all, the body does not want microbes because they are considered germs and the body's immune system fights them. (summary)

The Reciprocal Teaching would continue, with other students serving as discussion leaders of different sections. (One student could serve as discussion leader of the entire selection or the selection could be divided into sections with a different leader for each.) The teacher acts as coach and provides assistance where needed.

Link to Assessment

Students who lead the Reciprocal Teaching strategy gain an in-depth understanding of the content. Ideas clarified, predictions, questions, and summary statements might be shared in written form.

Reciprocal Teaching
Descriptors for Four Reading Attributes

When I <u>predict</u>, I:
- guess
- estimate
- assume
- imagine
- visualize
- infer
- speculate
- suspect
- believe
- forecast
- project
- envision

When I <u>clarify</u>, I:
- explain
- reread
- solve
- monitor
- refine
- simplify
- define
- describe
- illustrate
- sharpen
- remember

When I <u>question</u>, I:
- search
- ask
- investigate
- challenge
- quarrel with
- examine
- doubt
- quibble
- explore
- inquire
- probe
- dispute
- seek information

When I <u>summarize</u>, I:
- sum up
- conclude
- judge
- reread
- determine
- review
- surmise
- decide
- pull together
- deduct
- rundown
- organize
- tie together

 www.rachelbillmeyer.com • *Strategies to Engage the Mind of the Learner* • © 2006 Rachel Billmeyer

Reciprocal Teaching
Questions to Promote Thinking

Predicting
- What do you think will happen?
- What clues tell you what will happen?
- What will the author do or tell you next?
- What clues from the passage help you remember what has happened?

Clarifying
- I need help understanding this part of the section.
- Words I don't know or understand are . .
- Discuss and write down what the words mean.
- Use different words to figure out the meaning.
- Read ahead or reread to figure out the meaning.
- Add another example to figure out the meaning.

Questioning
- What questions do you have about the topic?
- Share what you think the author meant when . . .
- What did you think about as you read?
- Can you give another example for . . . ?
- What else do you know about this subject?

Summarizing
- Tell me about what you just read.
- What clues from the passage helped you organize your thinking?
- What is the most important part of the story?
- What are a couple of sentences that sum up the meaning of the entire passage?

Reciprocal Teaching
Student Worksheet

Predictions Made -

I think

I bet

I wonder

Questions Asked - (QAR strategy p. 141)

"Right There" Questions (literal)

"Think and Search" Questions (inferential)

"On My Own" Questions (application)

"Author and You" Questions (interaction)

Clarifications / Explanations Needed -

I did not understand the part where

I need to know more about

The section about_____ is confusing.

Summaries -

The important ideas in what I read are:

I can sum up the selection this way:

 www.rachelbillmeyer.com • *Strategies to Engage the Mind of the Learner* • © 2006 Rachel Billmeyer

Save the Last Word for Me

Why Use the Strategy

Many students do not find classroom discussions rewarding. They frequently comment that they do not feel safe sharing their ideas because it may not be correct or they don't want to compete with other students they perceive to be smart. When students have a structured reading strategy they are more able and likely to participate. The strategy Save the Last Word for Me (Vaughan and Estes, 1986) encourages reflective thinking while reading. When students reflect upon what they read they become thoughtful, active readers. Save the Last Word for Me is an excellent strategy to use when students need to think from multiple perspectives or connect ideas with experiences or prior knowledge.

Two benefits surface when using Save the Last Word for Me. Students are engaged before, during, and after reading a selection in a meaningful way, and secondly, the strategy incorporates a collaborative format for discussion. Each reader's ideas are heard and respected as they are discussed within the group.

How to Use the Strategy

1) Select and assign a selection for the students to read.
2) Explain that as they read the selection they must designate five statements that they would like to discuss. Suggest that students might use some of the following criteria when selecting a statement:
   • They agree or disagree with an idea.
   • It contradicts what they know.
   • There was a surprising turn of events.
   • An idea intrigues them and they want to think about it.
   • There is something they would like to try.
3) Show the students how to mark their statements. Options include highlighting the entire sentence, underlining it with a pencil, placing a post-it note by it, or place a checkmark in the column beside the statement.
4) Give each student five index cards, one for each statement marked. On the front of the card they write the statement as it appeared in the selection. On the reverse side they record personal thoughts to share. This part of the strategy might be assigned in advance.
5) Arrange students into small groups of four (this may occur the following day). Each student selects one of their five statements to share. One student in each group begins the sharing process by reading the statement to the group and showing them where the sentence is located in the selection. Once the statement is shared, the student is not allowed to say anything until all group members have talked about their thoughts. Group members are given time to think about their response and discuss their reactions. Once all ideas are shared, the student who initiated the statement responds, Save the Last Word for Me. The student turns the card over and explains the type of response chosen and what it says.

6) The discussion continues with the second student telling a designated statement and providing the "Last Word." Each student gets a chance to share one statement. If time permits, the students can select a second statement to share and repeat the discussion process.

When to Use the Strategy

Save the Last Word for Me strategy is appropriate for all grade levels and can be adapted to most subject areas. This strategy helps students read between the lines and react beyond the lines when reading narrative and informational text. In art, students can use the strategy as they observe and react to different artwork.

Link to Assessment

The strategy causes students to be reflective. As they read and respond to the selection, they are assessing their own beliefs about the topic. Students could use their five statements as prewriting ideas for a reaction paper.

Save the Last Word for Me
Student Copy

1) As you read the selection, mark five statements you want to respond to in one of the following ways:

- You agree or disagree with the idea.
- It contradicts what you know.
- There was a surprising turn of events.
- An idea intrigues you and you want to think about it.
- There is something you would like to try.

2) After you finish reading, write each statement as it appeared in the selection on the front of a 3" x 5" index card.

3) On the reverse side of each card write your personal response to be shared in a small group. This statement becomes the "Last Word" told in your small group.

4) Meet in a group of four to do the following:

- Determine which statement you want to tell first.

- Select a group member to begin the discussion process.

- Have that person read the statement from the front of the card and show where the sentence is located in the selection. Once the statement on the front of the card is shared, <u>this person may not say another word.</u>

- All group members are given an opportunity to tell their reaction to the statement. Each group member must participate.

- When all group members have shared, the person who wrote the statement can state the "Last Word" written on the back of the card.

- Continue with the second person in the group, repeating the process until all of the cards are completed.

Reference: Vaughan and Estes, 1986

How to Use the Strategy

1) Determine the selection students will read. Explain what a story map is and how it will be created using a circular formation (Routman, 1991). The story map will relate the main events of the story in sequence using pictures. Display an example of a story map using pictures and brief descriptions.

2) Read the selection aloud to the students or have them read it with a partner or independently.

3) As a class, discuss the main events of the story. Record ideas on chart paper or an overhead.

4) Discuss the sequence of the listed ideas. Write the first main event in the one o'clock position on the map and then draw an illustration.

5) Continue to draw the main events of the story in clockwise fashion, ending with the last main event and picture at twelve o'clock.

6) Encourage students to explain their decisions for sequencing the main events.

7) Create a kinesthetic activity by cutting the pictures with matching descriptive sentences into individual cards. Students read the story and sequence the main events, adding their own ideas as necessary. The picture/sentence cards can be placed in a Listening Center with a taped reading of the story. Students can listen to the story on tape and then reorganize the events of the story in chronological order. Students who created the original story map could serve as the checkers.

Benefits of the Strategy

- Teaches students how to sequence the events of a story
- Increases retention through drawing and visual imaging
- Allows the student to use different learning styles through sketching
- Highlights the main events of a story
- Provides an opportunity for a second reading of the story
- Incorporates decision making
- Creates independent readers

Motivation is what gets you started. Habit is what keeps you going.
- Jim Ryuh

Story Mapping

Name of the Story

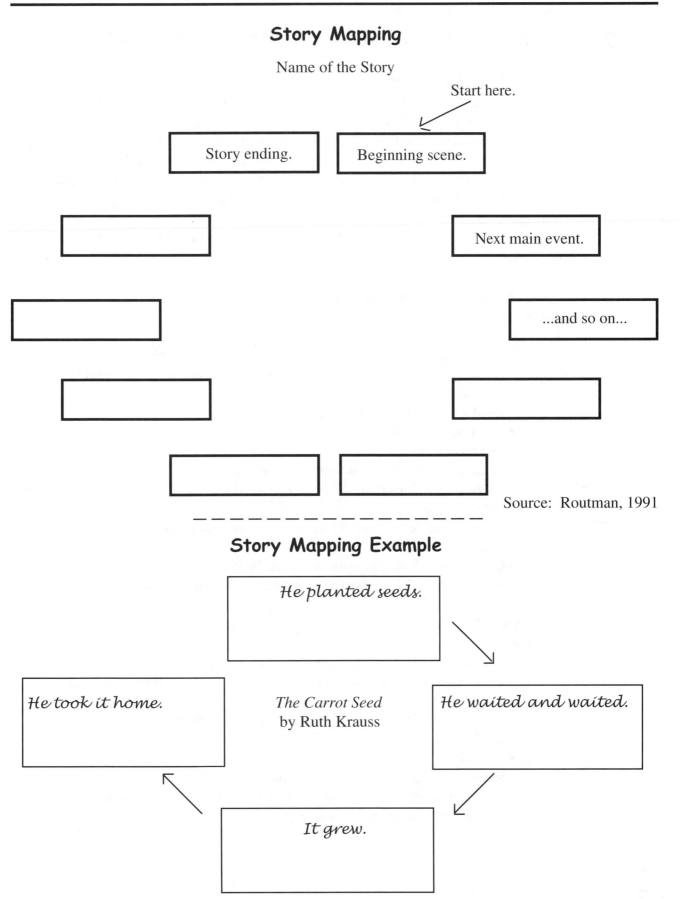

Start here.

| Story ending. | Beginning scene. |

Next main event.

...and so on...

Source: Routman, 1991

Story Mapping Example

He planted seeds.

He took it home.

The Carrot Seed
by Ruth Krauss

He waited and waited.

It grew.

Why Use the Strategy

Educators search for strategies that will increase comprehension skills of students. We know that if students are to understand and remember what they read, they need a structured approach for comprehending a selection. The Survey, Question, Read, Recite, and Review (Robinson, 1961) strategy provides that structure because it helps students organize information before, during, and after reading. The SQ3R strategy has a five-step study plan that incorporates important attributes for active reading: questioning, predicting, setting purpose, monitoring, and evaluating. The strategy can be utilized at all grade levels in all content areas.

How to Use the Strategy

Before Reading:

1) Survey the Information
   - Read the title, ask yourself what you know about the topic.
   - Survey the headings and subheadings and continue to assess what you already know.
   - Read the introduction and the summary.
   - Study all of the illustrations and graphic aids.
   - Establish a purpose for reading.
   - Make a list of unfamiliar words and terms.
   - Preview questions in the book, if provided.

2) Formulate Questions
   - Reread the title and turn it into a question to guide your thinking as you read.
   - Create and record questions about the headings and subheadings.
   - Formulate guiding questions about any illustrations or graphic aids.

During Reading:

3) Read
   - Read each section and answer questions formulated before reading.
   - Use context clues to write definitions to your list of unfamiliar words and terms.
   - Make connections between what you read and the illustrations or graphic aids.
   - Reread the headings, subheadings, and italicized words.
   - Reread the sections that were confusing or unclear.
   - Highlight ideas related to the purpose identified or record the idea on a post-it note and attach it to the page.

4) <u>Recite</u>
- Answer questions to yourself. Paraphrase with a partner or in writing.
- Study new vocabulary words and terms making connections to information read.
- Recall without looking at the book or notes and record learnings.

After Reading:
4) <u>Review</u>
- Review your purpose for reading the information.
- Reread your notes or highlighted statements.
- Revisit questions in the book, if appropriate.
- Test your understanding of new vocabulary words and terms.
- Discuss learnings with a friend and clarify answers to difficult questions.
- Write a summary of what was learned.
- Participate in a large or small discussion about the topic read.

When to Use the Strategy
The strategy can be used:
- To model for students how to activate thinking before, during, and after reading.
- As a helpful tool when students are assigned difficult reading material or lengthy passages.
- As a study tool to prepare students for a test.

Link to Assessment
The SQ3R strategy serves as an excellent self-assessment tool.   The strategy causes students to think at a higher level of processing as they assess how well they understand what is being learned during each of the five-steps in the study plan. Teachers can monitor student comprehension as the students progress through each step of the plan.

SQ3R Self-Assessment Guide

Reading Assignment_____

Did You . . .   **Check**

SURVEY

- Read the title, introduction and the summary
- Study the illustrations, graphic aids, new vocabulary
- Establish a purpose for reading

QUESTION

- Formulate questions about the title, headings, pictures, and charts that will guide your reading

READ

- Read to answer your questions
- Reread the sections that were confusing or unclear
- Write ideas related to the purpose on a Post-it note and attach it to the page

RECITE

- Answer the questions
- Study the new vocabulary words

REVIEW

- Review your purpose for reading the information
- Test your understanding of the new vocabulary word
- Write a summary of what was learned

REFLECT

- Record how the strategy helped you comprehend the selection

 www.rachelbillmeyer.com • *Strategies to Engage the Mind of the Learner* • © 2006 Rachel Billmeyer

Summary Wheel
"Pizza (Piece of) Thinking" Summary Wheel

Why Use the Strategy

The ability to summarize is an extremely complex, difficult task. Students are bombarded with information in each subject area and struggle with the assignment of organizing and condensing the information. In order to first make sense of the information and secondly to learn it, they must be able to synthesize the ideas using their own words. When students read social studies books they frequently complain that there are so many details to remember. They have a difficult time seeing the design in the abstract painting. Students need to know how to organize the key terms or concepts into essential categories and then summarize what each category represents. In the McREL study examining nine instructional strategies (2001), Bob Marzano states that summarizing ranked second for having a strong effect on student achievement. The Summary Wheel (Cutts, 2002) strategy teaches students how to organize understanding of key terms and ideas, to identify main ideas and supporting details, and how to organize thoughts into meaningful, succinct summaries.

How to Use the Strategy

1) Discuss the purpose and benefits of summarizing.
2) Use movies or a current topic to create summaries with the students.
3) Select a topic and passage for the students to read.
4) Assign students to look for key terms or "big ideas" as they read the passage.
5) Draw a large set of concentric circles on the chalk board. Select the key terms and record them on the ring created by the circle (the crust of a pizza).
6) Locate the center of the circles and draw radius lines to the edge separating the words (looks like a pizza).
7) Ask students to reread the passage a second time recording details for each "big idea" written around the circle.
8) Elicit details from the students and record them in the appropriate section of the circle (pizza topping for each slice).
9) Review the rules for summarizing:
    • Include only important information
    • Combine ideas when writing a summary
    • Add connective words for clarity and coherence
    • Use category terms instead of a list of words (e.g., use furniture for chair, sofa, table)
10) Review what a summary does not contain:
    • Your opinion
    • Material directly copied or quotes from the selection
    • What you think the author should have said
11) Model for the students how the information written on one section can be organized into a summary. The "big idea" (crust word) becomes the topic sentence. The details (topping words) become the supporting sentences in the summary.

12) Have students individually or in pairs select a section and create a summary. Check to see that each section is selected.

13) Illustrate summaries with a diagram or drawing. Students share their summary and illustration with the class.

When to Use the Strategy

This strategy can be used to help students summarize a video, a guest speaker presentation, or any selection assigned. A Summary Wheel can serve as an aid for organizing thinking when students are given a writing assignment requiring them to read from several resources. The strategy can serve as a graphic organizer.

Link to Assessment

In most state assessments students are asked to read and summarize their ideas about a given topic. This strategy can be used as a tool to prepare students for assessments.

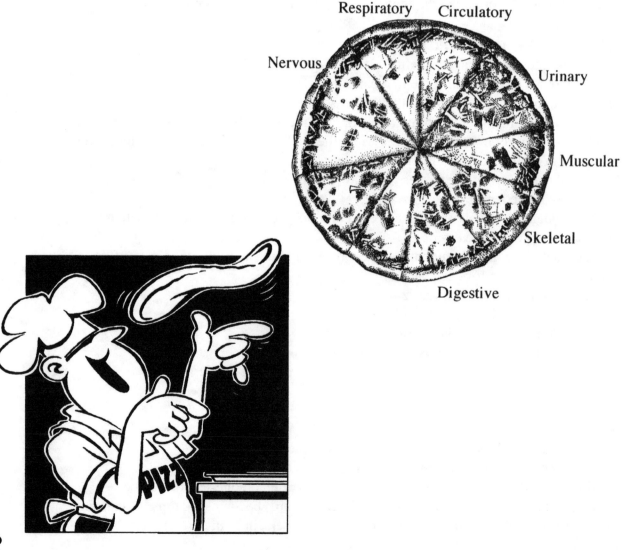

SUMMARIZING

Rules for summarizing:
- Include only important information
- Combine ideas when writing a summary
- Add connective words for clarity and coherence
- Use category terms instead of a list of words (example, use furniture for chair, sofa, table)

What a summary does not contain:
- Your opinion
- Material directly copied or quotes from the selection
- What you think the author should have said

Summary Wheel Example
"Pizza (Piece of) Thinking" Summary Wheel
Physical Education Fundamentals

Categories

1. Hand-eye Coordination
2. Batting Stance
3. Thinking Ahead
4. Positions
5. Calling for the Ball
6. Situations

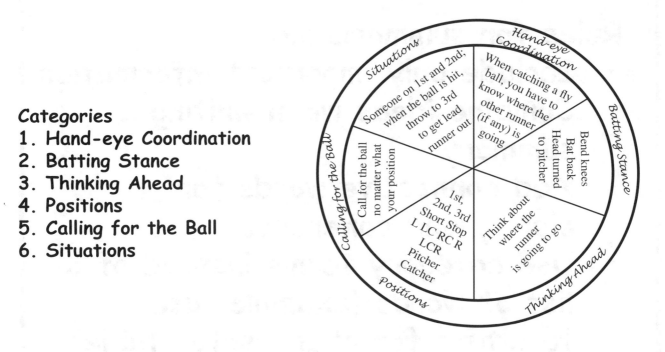

"Pizza (Piece of) Thinking" Summary Wheel
Vietnam: The Beginning Year (1965-1969)

Text Previewing

Why Use the Strategy

The text previewing strategy helps students understand the text features of the book and the resources used. Students spend a great deal of time interacting with textbooks. So it would be beneficial to spend time at the beginning and occasionally throughout the semester analyzing how the text is organized and how to use it effectively. Since teachers are familiar with their content and textbooks they sometimes assume that students will figure out the text. Yet, students lack the experience and background knowledge needed to understand the importance of charts and graphs, boldfaced vocabulary words, or the link between the words on the page and the graphics used in the book.

A math teacher shared with me that he had just begun using the Text Previewing strategy. When I asked him if it was worth taking class time to teach the Text Previewing strategy, he stated how amazed he was because students seemed to be more successful and independent. He concluded by saying that he was sorry it took him twenty-seven years to find out about this strategy.

How to Use the Strategy

1) Provide students with a graphic organizer or outline form of the "big picture" for the course of study. Have students look through all resources provided them. Explain the purpose of each book.

2) Guide students through the table of contents and explain how those ideas are related to the ideas represented in the "big picture." Allow students time to examine the major parts of the book: introduction, glossary, index, and appendix.

3) Preview the first chapter they will study. Read the title and the introduction aloud to the students. Ask them to summarize the main ideas.

4) Preview all headings and predict how the sections relate to the main ideas stated in the introduction.

5) Read the first sentence under each heading. Highlight critical words or phrases students must know in order to understand the concept presented in the chapter.

6) Examine all words in bold to determine if they are "critical words" students must learn. If "nice to know words" (words not necessary to understand the concept) are in bold, direct students to highlight all "critical words" using a colored highlighter.

7) Look at pictures, charts, and graphs in the chapter and explain how they are referenced in the text. Check to see if the explanation in the text is congruent with the explanation next to the picture, graph, or chart.

8) Examine the text for any special features. For example, an economics textbook frequently displays a small box with F.Y.I. in it and a tidbit of information. Have students read the information and determine its relationship to the information on the page and if it is information they must know. Explain the meaning of all acronyms.

9) Read the chapter summary aloud and ask the students to make connections between ideas in the summary and the main ideas discussed in the introduction.

10) Survey questions presented at the end of the chapter for appropriateness.

When to Use the Strategy

Spend the first week of class explaining and showing students how to use their resources. Periodically throughout the semester reinforce the ideas shared the first week of class. Examine each chapter or new resources for nuances that might interfere with student comprehension.

Link to Assessment

Knowing how to reference and use resources is an important lifelong skill. Assess students' ability to use material effectively as part of an assigned research paper or project. Assess how students' displays (science, technology) are explained.

Scavenger Hunt - Familiarize Yourself With The Text

• What is the title of the book?

• What do you learn about the book from the cover?

• Give the full name of each author. What does each author do for a living and how might their background influence their writing?

• What is the copyright of the book? How might that influence what is in the book?

• Examine the Table of Contents
   How many units of study are presented?

   How many chapters are in the book?

• What type of graphics are used? Maps, charts, pictures . . .

• What special features are presented in this book? List and describe them.

• How are new vocabulary words presented? What helps you determine if the words are "critical words" versus "nice to know words?"

• What is an Appendix? What kind of information is in the Appendix of this book?

• Where are the Glossary and Index? What type of information is presented in each? Give an example of how each works.

• Close the book and make a list of what you learned about the book so it will be a helpful learning tool.

Text Tagging

How to Use the Strategy

1) Select a passage for the students to read. Example: "Headaches"

2) Create questions or generalized statements about the passage. For example:

Question - What are some ways to prevent headaches?

Generalized Statement - People who suffer from chronic headaches can engage in preventive measures.

3) Introduce the students to the passage. Preview it with them building on their prior knowledge.

4) Present questions or generalized statements to the students as a handout, or on the overhead or chart paper.

5) Hand out sticky arrows to the students and explain how to tag the text while reading. Model how to place a sticky arrow on information relating to the questions or generalized statements.

6) Instruct students to work alone or in pairs and read the passage tagging the text (place sticky arrow).

7) Engage in class discussion about how students tagged the text for each question or generalized statement. To enhance thinking, have the students analyze why they marked that particular part of the text. Working in small groups, have students compare their taggings and discuss their answers.

8) To increase understanding about the ideas tagged, instruct the students to summarize the author's idea in their own words. Students select all or an assigned amount of ideas tagged and place a small Post-it note on top of the sticky arrow. Ask students to reread the idea tagged and then to rewite it in their own words on the Post-it note. This short extension activity assists students with the difficult reading attribute of summarizing.

9) Process the effectiveness of the strategy with the students. "How did the Text Tagging strategy help you understand what the passage was saying?" This can be completed through individual journaling with a follow-up discussion.

Text Tagging Alternative
Selective Marking for Focused Reading

Teach students to flag ideas while reading using a selective marking system. Throughout the article or in the margin they draw icons which represent certain ideas. Possible marking ideas are:

- Highlight/underline the main ideas and supporting details (color code)
- Place a star next to ideas they want to remember
- Circle key vocabulary words
- Summarize ideas in the margin or on a sticky note stuck to the margin

Teacher modeling is the key for student success with Focused Reading.

Example:

Focused Reading

+   **New information to remember**

?   **Idea needs clarification**

    Idea I will use

( )   **Information stretched my thinking**

Benefits of the Strategy
- Guides students thinking during reading
- Helps students remain focused while reading
- Causes more students to read the entire text
- Allows the kinesthetic learner to use manipulatives
- Encourages more students to engage in the follow-up discussion because they feel prepared having tagged or marked their text in advance
- Builds a reading community because students are actively engaged in the reading process

Why Use the Strategy

The Think-Aloud (Davey, 1983) strategy causes thinking, which is a covert process, to become overt. It is an excellent metacognitive strategy, causing students to think about their own thinking. Teachers model their thinking process by verbalizing their thoughts so students understand the type of thinking necessary to work through a specific process. For example, before reading a selection the teacher might say aloud to the class, "As I preview this passage I am wondering what enthymeme means, and I'm thinking I better find out so the passage will make sense." or "I'm mulling over a prediction for this reading. I'm thinking it will be about three different rain forests and what makes them different." A benefit of the Think-Aloud strategy is that it helps students understand how the mind constructs meaning when reading, as well as how it thinks through difficult spots. Struggling readers frequently do not understand how the mind is engaged when reading. They know how to decode the words but struggle with making any meaning in order to understand the gist of the passage. The Think-aloud strategy explicitly helps them understand what goes on in the mind of the reader.

How to Use the Strategy

1) Explain to students that reading is a covert (hidden) process and that they must take an active role in the reading process. Their brain needs to be actively engaged while reading. To demonstrate what that means, model the Think-Aloud process using a familiar and not difficult concept. The goal is to get the students to focus on the use of the strategy and not struggle with understanding the concept.

2) Read the selection aloud to the class, stopping periodically to think-aloud by:
   • Asking yourself the meaning of a word
   • Asking yourself questions
   • Making self-corrections
   • Modeling persistence, "I really need to concentrate."

Once the teacher has modeled the process several times, students work with a partner to practice the strategy. Elicit examples of student thinking to share with the entire group. Allow for group discussion so students fully understand the strategy.

3) Another way of using the Think-Aloud strategy is to read authentic text, such as feature newspaper articles or news magazines, with a small group of students. As each person takes a turn reading a paragraph, ask them how they are constructing meaning, the kinds of comprehension difficulties they are experiencing, and how they are attempting to resolve them. Students take turns revealing their thinking while reading. Other students may want to discuss or elaborate on a student's comments.

4) Provide students independent practice using a checklist to assess their progress.

When to Use the Strategy

The Think-Aloud strategy can be used to:

- model specific reading attributes ("I predict that. . ."),
- organize thinking using an organizational pattern,
- model thinking for planning and reflection,
- model thinking with different genres,
- model a problem solving process,
- think through math problems,
- decode an unknown word,
- organize information for a speech or a report, and
- figure out an analogy.

Link to Assessment

When assessing students, understanding their thinking process is important. Through the Think-Aloud strategy, thinking can be assessed.

Thinking from Different Perspectives

"I don't see the world as it is, but as I am."
- Thalmud

Why Use the Strategy

A reader's perspective and background knowledge about the topic determines how the selection is understood and interpreted. No two people read and interpret a passage the same way. For example, students who live on a farm or have visited a farm will interpret a passage about farming differently than students living in New York City. Thinking from Different Perspectives (McNeil, 1984) is a reading strategy which encourages students to read the same selection several times, each time thinking from a different perspective. The strategy causes students to analyze their own thinking while learning, as well as develop critical reading skills. Students learn alternative ways to analyze text, consider different ways of interpreting information, and develop empathy for different points of view. When students read from different perspectives, their comprehension and appreciation of the topic increases.

How to Use the Strategy

1) Assign a selection for students to read. The first reading is to help them develop an overall understanding of the selection or topic.

2) Identify different perspectives related to important concepts or ideas within the selection and display them on an overhead transparency, chart paper, or chalkboard. These become the different roles students assume when they reread the selection. Examples include:

- Students studying the Civil War are asked to think from the perspective of a person living in the South which could include a Confederate Army member, an Army general, a slave, or a plantation owner.
- Selections can be read from different economic, religious, or social perspectives, such as peasant, governor, president, doctor, Italian immigrant, or Communist leader.
- Novels in English can be read from the perspective of different characters.
- Perspectives in science include various chemical reactions, elements of nature (lake, fish, worm) or the point of view of a chemist or nuclear engineer.
- Issues or concerns within a family can be viewed through the eyes of different family members, including the cat and dog.

3) Model for students, using one of the listed ideas, how people think when analyzing a different point of view.

4) Organize the class into small groups and assign each group one role from the displayed list. Thinking from their assigned role, have group members discuss the needs and concerns of their particular perspective. Instruct students to record ideas on the Thinking from Different Perspectives Guide. Assist students as needed.

5) Have students reread the selection to look for specific statements that support their perspective. As they discover text statements, encourage them to discuss their reactions to each one. Group members will have their own interpretations. Students record the text statements plus their personal reaction on the guide.

6) After students have reread the selection, have them discuss if any important information was missing. Sample discussion question: "If they were to rewrite the selection what information would they include to support their perspective?"

7) Allow students to share insights gained when reading from different perspectives. Have students organize their thoughts, feelings, and impressions about the perspective they studied by writing a summary position statement on the guide.

8) Conduct a class discussion about the benefits of using the Thinking from Different Perspectives strategy.

When to Use the Strategy

Thinking from Different Perspectives can be used in all content areas with all grade levels. Assign groups of students different characters from a story and have them respond to each character from a different perspective. History offers students many opportunities to think from different perspectives. Not all history books are written from the same perspective; studying history in the North takes a different slant than history books written for the South. Thinking from different perspectives can foster creativity. Students can be encouraged to write from the perspective of others, as well as from worldly perspectives (Billmeyer, 2006).

Link to Assessment

State and national tests frequently include test questions requiring students to read, think, and write from the perspective of someone else. Providing this type of assessment as part of classroom instruction is beneficial. When students can respond to test questions thinking from a different perspective, they display a deeper understanding of the test content. Another option is a performance assessment in which the students role-play an assigned perspective. The assessment could be an impromptu situation or require students to prepare in advance.

Thinking from Different Perspectives Guide Example

Your Perspective on "Pharaohs of Egypt"

Possible roles: Pharaohs, common people/farmers, scribes, slaves, & governors

Needs

Control and power
Money and supplies
Respect and loyalty
Strong economy

Concerns

Collecting tax money
Flood water shared fairly
Drought = no crop = no trade

Read and React

Text Statements

Pharaohs were the most important people in Ancient Egypt & everything belonged to them.
Money did not exist then.

A Pharaoh is the child of the Sun God, Ra.

Your Reactions

They were the ultimate boss.

Pharaohs determined value & everyone's economic status.
Everyone had to follow the Pharaoh's orders or they were sentenced to death.

Summary Position Statement

My job as a Pharaoh is a very difficult one. I have incredible responsibility making sure our economy is successful. As a Pharaoh, I own all of the important land and control all of the tax dollars. It is my responsibility to keep track of all written documents. That includes all government orders. It is hard work!

Thinking from Different Perspectives Guide

Your Perspective on _____

Possible roles: _____

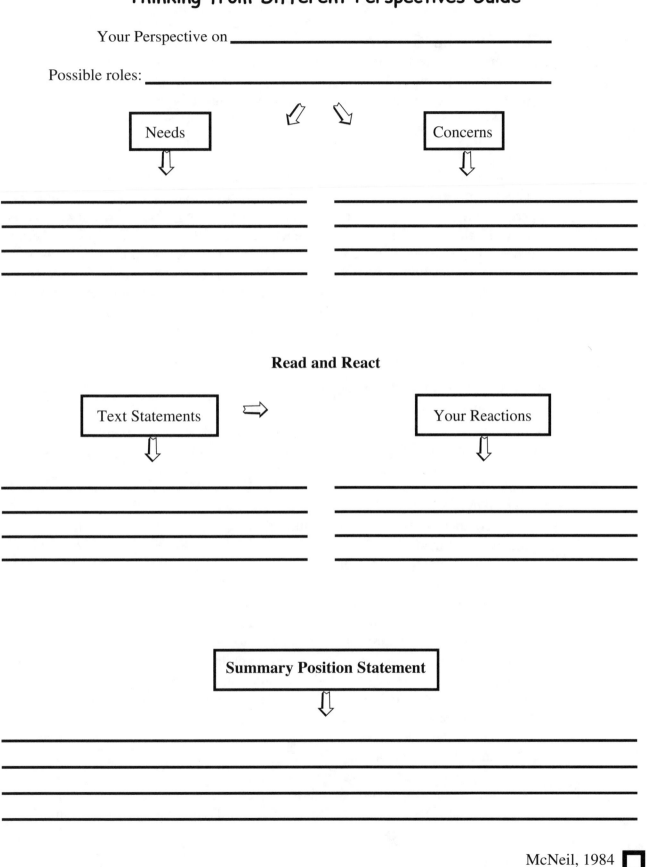

Needs   Concerns

Read and React

Text Statements   ⟹   Your Reactions

Summary Position Statement

McNeil, 1984

Why Use the Strategy

To summarize means to briefly restate the author's idea in your own words or to present the key points of a larger selection in a condensed form. Students struggle with summarizing because they tend to focus on interesting, exciting, or funny details. Summarizing information helps students integrate and reinforce new learnings, as well as create connections among new ideas and prior knowledge.

Many students prefer rehearsal of information which leads to rote learning and limits transfer of information from one situation to another (Friend, 2001). When students are required to summarize information, they must use the higher order thinking skills of analysis, elaboration, and paraphrasing. Students find elaboration difficult because in order to elaborate on a concept requires a thorough understanding of it. Thus, to summarize information learned is a difficult task. In order for students to remember, understand, and transfer information, they need to be skillful summarizers. Students need many opportunities and ways to utilize the summarizing process. The Window Pane Summary offers students another way to summarize information they are learning.

How to Use the Strategy

1) Clarify the purpose and benefits of summarizing.

2) Introduce to the students the concept they will be learning. Explain how to organize the information about the concept into major topics or categories. The Window Pane Summary is divided into the appropriate number of categories. For example, if students were studying *The Cold War*, the Window Pane Summary could be divided into six categories:
- Compare and Contrast with Other Wars
- Role of the United States
- Role of the Soviet Union
- Outcomes of the War
- Overall World Effects on Society Today
- Connections to George Orwell's novel *Animal Farm*

3) Assign students the appropriate information to study for each category.

4) Instruct students to skim the entire selection in order to gain an overall understanding of the topic and then to study in-depth the information for each category.

5) Select one category and model how to summarize the information and record it into the appropriate window pane.

Review the rules for summarizing:
- Include only important information
- Combine ideas when writing a summary
- Add connective words for clarity and coherence
- Use category terms instead of a list of words (for example, use furniture for chair, sofa, table)

ꝏ

Review what a summary does not contain:
• Your opinion
• Material directly copied or quotes from the selection
• What you think the author should have said

6) Students individually or in pairs select another category, study the necessary information, and create a summary statement. The teacher can also record a summary statement for each category. Students share their summary statements and compare them with the teacher's examples.

7) Summary statements are compared with the rules for summarizing and revised as necessary.

8) Once the Window Pane Summaries are developed, a conclusive summary statement can be created about the topic. For example, once students have developed summaries for the six categories about the Cold War, they can create an overall summary statement about the Cold War.

9) Students are now prepared to use the Window Pane Summary independently or working with a partner.

When to Use the Strategy

The Window Pane Summary can be used in all content areas at all grade levels. Young children can be provided a larger sheet of paper divided into the appropriate number of boxes and draw a picture to summarize the category idea. The strategy is especially helpful with content that is unfamiliar, abstract, consumed with details, or lengthy.

Link to Assessment

After studying a concept, students can use the Window Pane Summary as an assessment tool. They can be provided the handout with the appropriate numbers of window panes and asked to summarize each category for the topic studied. Students can use the Window Pane Summary to organize their thinking when assigned a "constructed response" test question.

Window Pane Summary

Concept - <u>Cold War</u>

Compare and Contrast with Other Wars	**Role of the United States**
Role of the Soviet Union	**Outcomes of the War**
Overall World Effects on Society Today	**Connections to George Orwell's Novel *Animal Farm***

Write to Learn

Why Use the Strategy

Much writing in school tends to be for the purpose of evaluating the correctness of students' writing or what students know about a specific topic. Students respond in writing to prescribed questions with correct information. Just as no coach is present every minute of a player's independent practice and no band director sits through each musician's individual practice, the Write to Learn strategy is evaluation-free. It allows students to think critically, explore and experiment with ideas, and to internalize the content in a different way. The students are free to express personal ideas, concerns, and questions about the concepts they are learning. This free flow type of writing encourages students to get their ideas down without worrying about correct punctuation, grammar, or spelling. Teachers frequently use Response Journals, Reading Logs, or Learning Journals as a means for free writing.

How to Use the Strategy

1) Select a specific concept students will learn to introduce the Write to Learn strategy. If students are not used to free writing, they will struggle with what to write. Selecting a topic students enjoy or are curious about will increase their desire and ability to free write.
2) Create a schedule for writing so it becomes a regular part of the learning process.
3) Encourage students to record their ideas in different ways; graphic organizers, sketching and drawing, or outlining.
4) Ask students periodically to share their entries with a partner, in small groups, or with the entire class. When students share how they write to learn, they begin to analyze the different approaches available for learning information.

When to Use the Strategy

Write to Learn can be used in any content area at any grade level. When students struggle with specific concepts, writing to learn can be very helpful. Response Journals can be used to show progress in learning. If students date each entry before recording their thinking about the concept, they can analyze their thought process throughout the unit of study. Students can review journal entries when preparing for a test or use them to help peers understand difficult content.

Write to Learn Examples

Response Journal for Science 1

Student Name_____   **Topic:** Climate, Section 1-1

I developed the book questions but have these extra questions I'm interested in.
- *Is CO2 also in the air we breathe inside buildings?*
- *Since there is a rise in CO2 will the food we eat be affected and toxicate us?*
- *What is El Nino?*
- *As a scientist do you come up with everything yourself? The process of doing research, experiments, and analyzing?*
- *Does El Nino affect everywhere at once or does it just affect places as the current travels?*

Topic: Climate, Section 2-1
This stuff on climate isn't half bad. Here are some things I learned. The climate is affected by two basic factors: temperature and precipitation. Latitude, elevation, and the presence of ocean currents are 3 factors of temperature and prevailing winds and mountain ranges affect precipitation.

Reading Log for Language Arts

Book/Story Title_____**Author**_____**# Pages**____**Started___Finished**

A Time for Dancing   Davida Hurwin   257   August 27

Reactions: Monday 8-30-99
This book is very interesting. It's about this girl and her mom and how her mom spends a lot of time with her boyfriend and that she likes to go to parties and hang out with friends. This is it so far.

Reactions: Tuesday 8-31-99
The book is starting to get more interesting. This girl has something wrong with her but she wouldn't tell anybody. Also her boyfriend dumped her for somebody else, and she hasn't gotten over that. She is trying to find a way to get him back.

Reactions: Wednesday 9-1-99
The book keeps going back and forth between the characters so I get confused, but the girls' names are Jules and Sam. Jules is the one having problems.

Reactions: Thursday 9-2-99
They have been to 13 doctors and every doctor has told them the same thing and they take x-rays and shots and everything like that from every doctor. Her mom is tired of it so she is demanding to know what is wrong with her daughter.

Section 4 - Questioning Strategies
Thinking, Processing, Reflecting through Questioning

"Once you have learned how to ask relevant and appropriate and substantial questions you have learned how to learn. This is what we need to teach in our schools. Students are too often restricted to the process of memorizing (partially and temporarily) somebody else's answer to somebody else's question."

- Neil Postmam

Rationale

"What good questions did you ask today?" was a regular conversation between Isidore Rabi, a noted scientist, and his mother at the end of a school day. Isidore's mother encouraged him to ask good questions, and for that reason he credits her for his becoming a Nobel Laureate in physics.

As you reflect on the good questions you might have asked today, what thoughts come to mind? Possible reactions might include, "Do I have a questioning mind?" or "Do I encourage students to ask questions?" or "What types of questions develop a questioning mind?" or "What are the benefits of asking questions?" Questioning can be a quest or a journey in search of unknown information. Through questioning students become information seekers and users who learn more about themselves and the content being studied. Questions can enrich students' learning about the content as well as cause students to focus on themselves as productive learners (Enlighten Your Thinking Questions, p. 138).

Questioning plays a critical role in classroom instruction. Research highlights the positive effects that effective questioning has on students' comprehension and retention of information (Anderson and Biddle, 1975). Effective questions involve a variety of cognitive processes such as memory, divergent thinking, convergent thinking, and evaluative thinking. Research supports the use of lower-level, concrete questions ("Who are the main characters in the story?" and "How much allowance do you receive weekly?") as well as higher-level questions ("How are the two characters alike and different?" and "What advertising and marketing strategies affect you the most?"). Thought-provoking questions serve as the basis for elaborative and reflective thinking.

Thought-provoking questions can transform students from passive learners to active, curious learners, whether the questions and answers are overt or covert. Students not only benefit from answering questions provided by the teacher or text, but from formulating their own questions. Self-questioning is an important learning activity because students are searching for answers they want to know.

"Question generating gives the students an opportunity to identify the kind of information that provides the substance for a good question, to frame that question, and then to engage in self-testing. The student becomes much more involved in the activity and in the text when they are posing and answering the questions and not merely responding to teacher or text questions."

- Annemarie S. Palinscar & Ann L. Brown, 1986

Asking thought-provoking questions is not an easy task; students need to be taught how to formulate questions that elicit, extend, and deepen thinking. For example, the novel approach for reading incorporates small groups of students reading the same story with one student serving as the discussion leader. The effectiveness of the discussion leader's role is based on the quality of questions asked. Group members are actively engaged in discussing the book when the questions cause them to think, analyze, and evaluate the story read. Student-generated questions help students see content in new and different ways.

It is important to pay attention to behaviors that enable students' thinking when questioning. Consider the following when using questioning strategies:
- Questions should be prepared in advance so the appropriate levels of thinking are incorporated and so that questions are congruent with the objective of the lesson.
- Wait time is an important part of questioning. Students need time to think and formulate their answers to questions. Higher-level questions require more wait time. There are two wait times; the first requires at least five seconds of thinking after the question is asked and the second requires five seconds of wait time after the student responds to the question, allowing for further elaboration.
- Answers to questions are provisional. Right or wrong; every answer is only the first step towards a more meaningful, more fully developed answer. Speech and writing are the audible and visible edges of thinking.
- The most important part of the questioning process is the teacher's response to the student's answer. Every answer is a gift. The quality and quantity of future gifts depends on how we treat this gift here and now.

Questioning strategies included in this section.

		Page
• Chat and Go Questions	. . . . .	133
• Concept Question Chain	. . . . .	136
• Enlighten Your Thinking Questions.	. . .	138
• Question-Answer Relationships	. . . .	141
• Unwrap Your Thinking Questions .	. . .	145
• Questioning the Author	. . . . .	147

Chat and Go Questions

How to Use the Strategy

1) This is a fun way to get students into informal conversations about their readings. Record open-ended questions on individual slips of paper; fold and place them in a basket. Or make one set of questions per table group (examples below).

2) Next, ask students to think about a selection read recently, one they want to share.

3) Organize students into groups of three to four.

4) Instruct each student to draw a question from the basket, to read it, and to prepare a response to share about their selection. If a student draws a question that is not relevant, have them draw again.

5) Review active listening and inquiry skills with students. Model the process with a personal selection. Share the selection, read the question to the class, and share the responses. Allow students to ask inquiry questions about the selection.

6) Instruct students to share their questions and responses with group members who listen and ask questions.

7) While students share, the teacher circulates to listen in on conversations.

8) As a closure, ask several students to share their questions, the selection read, and their responses to the questions.

Benefits of the Strategy

- Provides an opportunity for students to have informal conversations
- Focuses on the importance of questioning when reading
- Strengthens active listening and inquiry skills
- Encourages students to read and explore new books, authors, and topics

Sample questions

What do you think are the main ideas of the selection read?

What are the high points of interest within the selection for you?

Did you find the reading predictable? What clues were you given?

What is your overall feeling after reading the selection?

What passages from the selection helps listeners understand the main ideas?

How were the characters depicted within the selection? What are your impressions about them?

What may be causing the main character to behave as he/she is?

What is your overall opinion of the selection? Would you encourage someone else to read it? Why, why not?

Describe the setting of the selection. How is it important to the story?

What characters did you learn the most from? What did you learn?

In what ways did your thinking change as a result of reading the selection?

Compare this book or selection to another one you have read recently.

What are your thoughts about the author's style of writing?

If you could be any character in the story or selection which one would you be? Why?

What did you notice about your thinking as you read this selection?

What events from the selection reminded you of your own life? Elaborate.

Were the events in the selection realistic? Why or why not?

What thoughts did you take away as a result of reading the selection? What idea from the selection do you remember most clearly?

Explain or describe the results of a particular character's actions. Be specific. What is your response to this character's actions?

How would you rate this selection on a scale of 1 - 10 with 10 being the highest rating? Explain the reason(s) for your rating.

What changes would you make if you were the author of the selection? Where would you include more details? fewer details?

What is your impression of the author?

What is the theme of the selection? How can you apply this theme to your own life?

If you were asked to do a press conference about the selection, what information would you share with reporters so they could write a news story? Remember: Who? What? Where? When? Why?

How would you compare this selection with a previous reading? What similarities or differences can you identify?

Which character are you most like? Why? Least like and why?

How might this reading influence your life?

If you were asked to advertise this selection, what would you say or show in the display?

In what ways is this selection similar/different to what you usually read?

If you owned a bookstore, would you stock this selection? If so, how would you promote the sale of it to your customers?

What type of reading do you find most satisfying? How is this selection like or unlike what you find satisfying to read?

Concept Question Chain

"There are one-story intellects. Two-story intellects.
And three-story intellects with skylights.
All fact collectors who have no aim beyond their facts are one-story men.
Two-story men compare, reason, and generalize,
using the labor of fact collectors as their own.
Three-story men idealize, imagine, predict. . .
Their best illumination comes from above the skylights."

- Oliver Wendell Holmes

Why Use the Strategy

A questioning mind enhances learning. Questions help students anticipate meaning, search for information, modify ideas, and elaborate upon ideas presented. When students are provided a scaffold or framework for learning new information their learning is enhanced (Vygotsky, 1978). The Concept Question Chain (Johnson, 1992) provides students with a framework for learning through chains of questions about a specific concept. The questioning chain, which consists of literal, interpretive, and applied questions about a concept, helps students recognize the relationship among ideas. This strategy, which is similar to the Question-Answer Relationships strategy (p. 141), causes students to think about a concept from different levels of cognitive processing. As students become confident with different levels of questioning, they can transfer the questioning chain process to other learning situations.

How to Use the Strategy

1) The teacher begins by explaining the benefits of questioning. It is important that students understand there are different types of questions (literal, interpretive, and application), each causing the brain to think differently. For example, what do you notice about your brain as it processes each set of questions?

> • "Who is President of the United States?" and "In the story, *Goldilocks and the Three Bears*, what were the three bears eating for breakfast?"
> • "How does George W. Bush's performance as president compare to his father's as president?" and "Why was baby bear so upset when he came home?"
> • "What if Al Gore had been elected president of the United States instead of President Bush?" and "Why is it wrong to go into someone's house when they are not home?"

The first set of questions require literal thinking; the brain is searching for one right answer. The second pair of questions requires your brain to interpret information, drawing upon different sources of information. Perhaps you used a Venn diagram to organize your thinking. Maybe you needed more wait-time with these questions. The last set of questions requires your brain to hypothesize, speculate, and use your own background knowledge. Application questions can require even more wait-time than the other types of questions.

2) Select a unit of study and important concepts students need to understand. Examples:
- A farm unit may focus on crops, animals, and machinery.
- A jazz unit in music may include the history, famous musicians, and characteristics.
- An architecture unit could include design and perspective.

3) Select a concept and create a chain of questions about it. The concept provides the framework for writing the three levels of questions. Begin with the interpretive level questions because this level provides direction for developing appropriate literal and applied questions. Examples: What animals are raised on a farm in Iowa? How do farm animals compare to zoo animals? How do people who live in the city benefit from farm animals?

4) Prepare students for the unit of study and any related reading.
- Pull forward the students' background knowledge.
- Set a purpose for studying the unit and for assigned reading.
- Introduce new vocabulary words or terms by recording them on a "word wall" or chart paper so students learn to use them in their everyday language.
- Provide an example of each level of questions to serve as a guide for study.
- Assign the reading and ask students to focus on the specific concept.

5) Have the students read the selected text and encourage note taking if appropriate.

6) Conduct a guided discussion to help students understand and apply the concept being learned and to provide an opportunity for them to interact with the different levels of questions.

7) After the discussion, have students create a graphic organizer depicting their understanding of the concept.

8) Process the Concept Question Chain with the students. Ask students to discuss the questions that made them think and/or understand the concept. Have them create new questions that would be helpful in future readings.

When to Use the Strategy

The Concept Question Chain actively engages students when learning any concept. The strategy can be used as a framework for reading informational and narrative text. Questions can be used to activate thinking before, during, and after reading or as a study tool to prepare for testing.

Link to Assessment

The Concept Question Chain serves as an excellent self-assessment tool. The strategy causes students to think at higher levels of processing as they assess how well they understand concepts taught in any unit of study. Teachers can monitor student comprehension as they reflect upon their learnings. This strategy helps a teacher analyze the student's ability to apply information learned.

How to Use the Strategy

Art Costa and Bena Kallick (2000) identify sixteen habits of mind which are broad, enduring, and essential life span learnings appropriate for students and adults. They believe that by teaching these habits of mind students will be able to draw upon them when faced with challenging situations. Questions were developed for all sixteen habits of mind. This is not intended to be a conclusive list. Questions can be adapted for all grade levels. Some questions focus specifically on reading projects while others can be used for all aspects of student learning. To create the "Enlighten Your Thinking" activity, copy the questions on light bulbs (p. 140). Questions can be used as an introduction to a lesson, during, or as a closure activity. Place a set of laminated lightbulbs on rings or in a basket for easy access.

Benefits of the Strategy

- Provides an opportunity for students to have informal conversations
- Teaches students about the importance of the habits of mind
- Strengthens active listening and inquiry skills
- Reinforces the importance of thinking about difficult situations in different ways

Sample questions:

Persisting

Which character(s) showed persistence by seeing tasks through to completion?
What strategies helped you to complete your project?
Give examples of strategies you used to remain focused on your work.

Managing Impulsivity

What information did the author provide that kept you wondering and thinking about the character?
What benefits did you find from preparing more than one draft of your work?
When you find yourself tempted to hastily turn in your work, what strategies or alternatives do you consider? Why?

Listening With Understanding And Empathy

If you were _____, how do you think he/she would feel about the statement?
What strategies do you employ to aid in listening to others?

Thinking Flexibly

What other solutions could be tried to solve the problem presented in the selection?
What options did you consider when deciding how to present your information?
As you complete group projects, what strategies did you use to see others' perspectives?

Thinking About Thinking

What feelings were you noticing as you read the story?
How did the author cause you to think? To feel?
How did you arrive at the answer?

Striving For Accuracy

How did the author show exactness in his work?
Give examples of the author's accuracy in representing the setting and time of the story.
What details could the author give to make it clearer or more precise?
What strategies do you use to ensure the accuracy of your report?
What benefits do you receive from checking and rechecking your work?

Questioning and Posing Problems

How did the author raise questions in the selection?
What problems did the characters need to solve?
What questions came to mind as you read the selection?
What data or information will be necessary for you to find a solution?

Applying Past Knowledge to New Situations

What prior knowledge did the main characters have?
What experiences contribute to the author's writing?
How does the story relate to events or experiences that you have had?
What have you learned from this?
As you look at past projects that have been successful, what strategies will you repeat to continue that success?

Thinking and Communicating with Clarity and Purpose

In what ways did the author present the plot so that it was clear to you?
Are any parts of the plot unclear to you? Give examples.
Give examples from the book that show precision in language.

Gathering Data Through All Senses

In what ways did the author use the senses to tell the story?
Give examples of strategies you used to heighten learning through all your senses.

Creating, Imagining, Innovating

How did the author's work spark your imagination?
Imagine that you are _____. How would that feel?

Responding with Wonderment and Awe

What about this story intrigued you?
In what ways have your emotions influenced your analysis of the story?

Taking Responsible Risks

What kinds of risks did the main character(s) take? Why?

What good or bad outcomes resulted from the risks taken?

In what ways did you try something new when preparing your story?

Finding Humor

Give examples of the author's use of humor in the story.

As you reflect on your project, what brought you humor?

How did the use of humor help you while completing your project?

Thinking Interdependently

Give examples of the characters' interdependence with each other.

How did each character contribute to finding a solution or resolution?

Describe the benefits you have found in working with others.

Remaining Open to Continuous Learning

What did you learn from the author?

Give examples of evidence that the characters never stopped learning.

What new learning will you carry forward to your next assignment?

How has feedback contributed to your learning?

Enlighten Your Thinking

Insert questions in a text box within the light bulb center.

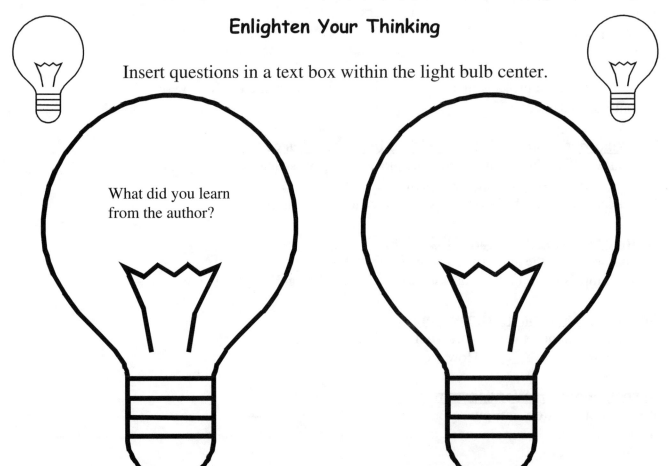

What did you learn from the author?

Question-Answer Relationships (QAR)

Why Use the Strategy

The Question-Answer Relationships (Raphael, 1986) strategy helps students make connections between information in the selection and their prior knowledge. Reading comprehension increases with the use of this strategy because readers are asked to think at various levels of cognitive processing. The strategy encourages the reader to think about the selection from four perspectives: entering the text, moving through the text, moving beyond the text, and carrying on a mental dialogue with the author. Students who use this strategy learn to recognize the different types of thinking needed when answering questions. Thoughtful questions cause readers to anticipate meaning, to search for information, to modify ideas, and to elaborate upon the ideas presented in the selection (Reciprocal Teaching, p. 102).

Another benefit of the QAR strategy is that students can learn to ask the four different types of questions, and the questioning process can be transferred from teacher to learner. This allows students to become independent strategic readers by formulating their own questions while reading.

How to Use the Strategy

1) The teacher explains that answering questions about selections read requires the reader to use information found in the book and information from their own background of experience. Provide an overview of the four different types of questions. Help students understand that the first two types of questions are text-based because the answers are found in the text.

Text-Based Questions or "In the Book"

• <u>Right There</u> questions require a literal-level response. The answer is easy to find because it is explicitly stated in the text. The words used in the question and the words found in the sentence to answer the question are Right There. Right There questions usually require a one word or short response and begin with words like who, when, or where. Because these questions usually elicit one right answer they require a minimal amount of teacher wait-time or student thinking. Examples of Right There questions are: "Who is president of the United States?" and "Where did the acupuncture technique originate?"

• <u>Think and Search</u> questions require more inferential thinking. This type of question asks the reader to interpret or analyze information read and then organize ideas from various sentences in order to formulate the answer. Students will find answers located in the text but first must "Think" how the information in the text is connected and then "Search" through the selection to determine what information will answer the question. Sentences beginning with words like describe, explain, or analyze may signal to the reader that this is a Think and Search question. Examples of the questions are: "Describe the similarities and differences between the drama, Romeo and Juliet, and the movie." and "Explain how the reading strategies described in the article might benefit your students."

The next two types of questions ask students to use information pulled primarily from their own background knowledge. These questions require them to hypothesize answers based on personal information. Answers are found in the mind of the reader.

Reader-Based Questions or "In My Head"

• <u>On My Own questions</u> ask students to speculate or hypothesize and apply the information to their own experiences. This type of question requires more think time because often there is no right or wrong answer. The question "What if all teachers incorporated reading strategies in their teaching?" asks the reader to speculate and to go beyond the selection read, using prior knowledge to formulate a response. On My Own questions can be useful in activating background knowledge prior to reading. Question starters include: What if? How might? and What can?

• <u>Author and You</u> questions require students to interact with ideas presented by the author. Students need to think about what they know about the topic, what the author is saying in the text, and how the two are related. For example, the selection discusses the acupuncture technique and the Author and You question might be: "When do you think acupuncture should be used?" Author and You questions may begin with words or statements such as: How will? Where could? and What would?

2) The next step is to model the Question-Answer Relationships process:
  • Read a selection to the students.
  • Ask a question about the selection.
  • Share the answer to the question.
  • State the type of question and give an explanation for the answer.

3) Instructional considerations when teaching Question-Answer Relationships include:
  • Instruct students how to tell the difference among the four Question-Answer Relationships.
  • Give students feedback.
  • Progress from shorter to longer and easier to more difficult selections and/or more complex questions.
  • Build independence by beginning with the large group, moving to small groups, and finally to independent activities.

When to Use the Strategy

Use the Question-Answer Relationship strategy to:
  • Prepare students for standardized testing.
  • Develop understanding of informational and narrative text.
  • Provide an opportunity for students to create questions about the selection read.

Link to Assessment

Assessment practices in standardized testing includes the four types of questions. Secondary students preparing for the SAT or ACT college entrance exam may find this strategy helpful.

Question-Answer Relationships Visual Organizer

In the Book QARs
Right There

The answer is easy to find because it is explicitly stated in the text. The words that make up the question and the words that answer the question are right in the same sentence.

For example: "What nations of Native Americans lived primarily on the Great Plains?"

In My Head QARs
Author and You

The answer is not found in the text but in the reader's head. The reader needs to think about what he or she knows about the topic, what the author is saying in the text, and how the two are related.

For example: "What seem to be the most crucial questions to be asked concerning global warming?"

Think and Search

The answer is in the selection but the reader needs to find it by using inference skills. The reader needs to think about what the question is asking and then search for the answer. The answer is found by gathering information from more than one sentence or paragraph.

For example: "How did pioneers in our state overcome hardships to build life as we know it today?"

On My Own

The answer is not found in the text but in the reader's own background knowledge. Questions might be used to activate background knowledge prior to reading or to assist in applying new information to one's own experiences.

For example: "Considering the problems Gene is having with bullies on his walk to school, what suggestions do you have for him?"

Question/Answer Relationships Worksheet

In the Book Questions

Right There Questions
  Cue Words: Who, When, Where, Identify, List

Think and Search Questions
  Cue Words: Compare, Predict, Draw Conclusions

In My Head Questions

Author and You Questions
  Cue Words: Interact, Relate to, Connect, Associate

On My Own Questions
  Cue Words: Speculate, Apply, Hypothesize, Explore

Question-Answer Relationships (QAR)

"Unwrap Your Thinking" Questions

Below are sample questions for the four areas of the Question-Answer Relationships strategy. Select questions appropriate for your age group, reword questions as necessary, or substitute ideas for underlined ideas. To create the "Unwrap Your Thinking" activity copy the questions on candy wrappers (p. 146). Run each set of questions on a different color of paper. Questions can be used as an introduction to a lesson, during the lesson, or as a closure activity. Place a set of laminated candy wrappers on rings or in a basket for easy access.

Right There (green paper)

Who is the main character?
When did the story take place?
Who is (are) the author(s)? Who is the illustrator?
When did _____ happen?
Who was in charge of _____?
How many characters were in the selection?
Define critical words in the selection.
What is the origin of <u>jazz</u> music?

Think and Search (blue paper)

What was the main cause of _____?
Retell the story or event in your own words.
How could you summarize the main idea?
Tell in your own words the theme.
Explain vocabulary words that are important in understanding the selection read.
Find two examples for _____.
For what reasons would the author explain _____ in the way he did?
Compare two ideas discussed in the passage.
How did the selection pique your interest?
What is the essential characteristic of an <u>equation</u>? Provide an example.
What impact did the Transcontinental Railroad have on the West?
Why is <u>cell division</u> an important science concept? Explain how the process works.

Author and You (red paper)

In what ways did you agree with what the author said?
How did the author cause you to think? To feel?
How would you describe the author's style of writing?
What features of this author's writing might you incorporate in your own writing?
What did you learn from the author?
What might be the author's reason for explaining the situation as she did?
What is the author telling us about _____?
What questions would you like to ask a composer of <u>jazz</u>?
What would you like to say to the illustrator about his/her choice of pictures?

On My Own (yellow paper) see p. 146

On My Own (yellow paper)

How does this story mirror experiences that you or others you know have had?

How might this information be useful to you?

What if this situation or the main character existed in your life?

In what ways are events shared in this selection still evident today?

What do you predict will happen next, based on what you read?

What do you predict will happen in ten years as a result of _____?

What assumptions and beliefs inform your attitude toward <u>stem cell</u> research?

What are your thoughts about capital punishment for drug dealers?

How would you describe each candidate's political platform?

How has <u>jazz</u> influenced other music and society?

Candy Wrappers for "Unwrap Your Thinking"

Insert questions in a text box within the candy wrapper's center.

Retell the story or event in your own words.

Questioning the Author

Why Use the Strategy

In many subject areas, students have difficulty reading and understanding their textbook. Students do not stop to think that authors are actual people who can write poorly or without clarity. All too often students are blamed for not reading the text and rarely is the text criticized. As a result, some students read in a perfunctory manner, some do not read at all, depending on the teacher for information, and some just give up, thinking they are not capable. Questioning the Author (Beck, McKeown, Hamilton, & Kucan, 1997) is a strategy that helps students construct meaning while coping with challenging text. This strategy helps students analyze what the author is saying versus accepting just what the textbook states. A benefit of Questioning the Author is that it keeps the reader's mind actively engaged during reading. The student addresses clarity issues by asking author queries while reading. Queries differ from questions in that they are not asked specifically about the information, but rather about the author's meaning or intentions. Questioning the Author is an excellent strategy to help students become independent and critical interrogators of the text (Silver, Strong, & Perini, 2000).

How to Use the Strategy

1) Lead a class discussion about selections read that were very hard to read and understand. Share examples with the students. Ask the students to explain strategies they use to help them understand what the author is trying to say.

2) Explain to students that authors are actual people and that their writing is not always clear or easy to understand. Select a textbook and have the students examine the backgrounds of the authors. Instruct them to check where the authors are from, their credentials, and what perspective they bring to the writing: teacher, university professor, eyewitness, or expert on the topic.

3) Preview a selected text with the students. Determine key points students must understand. Highlight critical vocabulary words. Instruct students to read a section of the text.

4) After reading the section, open a discussion using "author queries."
   - What is the author trying to say?
   - How does this compare with what the author already said?
   - What does the author think we already know?
   - Why is the author telling us this information now?
   - What do you think the author wants us to think, feel, or do?
   - What would you like to ask the author?
   - What is the author's explanation for why this happened?
   - Why do you suppose the author said it that way?

5) Model for students how a strategic reader uses the "author queries" to make sense of confusing text. Teach the students how to refer to the text for clarification of key points. Stress to the students that the strategy causes them to be metacognitive, to think about their comprehension while they read. Have students discuss the meaning of the text using the queries.

6) Have the students reflect on the Questioning the Author process and discuss the benefits of the strategy.

When to Use the Strategy
The strategy can be used in any subject area at an grade level. Questioning the Author is very helpful when the text is poorly written or when students find the topic very challenging.

Link to Assessment
In any test situation, students need to know how to "Question the Author." If students use queries during reading, they are more efficient and perform better on timed tests.

"Author Queries"

- What is the author trying to say?
- How does this compare with what the author already said?
- What does the author think we already know?
- Why is the author telling us this information now?
- What do you think the author wants us to think, feel, or do?
- What questions would you like to ask the author?
- What is the author's explanation for why this happened?
- Why do you suppose the author said it that way?

Section 5 - Graphic Organizers   Notes:

"A picture is worth a thousand words!"

Rationale

Graphic organizers are holistic, visual representations of concepts, facts, and details, and their relationships within an organized structure. They help students think visually about their own thinking. Organizers are designed so students can identify details, the relationship among the details, and the connection to the whole. Some benefits when using a graphic organizer include the following:

- encourages nonlinear thinking,
- emphasizes categorizing of information versus fragmented ideas,
- displays entire concept or process on one page of paper,
- illustrates the relationship between and among ideas,
- supports visual learners,
- provides students one more means for analyzing and constructing meaning,
- increases clarity, understanding, and retention of information,
- supports tactile learners,
- represents abstract ideas in concrete form, and
- develops higher level thinking skills and processes.

Graphic organizers exist in a variety of forms, such as Venn diagrams, time lines, flow charts, mind maps, and fishbone diagrams. The story elements from narrative text are frequently displayed through story map graphic organizers. Authors use graphic organizers called organizational patterns to assist the reader's thinking. Common purposes for organizational patterns are to clarify and depict cause/effect, compare/contrast, description, goal/action/outcome, problem/solution, and sequence chains.

Graphic organizers are beneficial for elementary children as well as college age students. They can be incorporated before, during, and/or after instruction. At the beginning of a unit of study a graphic organizer can be used to activate prior knowledge, to provide a conceptual framework for integrating new information, or as an advanced organizer to overview a larger body of content. During instruction, they serve as a note-taking device to help students actively process and reorganize information. As an end product graphic organizers can be used to summarize learning, encourage elaboration of learning, organize ideas for writing or speaking, provide a structure for review, or to assess the degree of student learning.

Graphic organizers can facilitate small group discussion by providing a means for students to analyze and compare their information and perceptions. They can also be used as a visual reference for rich class discussions. Students discuss the concepts learned and cite specific related examples. Whole class organizers can be developed on chart paper and referred to in subsequent or parallel units of study. For example, a timeline from Johnny Tremain can accompany a social studies unit on the American Revolution.

Graphic organizers need to be taught and modeled by the teacher. It is important to explain the purpose of the graphic organizer and provide opportunities for guided practice. The goal is to have students select and use graphic organizers independently. When students select a particular structure to organize their learnings they should ask themselves questions such as: "Is the author comparing and contrasting two situations?" or "Does the text present a sequence of events?" or "Is information presented in a hierarchy?" Teachers can help students learn how to use graphic organizers by using the following steps.

Teaching Graphic Organizers

"The difference between good and poor learners is not the sheer quantity of what the good learner learns, but rather the good learner's ability to organize and use information."

- Frank Smith

1) Explain the concept of graphic organizers and the purpose for using one.
2) Select a specific graphic organizer and describe its purpose and structure.
3) Describe and model how to use the organizer, first with familiar then with new information.
4) Instruct students to use the organizer first with familiar information and then with new material.
5) Reflect on the use of the organizer by sharing examples and benefits.
6) Provide opportunities for students to use graphic organizers and to reflect on the benefits.
7) Encourage students to construct their own graphic organizers.

- Adapted from Jay McTighe

Graphic Organizers included in this section.

		Page
• Semantic Mapping		151
• Story Mapping for Narrative Text . . .		153
• Thinking/Writing Patterns and Organizational Patterns for Informative Text .		159

Semantic Mapping

Why Use the Strategy
Semantic mapping (Johnson and Pearson, 1984) shows the relationship among key concepts and related technical terms in a text passage. Concepts are graphically organized into categories which helps the students visually see how the ideas are related. Semantic mapping is used as a prereading, during reading, and after reading activity. As a prereading activity, students are asked to pull forward their prior knowledge about the topic and then to complete and correct the map during reading. As an after reading activity, the map can help the students synthesize and evaluate the information read.

How to Use the Strategy
1) Model how to use the strategy. Select a topic recently studied and write the key concept or theme word on a chart or chalk board. With the students brainstorm and record words which relate to the key concept. As ideas are shared, ask students to explain their thinking, rationalize their beliefs, and make connections to prior knowledge.
2) Create a web or map. Write the concept in the center circle and organize the brainstormed ideas into categories, writing them on spokes coming from the concept.
3) When students understand the semantic mapping strategy, give them a concept they will study next. In small groups ask them to brainstorm and categorize ideas relating to the topic. As a large group, discuss ideas and create one semantic map. The map can serve as a diagnostic tool.
4) As the students study the topic, they can add, delete, or elaborate on ideas written on the semantic map.

When to Use the Strategy
Semantic maps can be used in any content area. They can be used as a prereading activity in which the students predict what they can learn about the topic to be studied. It works well as an introduction to a unit of study previewing important vocabulary words about the topic. Semantic mapping can be used as a review activity in which the students map key concepts learned and indicate the relationship between the ideas and related technical terms.

Link to Assessment
A semantic map can be used as an assessment tool. Students can create a written explanation to accompany their map to explain their thinking when developing a map.

Semantic Mapping Examples

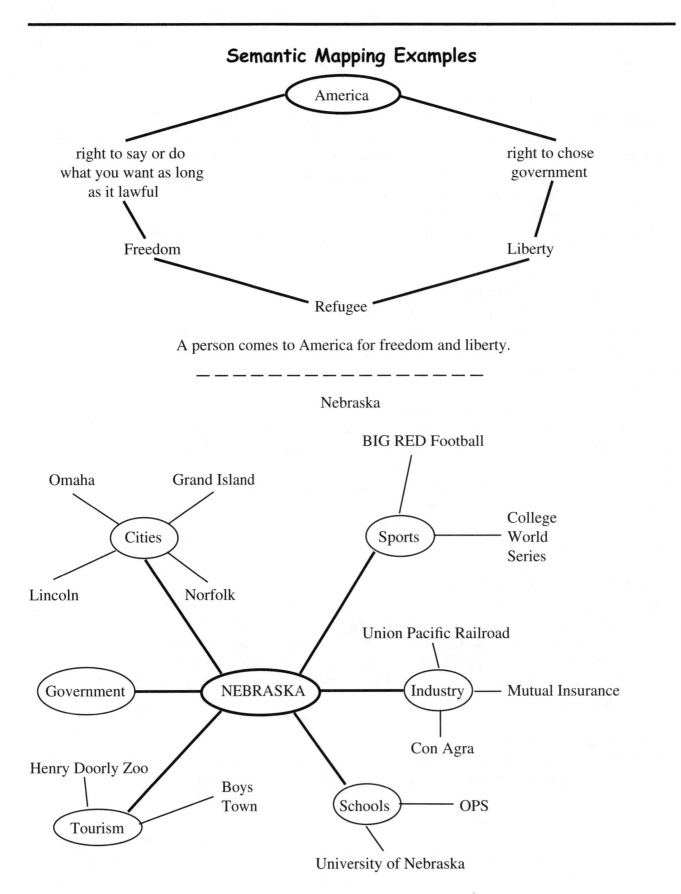

A person comes to America for freedom and liberty.

— — — — — — — — — — — — — — — — —

Nebraska is a safe, comfortable place to live.

Story Mapping for Narrative Text

Why Use the Strategy

A story map is a visual representation of the structure of a story. It includes all story elements: setting, characters, events, problem, solution, and theme. A story map helps the student understand the relationships among all the parts. When students use a story map they have a better understanding of the story. Explaining and sequencing the events in a story become easier for the student.

How to Use the Strategy

1) Select a story for students to read, preferably one in which all story elements are obvious.
2) Review the story elements with the students.
3) Read the story aloud or have the students read it silently.
4) Construct a story map on chart paper, overhead, or chalkboard. After reading the story complete the story map.
5) Assign another story and have students complete the story map individually or in pairs.
6) Teach the different forms of story maps to the students. Allow them to select the story map which appeals to their learning style.
7) Share and discuss student examples of story maps.

When to Use the Strategy

Story maps can be used with any selection when studying narrative text. Students can create their own story map after reading a story.

Link to Assessment

When students complete a story map the visual product can serve as the assessment tool.

Narrative Text
Story Plan

Title: _____

Author(s): _____

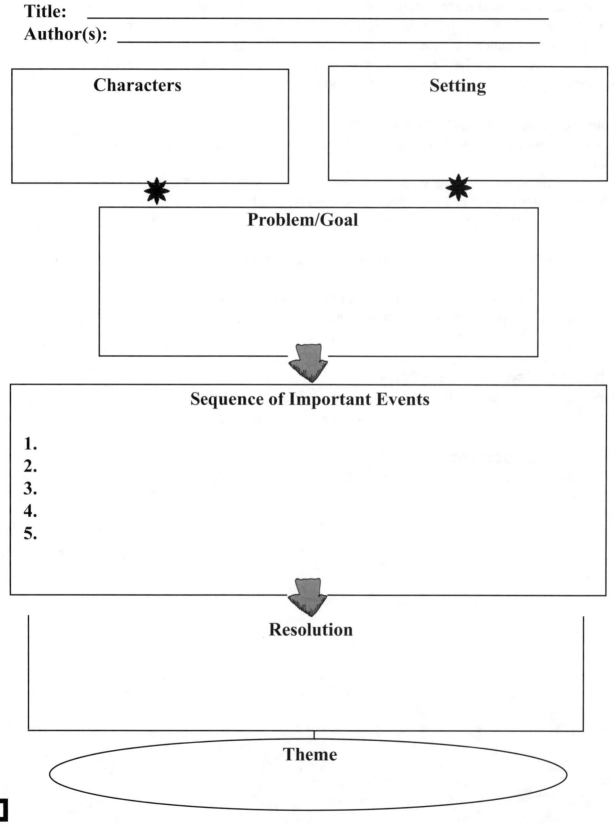

Characters

Setting

Problem/Goal

Sequence of Important Events

1.
2.
3.
4.
5.

Resolution

Theme

Narrative Text Story Mapping

Title
Author(s)

Elements

Main Characters	Other Characters

Setting

Where
When

Events/Action

Beginning	Middle	End

Problem - Goal	Solution

Theme

Narrative Text Story Map

★ TITLE: _____

☺ AUTHOR: _____

SETTING: _____

⌂ _____

○ TIME:

CHARACTERS:

PROBLEM:

✴ EVENT 1

✴ EVENT 2

✴ EVENT 3

✴ EVENT 4

✴ EVENT 5

SOLUTION

⬡ THEME

Narrative Text Visual Story Mapping

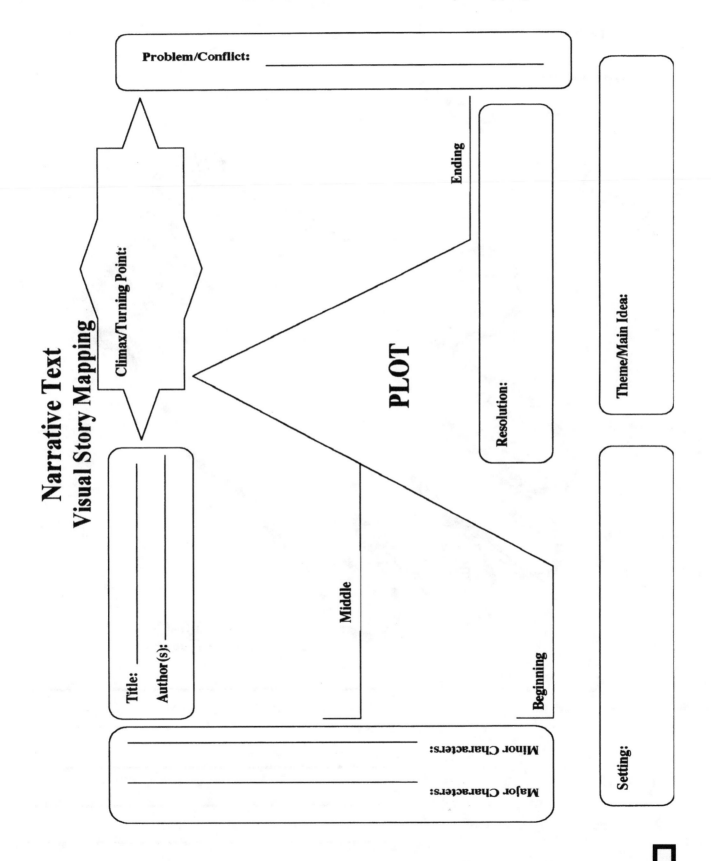

Narrative Text Visual Story Mapping

Problem/Conflict: _____

Climax/Turning Point:

Ending

PLOT

Resolution:

Theme/Main Idea:

Title: _____

Author(s): _____

Middle

Beginning

Minor Characters: _____

Major Characters: _____

Setting:

Narrative Text Story Imprint

Title:

Author(s):

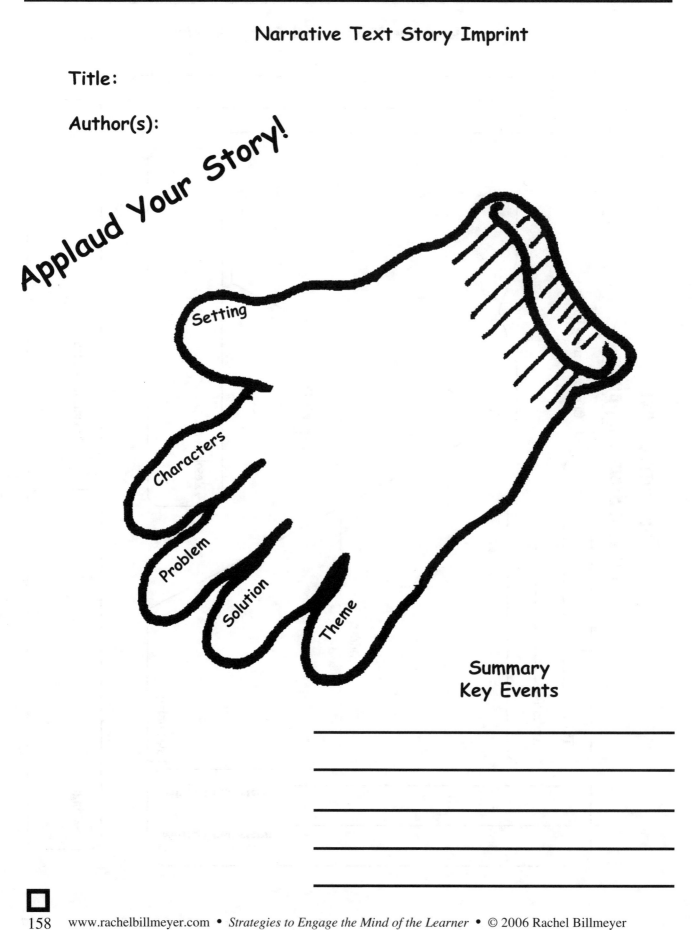

Applaud Your Story!

Setting

Characters

Problem

Solution

Theme

Summary
Key Events

_____

_____

_____

_____

_____

Graphic Organizers for Informative Text

This section includes informational text Thinking/Writing Patterns (p. 161-163) and six organizational patterns authors use to structure informative text (p. 164-172).

- **cause/effect**: establishes a causal relationship showing that things or events occur as a result of certain conditions

- **compare/contrast**: establishes a mental frame about multiple topics by highlighting the similarities and differences

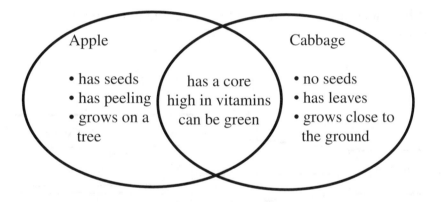

- **concept/definition:** highlights the importance of a specific concept by listing characteristics with examples

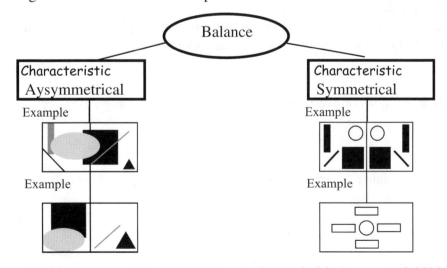

- **goal/action/outcome**: organizes thinking about a particular goal by arranging information into an action plan

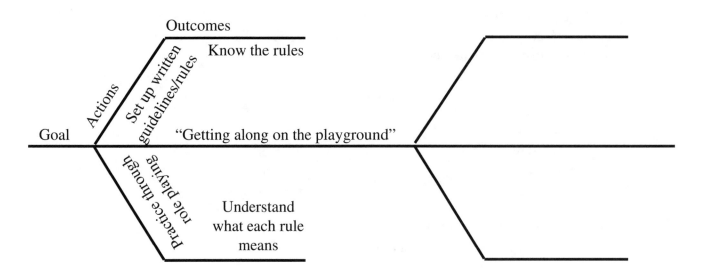

- **problem/solution**: identifies a specific problem needing to be solved and describes possible solutions

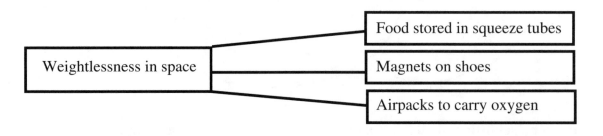

- **proposition/support**: establishes a specific viewpoint about a topic, creates a hypothesis statement, and organizes categories of information which support the statement (See Proposition/Support strategy p. 91-94 for an example.)

- **sequence**: arranges ideas or events into a series of events or a logical order

Food Chain

Sunlight ⇒ Green plants absorb sunlight ⇒ Animals eat plants ⇒ Humans eat animals

Informative Text Thinking/Writing Pattern

Concept(s)	Main Ideas	Supporting Details

Vocabulary Words

"Must know words"	"Nice to know words"

Informative Text Thinking/Writing Pattern

Concept: _____

**Theme/
Focusing
Statements**

**Main
Ideas**

- •
- •
- •

**Supporting
Details**

- •
- •
- •

Vocabulary Words: **Reader Aids:**

 www.rachelbillmeyer.com • *Strategies to Engage the Mind of the Learner* • © 2006 Rachel Billmeyer

Informative Text Thinking/Writing Pattern (Outline)

Concept: _____

Topic/Theme   I. _____

      Main Idea   A. _____

        Supporting   1. _____
        details   2. _____
                      3. _____
                      4. _____

      Main Idea   B. _____

        Supporting   1. _____
        details   2. _____
                      3. _____
                      4. _____

– – – – – – – – – – – – – – – –

Topic/Theme   II. _____

      Main Idea   A. _____

        Supporting   1. _____
        details   2. _____
                      3. _____
                      4. _____

      Main Idea   B. _____

        Supporting   1. _____
        details   2. _____
                      3. _____
                      4. _____

Cause/Effect
Topic

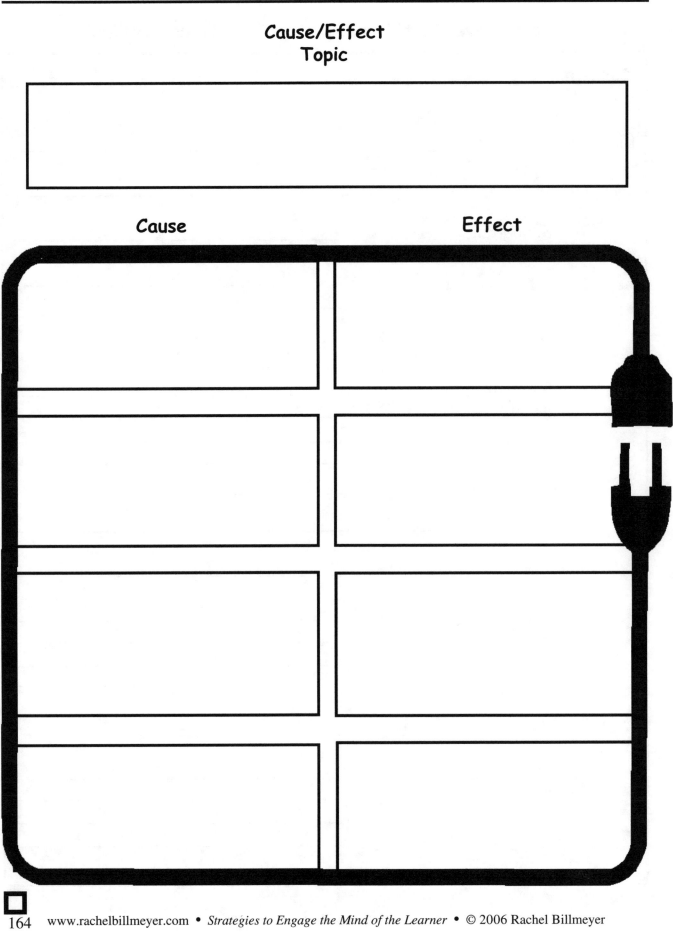

Cause   Effect

Cause/Effect Organizational Pattern

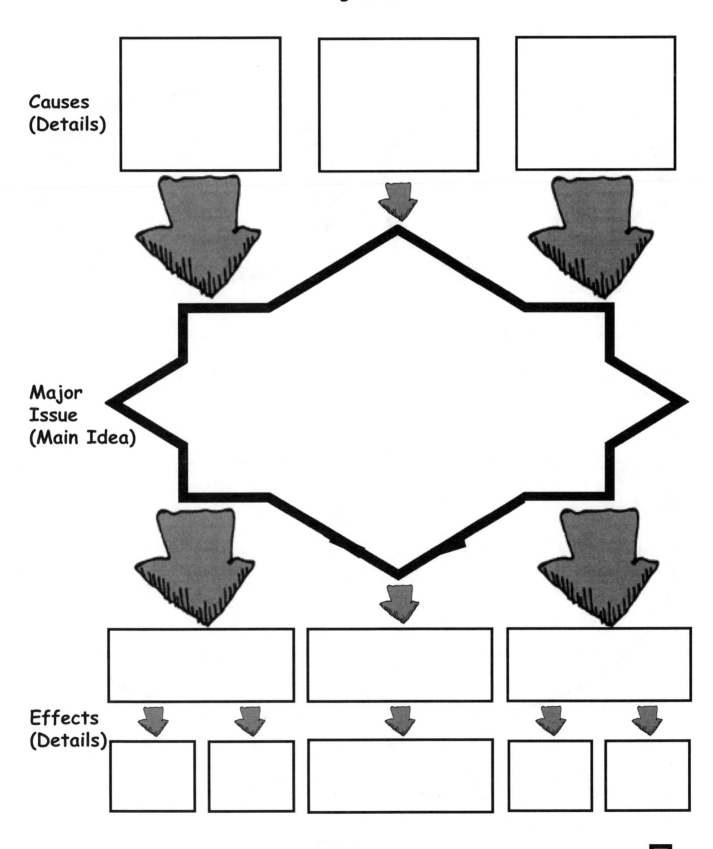

**Causes
(Details)**

**Major
Issue
(Main Idea)**

**Effects
(Details)**

Compare/Contrast

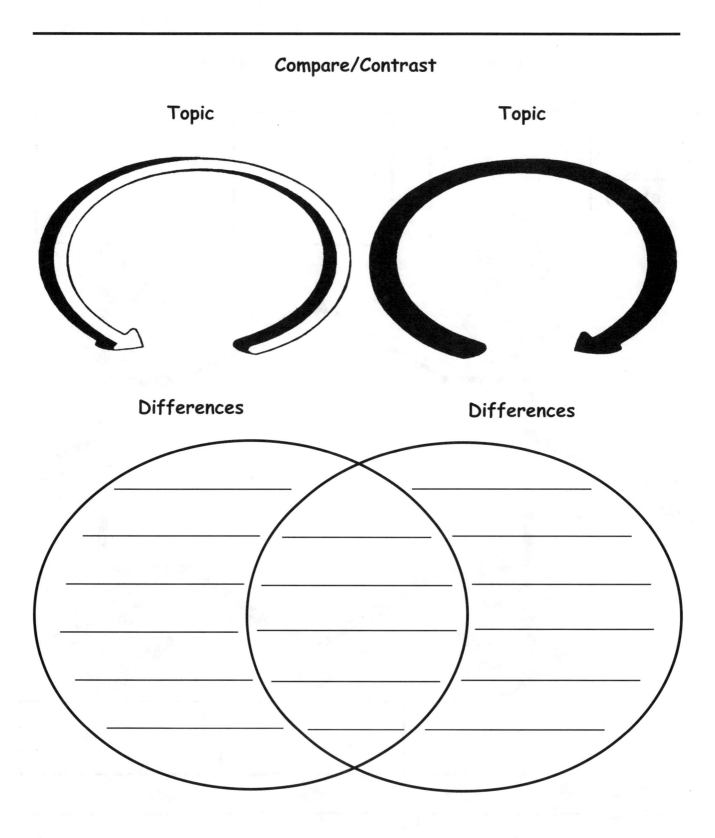

Topic   Topic

Differences   Differences

Similarities

Compare/Contrast

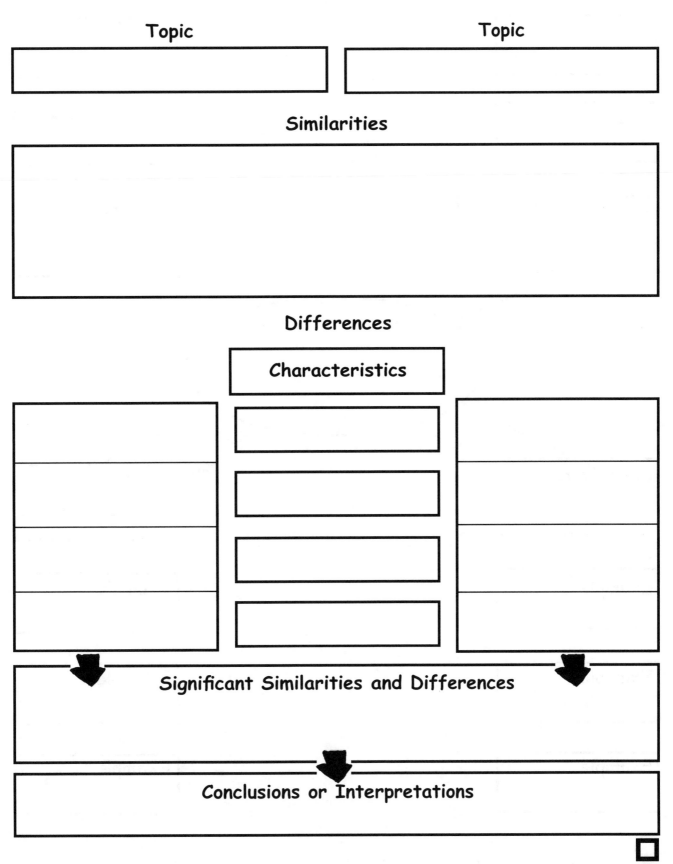

Topic

Topic

Similarities

Differences

Characteristics

Significant Similarities and Differences

Conclusions or Interpretations

Concept/Definition

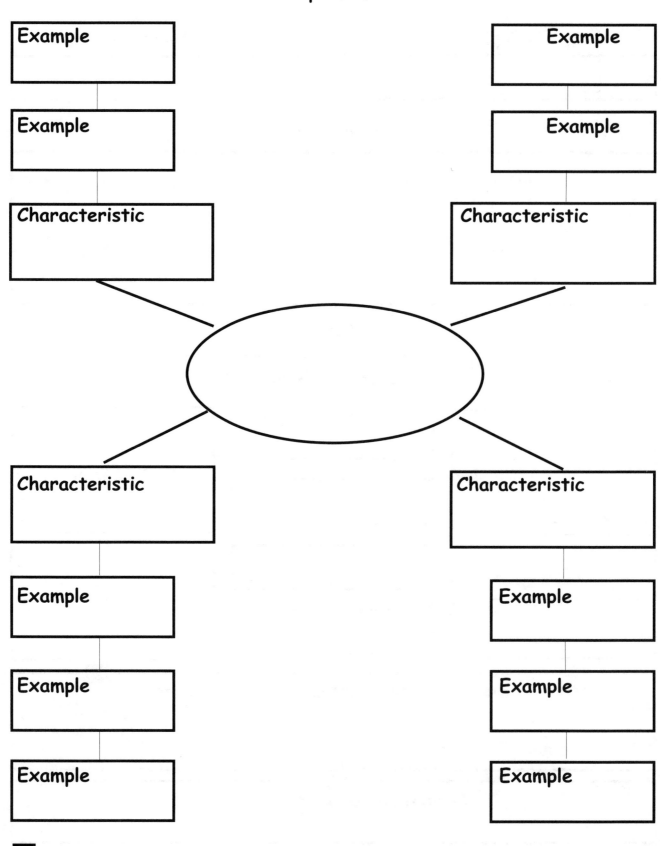

 www.rachelbillmeyer.com • *Strategies to Engage the Mind of the Learner* • © 2006 Rachel Billmeyer

Goal/Action/Outcome

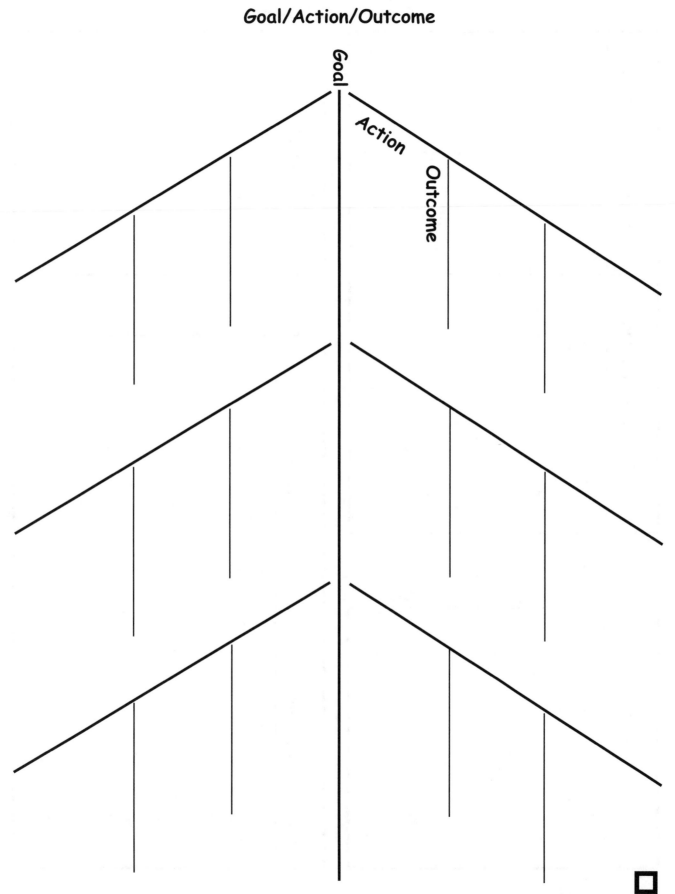

Problem/Solution

	Problem Solutions	Pros	Cons

Goal(s)

Problem

Rationale

Decisions

Problem/Solution

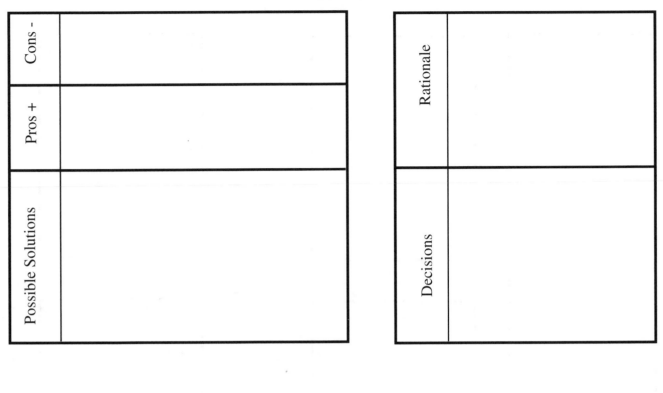

Cons -	
Pros +	
Possible Solutions	

Rationale	
Decisions	

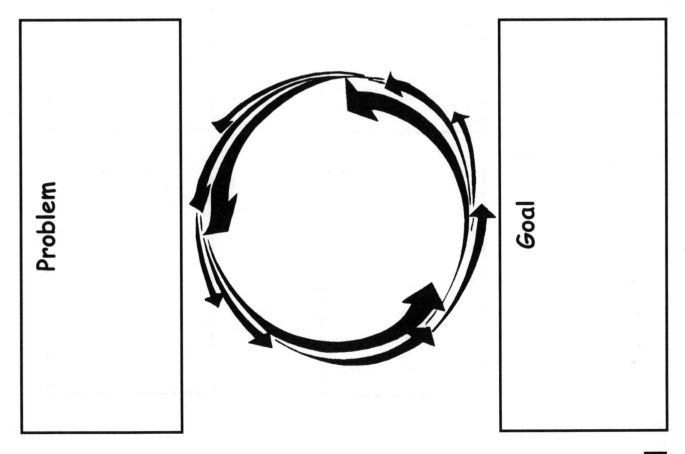

Problem

Goal

Sequence Chain

Sequence Chain for...

Section 6 - Information-Building Strategies

Rationale

Information-Building Strategies extend learning in two ways. Students extend their knowledge about content by recalling, analyzing, and evaluating information studied, as well as experience collaborative learning situations. When students examine the knowledge through interactive activities, learning becomes more meaningful. Each activity has a specific function. For example, some activate prior knowledge, others encourage brainstorming for new ideas, while others involve a review of information previously studied. Different methods of reviewing information encourage different ways of thinking about the concepts studied.

Information-Building Strategies promote individual accountability and positive interdependence. One of the principles of learning from Chapter 2, A Strategic Learner Collaborates with Others to Learn, states that learning is a socially interactive process (Vygotsky, 1978) and that students must be given opportunities to work with each other. These strategies fulfill that need. Most of the activities provide an opportunity for individuals to examine their own thinking before they are asked to work with others. Through cooperative activities students enhance their understanding of the content, learn how other students think, and increase their retention.

Information-Building strategies included in this section.

	Page
• Carousel Brainstorming	174
• FIRST-MIDDLE-LAST Word	175
• Four Corner Challenge	176
• Give 1 to Get 1	177
• Idea Exchange	180
• L.E.T.S. Connect	181
• Numbered Heads Together	183
• Paired Verbal Fluency	184
• Stir-the-Class	185
• Synectics Search	186
• Teammates Consult	187
• Walk About Survey	188

Carousel Brainstorming

Carousel Brainstorming is a fast-paced interactive strategy in which small groups of students rotate around the classroom responding to statements on posted chart papers. Carousel Brainstorming can be used in any subject at any grade level.

How to Use the Strategy

1) Determine the topic for students to analyze and specific statements for brainstorming. Examples include: reviewing questions for an exam, brainstorming different ideas about a selection read, recording ideas for the different story elements (plot, characters, setting), using different approaches to solve problems, or brainstorming ideas for a creative writing exercise.

2) Post large sheets of chart paper on the walls around the room with a different question or thought provoking statement written on each sheet. If walls are not available place paper on tables or the floor.

2) Divide the students into small groups and give each group a different colored marker. There needs to be the same number of groups as there are chart papers.

3) Have each group stand in front of a sheet of paper, select a recorder, and read the statement on the chart paper.

4) Each group has two to three minutes to brainstorm responses to the statement or question listed. The student with the marker records all ideas shared. Responses can be illustrations, especially when used with young children.

5) After the two to three minutes, signal for groups to stop recording and "carousel" to the sheet on their right.

6) Repeat the process until each group has responded to statements or questions on each chart paper.

7) Each group will end up where they started and have the opportunity to read all of the responses and/or examine illustrations.

8) Have each group categorize the responses and delete the repeated comments or ideas.

Benefits of the Strategy
- Keeps students focused and involved as they discuss and record ideas
- Fosters a collaborative environment
- Encourages critical thinking about a topic
- Involves different learning styles
- Incorporates movement
- Creates motivated learners

FIRST-MIDDLE-LAST Word

FIRST-MIDDLE-LAST Word (Wellman and Lipton, 1998) focuses on acronyms to organize thinking before, during, or after learning. Students record ideas for each letter of the concept studied.

How to Use the Strategy
1) Determine the concept or topic students will analyze.
2) Write the word vertically down the side of an overhead or chart paper.
3) Have students work individually or with a partner to record key ideas or important information about the topic. To promote deep thinking, encourage students to create a short phrase or sentence about each letter of the word.
4) When students have completed their word, have them compare ideas with another person or pair.
5) Have the students add, change, or delete information. Students can record responses on acetate to be shown on the overhead or write on chart paper and display on a bulletin board.

Benefits of the Strategy
- Activates prior knowledge
- Helps students summarize essential information
- Serves as an opening or closing activity
- Causes students to monitor learning throughout a unit of study
- Provides a note taking structure in which students record ideas for each letter while reading, watching a film, or listening to a lecture
- Serves as an assessment tool

First Word Example

Instructions: Step 1 - along the left side of the page, the term "farm" is spelled out. To the right of each letter, write a phrase or sentence that helps to describe the farm. When finished, complete Step 2 at the bottom of the page.

F - Families sometimes live on farms.
A - Animals like cows, pigs, and chickens live on farms.
R - Red barns are often seen on farms.
M - Most of our food is grown on farms.

Step 2 - on the back of this page, use the phrases/sentences that you have written above to write a summary paragraph(s) about the farm.

Four Corner Challenge provides the students an opportunity to explore a topic of interest. Students engage in conversation with classmates who select the same corner topic.

How to Use the Strategy

1) Determine four topics about a unit of study which will challenge students' thinking. For example: analyze problem solving alternatives, brainstorm proposition with support for a research paper, recall related facts, or present perspectives of a debate topic.

2) Record one topic per chart paper and post a chart in each of the four corners of the room. Determine discussion questions that focus and challenge students' thinking about the topics. Record the questions on chart paper or an overhead transparency. Questions can be general to all four topics or specific to each one.

3) Explain the four corner topics and discussion questions. Model how to use effective communication skills and then have the students move to a corner of choice.

4) Using the posted discussion questions, students challenge each other's thinking about the topic. For accountability, students could be expected to record the answers to the questions.

Option - If Four Corner Challenge is used to access prior knowledge or as a prereading activity, have students revisit their corner topic during and/or after the lesson to elaborate on previously discussed ideas or to add new ideas.

Benefits of the Strategy

- Provides students an opportunity to explore a topic of choice
- Allows students to collaborate and learn with peers
- Involves movement
- Encourages use of effective communication skills

Example: **Rocketry**

What were some of the major challenges the space program has faced in rocketry? How did they solve (or are they solving) the challenges?

Proposition: *German advances in rocketry during World War II formed the basis for modern day rocket technology.*

Important facts, events, and dates regarding rocketry.

Rocketry is the "travel of the future."

Give 1 to Get 1

Give 1 to Get 1 is an interactive strategy that provides students an opportunity to exchange ideas about a topic before, during, or after learning. This barter system activity engages all students in the learning process.

How to Use the Strategy

1) Select a topic of focus and determine what information students will give in order to extend their knowledge about the topic.

Examples:
- Exchange ideas about the interpretation of an assigned article. (I think the author wants us to believe/think. . .)
- Brainstorm writing ideas for a research paper. (remember to state as a thesis, for example, Human settlement is putting Polar bears at risk.)
- Review learnings from a unit of study. (something I want to be sure to remember is. . .)
- Build prior knowledge about a topic to be studied. (one thing I know about snakes is. . .)
- Exchange specific ways to implement an idea. (I think one way to make this successful is. . .)
- Provide an opportunity for a mini-reflective conversation about a learning. (an interesting thought I have is. . .)
- Develop questions as a review guide for a unit of study. (one thing I wonder about or one question I have is. . .)

2) Prepare a worksheet consisting of nine to twelve boxes. For younger children three to six boxes is sufficient.

3) Explain that the Give 1 to Get 1 strategy consists of three parts.
- Part I: requires the students to record three of their own ideas about the topic of study
- Part II: involves students exchanging ideas with each other
- Part III: provides an opportunity for small groups of students to review ideas gained when working with peers

4) Part I: Give students the prepared worksheet and instruct them to record three ideas related to the assigned topic, one idea per box.

5) Part II: Instruct students to get up and mingle with different students in order to give and get ideas. Students give an idea from their worksheet, their partners record the idea, and then reverse roles. Students get only one idea from each partner and each recorded idea must be different. Encourage students to exchange ideas with students with whom they don't regularly have the opportunity to talk.

6) Part III: After students give and get ideas, have them discuss their ideas in small groups. They can share ideas they found to be most helpful, unique, different, thought-provoking, or interesting depending on the topic shared. If students did not

~~~ fill each box, they can record more ideas at this time. Conclude with a large group discussion of the ideas.

Benefits of the Strategy
- Builds a reflective community of learners
- Activates or assesses prior knowledge about a topic
- Serves as a pre-reading, during reading, or after reading activity
- Causes students to be active listeners
- Allows students to learn from each other
- Provides an opportunity for independent thinking, partner sharing, and large group reflection

Example

I think the author wants us to believe/think. . .	Now that I have read this, I wonder. . .	I want to be sure to remember. . .
One thing I already know about this topic. . .	One question I have is. . .	An interesting thought I have is. . .

Option
Provide each student with an index card and instruct them to record one idea about the selected topic on it. Students Give 1 to Get 1 by walking around, exchanging cards with other students, and discussing the idea written on the card.

Give 1 to Get 1

Idea Exchange

The Idea Exchange is a quick interactive strategy for gathering information about a specific topic. The strategy focuses on active listening as students exchange thoughts and ideas with classmates.

How to Use the Strategy

1) Select a topic that requires ideas from all students such as class problem and/or issue needing a solution.

2) Discuss the five steps of the Idea Exchange:

- Individual Response - students respond to a sentence stem such as "A safe classroom looks/sounds like. . ." and/or "Specific ways to create a safe classroom are. . ."
- Mingle, Share, Listen - students walk around exchanging ideas in conversations. During this step students are actively listening to each other so that they remember what was said.
- Remember & Record - students return to their seats and write what they heard.
- Table Group Discussion - when all students are finished recording they collaborate to create a group list of the ideas.
- Large Group Synthesis - chart the final compilation of ideas and post for future reference.

Benefits of the Strategy

- Encourages open-ended thinking
- Creates a risk-taking environment for learning
- Allows students equal access and responsibility in brainstorming ideas about a possible topic
- Causes independent and interdependent thinking
- Incorporates active listening skills
- Builds collective wisdom of the group

L.E.T.S. Connect

The L.E.T.S. Connect (Cutts, 2002) strategy engages the mind of the learner throughout a read aloud or a video. Periodically the activity is stopped so paired learners share with each other what they are thinking about the topic at that moment.

How to Use the Strategy

1) Select a book or selection to read aloud or a video to show the students.

2) Review with students the importance of thinking about what they are learning before, during, and after when reading or watching a video.

3) Explain the strategy, L.E.T.S. Connect to the students. State that L.E.T.S. Connect is an acronym which means:

> L = Listen to the selection
> E = Engage with the content
> T = Think about the ideas and details, vocabulary, or sequence of events
> S = Say something to your partner about your thoughts
> Connect = Do all of the above steps and connect with the author, content, and other students' thoughts. Connections are any related thoughts that enter the listener's mind.

4) Organize students into groups of two or three.

5) Before reading a narrative, state to the students, "L.E.T.S. Connect with the selection by sharing predictions about the story based on the title, the book cover, the author's name, or background knowledge." When reading informative text, students can predict by perusing graphics, bold face type, or previewing study questions.

6) Read the selection aloud to the students and at various predetermined points stop reading and announce "L.E.T.S. Connect." At this point students say something to their partner about the connections they are making with the selection.

7) After reading the selection, instruct the students to make a final connection by creating a summary statement about the entire selection.

8) A written culminating activity could be a summary written by an individual or group of all the shared connections.

Option

"L.E.T.S. Connect" motivates students to actively construct meaning while reading through the use of different processing skills. For example, the strategy could be used to reinforce story elements. Before reading, review the story elements with the students. Distribute a story map of the story elements and explain to the students that they will complete the map individually or with a partner after the selection has been read. At key points during the reading, stop and say "L.E.T.S. Connect" and have the students link their comment to a story element. After reading the story, the students complete their story map and share them with other students. The story map is an assessment tool.

⌘ Option

L.E.T.S. Connect can be used for informational reading such as during a science experiment. During the experiment the teacher stops periodically and asks the students to connect by saying what might happen next in the experiment.

Benefits of the Strategy

- Provides an opportunity for the teacher to read aloud to students, setting the pace and stopping points for making connections
- Allows the listener an opportunity to discuss thoughts, connections, or personal experiences during the reading
- Causes students to be actively engaged and monitors their thinking throughout the entire selection
- Makes the final summary statement easier for students to develop when relating thoughts throughout the reading
- Extends thinking and understanding for both narrative and informational text

Numbered Heads Together

Numbered Heads Together (Kagan, 1992) is an effective structure that develops cooperative groups, as well as individual accountability. Working in small groups, students pool their ideas about a question posed by the teacher. After an appropriate amount of time for heads together, one student is responsible for explaining the group's answer to the class.

How to Use the Strategy

1) Create teams of three to five students and assign each team member a different number from one to five.

2) Assign each team a letter of the alphabet. Matching letters are placed in an envelope for the teacher to use when calling for a specific student response.

3) Select a topic for students to review, create questions about it, and record them on chart paper, an overhead, or the chalkboard. Questions can range from basic recall of information to open-ended processing questions. Share the first question with the students.

4) The teacher says "Numbered Heads Together" and each team of students pools ideas that answer the question.

5) After an appropriate amount of time, the teacher reminds the students that each team member must be prepared to reveal the group's response to the question.

6) The teacher calls a number from one to five and all students with that number stand up. Next, the teacher selects a letter from the envelope and the student standing at the table group with the matching letter states the group's response to the answer.

6) If the answer is incomplete or incorrect, another person standing is called on to give the answer ("and does group x have any corrections or additions?"). If open-ended questions are asked, all students standing might state the team's response.

Benefits of the Strategy

- Develops collaborative teams as well causes individual accountability
- Encourages active listening
- Serves as a quick review of information learned
- Works as an assessment tool, have each team member submit written responses
- Allows teams to compete with each other, which is motivating for some learners
- Provides an opportunity for students to interact with a topic at different levels of cognitive complexity

Paired Verbal Fluency

Paired Verbal Fluency is a quick, interactive strategy in which students exchange ideas about a selected topic with a partner. Each student has three opportunities to talk freely with the same partner about a selected topic.

How to Use the Strategy

1) Structure the classroom so that students can work comfortably in pairs and have the pairs decide which partner will be #1 and which person will be #2.

2) Assign the topic and have each pair discuss by taking turns. Student #1 talks for 60 seconds uninterrupted to student #2. Partners listen carefully so as not to repeat ideas shared. After 60 seconds, the teacher signals so student #2 can talk about the topic for 60 seconds uninterrupted while student #1 listens. The exchange of ideas continues for three rounds with each round using less time.

3) Explain that the teacher is the time keeper so students can focus on sharing ideas and active listening. Possible time frames for exchanging ideas are 60, 45, and 15 seconds. The timing of the rounds depends on the age of the students, dynamics of the class, and knowledge of the content.

4) Introduce the Paired Verbal Fluency strategy to students by using a familiar topic, such as personal interests, reactions to a current event, or rules of a game.

5) After the three rounds of sharing, students independently or with their partners could record ideas exchanged. Lists can be used for class discussion, to review for a test, or keep them for future reference.

6) The Paired Verbal Fluency strategy works well at the end of a unit just before taking a test. Students would have the opportunity to talk with a partner about their learnings which can relieve test anxiety.

Benefits of the Strategy

- Stimulates thinking before writing about an assigned topic
- Helps students recall prior knowledge about the topic or unit of study
- Works as an anticipatory set to get the students focused on the topic
- Prepares the students for large group class discussions
- Provides opportunities for students to practice sharing ideas and opinions
- Serves as a study tool to review information before testing

Stir-the-Class

"If ever I am a teacher, it will be to learn more than to teach."
- Dorothee DeLuzy (1747-1830)

Stir-the-Class (Kagan, 1992) is a fast-paced, communication strategy in which small teams of students stand together and brainstorm answers to a question posed by the teacher. Student are stirred after each question to the next group in order to exchange brainstormed ideas.

How to Use the Strategy

1) Create teams of three or four students and assign each student a number, one-four.

2) Have the teams stand together and form a circle of teams around the room.

3) Display prepared questions on the overhead and reveal the first one for the teams to discuss. Types of questions can range from recall of information to open-ended processing. (Explain the Steps of the Scientific Method used in the experiment. What are the steps in the Scientific Method? What are the primary and secondary colors on a color wheel? What makes them primary or secondary? In what ways does/ can knowing the color wheel help you as an artist?)

4) Teams huddle to discuss the answer to the question.

5) Select a number from one-four by spinning a spinner or drawing a card. Stir-the-Class by having the team member with the selected number rotating clockwise to the next group.

6) Instruct the new team member to explain to the new group ideas discussed for the first question.

7) Present the next question to the new groups, they discuss it, a new card is drawn, and that team member rotates to share.

8) Process continues until all questions have been discussed.

9) End with a two-prong process question:
   • How did this strategy assist your learning of this content?
   • In what ways did this strategy benefit you as a learner?

Benefits of the Strategy
   • Creates interdependence
   • Builds individual accountability
   • Involves movement and creates motivated learners
   • Focuses on verbal responses which encourage active listening
   • Allows students to process information at different cognitive levels

Synectics Search is a communication strategy which causes the brain to think about an issue or topic in a different way. The strategy activates fluid and creative thinking because it causes the brain to compare two things that would not ordinarily be compared.

How to Use the Strategy

1) Select the variation appropriate for the situation.
- Compare selected concept with a broad category or a specific item
- Compare a selected concept with a specific item, for example, "A scientist is like a bank account because. . ."
- Select a concept and a broad category: "Reading is like (summer activity) because. . ." Elicit four different items within the category. For example,

boating	fishing
gardening	golfing

- Select two items to base comparison on: "Creative writing is more like (pasta/ice cream) because. . ."

2) Create teams of three or four. Ask one person within the team to be a recorder.

3) Show the chart displaying the sentence and box if appropriate.

4) Explain the concept and the topic to use for the comparison. Model one example.

5) Allow three to four minutes for the groups to brainstorm with the recorder writing down all ideas. Ask each group to select a favorite sentence to share with the entire class. Share and enjoy.

Benefits of the Strategy

- Causes the brain to think in pictures instead of words and analytically rather than literally as it searches for connections
- Makes complex ideas easier to understand
- Serves as a useful tool for explaining unfamiliar ideas to students
- Serves as a prewriting activity
- Provides opportunities for brainstorming
- Encourages students to think at a higher level of processing
- Helps students create explanations of a learned concept

A Cell is Like a Factory - Example

Cell Part	What it Does	Factory Analog
cell membrane	outer boundary/lets things in & out	walls and door
cytoplasm	gel-like material/fills cell	air
nucleus	directs cells activities	main office
chromatin	DNA - coded information	boss, computer files

Teammates Consult

Organizing students into groups does not always guarantee they will work cooperatively. Teammates Consult (Kagan, 1992) is a cooperative structure which focuses on positive interdependence. This unique strategy forces students to verbally frame their thinking or develop answers to questions with team members before independently recording them.

How to Use the Strategy

1) The teacher selects and prepares a worksheet about a topic for study, such as a set of math problems, a lab report, discussion questions for a social studies passage, or a novel in English. For example: The steps we must remember in doing long division are. . . We will be accurate and efficient in doing long division if. . . Give examples of fate and coincidence in Hardy's Return of the Native. Why do you think Hardy uses so much fate and coincidence? What does it say about his view of the world of his time?

2) Students are organized into teams of three or four. Each student receives a copy of the worksheet and as a team they discuss their assigned task. The teacher answers questions the teams have about the task.

3) Students are instructed to put their pencils or pens in the center of the team's work space. Providing a pencil holder, such as a glass, can, or beaker formalizes this step.

4) One student is selected to read the first statement on the worksheet to group members.

5) Teammates consult to determine answers or frame thinking. If appropriate, remind students to refer to their text materials and/or notes.

6) The student sitting to the left of the reader facilitates the discussion and checks to see that all the teammates understand and agree with the statement or answer.

7) When there is agreement, teammates pick up their own pencils or pens and write the answer on their own worksheet.

8) Individual teams move on to the second statement on the worksheet. The facilitator becomes the new reader. Pens or pencils are returned to the middle of the work space. Students continue the process remembering to rotate roles until all of the problems or questions are answered.

Benefits of the Strategy
- Fosters independent and interdependent thinkers
- Develops a collaborative environment
- Allows students to pool ideas before recording a response
- Encourages active listening

Walk About Survey

The Walk About Survey is a three part strategy which causes students to independently respond to a topic, survey classmates for their ideas, and end with a small group discussion. The strategy involves all students in generating new ideas, processing past learnings, synthesizing information, and sharing current thoughts and understanding about a topic.

How to Use the Strategy

1) Determine the topic students will survey and three specific categories to guide the their thinking about the topic. Examples include:
- recollections about the topic,
- understandings gained,
- connections made to other topics or the real world,
- observations made during the unit of study,
- applications made, and
- insights acquired.

If students are reading a novel, the ideas can center around impressions before reading, during reading, and after reading.

2) Organize students into small groups.

3) Give each student a copy of the Walk About Survey. Explain the purpose of the strategy and the three different responses students are to make about the topic. Overview the three parts of the strategy:

Part I: Individually record three ideas

Part II: Survey classmates, excluding group members

Part III: In small groups compare and categorize learnings, search for themes, and prepare to report findings to the entire class.

4) Part I: Instruct students to individually record one idea for each category in the boxes on the left side of the survey labeled "My idea. . ."

5) Part II: Have students walk about to survey other students, excluding group members, using the following process:
- Student tells one idea to another classmate, partner listens, restates idea heard, and writes idea in the appropriate box on the survey.
- Student telling the idea reads what partner wrote and then signs his name on the line in the same box. Student signature provides accountability as well as a future reference for more information.
- Students reverse roles and continue to survey other classmates. Students may record only one idea from each person.
- Students continue to survey classmates until all boxes contain one idea or the time is up. The time frame varies from ten to fifteen minutes.

6) Part III: Have students return to their small groups and exchange ideas captured. Students can record new ideas in empty boxes. The small group discussion can focus on categorizing ideas collected into themes, and/or exploring and elaborating on ideas gathered.

7) Discuss ideas organized in their small group with the class.

Option

Use three levels of questioning from the Question-Answer Relationship strategy (p. 141). Students develop one question about the selected topic for each level of processing: "Right There"/literal, Think and Search"/inferential, and "On My Own"/ application. Students walk about to survey and record questions from their class-mates.

Option

Students select a book they have read and record one idea about the characters, plot, setting, problem/solution, or theme in the "My idea..." box. Students survey each other sharing ideas about the books they have read.

Benefits of the Strategy

- Engages the mind of the learner before, during, or after learning
- Encourages students to respond at different levels of cognitive processing
- Serves as a tool for organizing prior knowledge or as a prewriting activity
- Involves students as independent and interdependent learners
- Incorporates productive communication skills: active listening, and restating
- Involves movement
- Adapts to all grade levels and all content areas

Book Survey Example

Selection Read

Setting			
	Book Signature	Book Signature	Book Signature
Characters			
	Book Signature	Book Signature	Book Signature
Theme			
	Book Signature	Book Signature	Book Signature

Walk About Survey
(Add three categories to focus thinking)

Survey Topic:

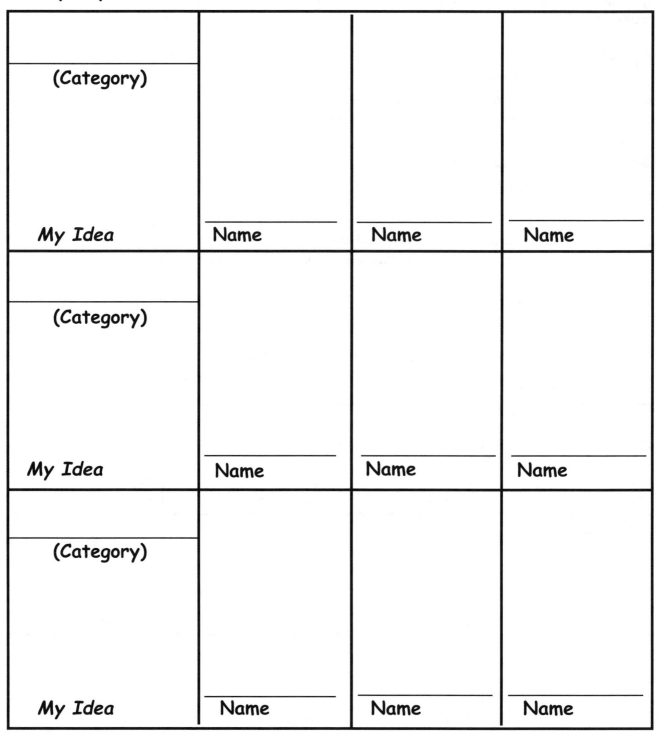

(Category)			
My Idea	Name	Name	Name
(Category)			
My Idea	Name	Name	Name
(Category)			
My Idea	Name	Name	Name

Section 7 - Discussion Strategies   Notes:

*"The goal of education should be to produce critical thinkers in the strong sense.
Strong sense critical thinkers are those who use certain intellectual skills
(such as clarifying issues, detecting faulty reasoning, etc.)
in the pursuit of certain values (such as truth, open- or fair-mindedness, rationality,
clarity, autonomy, and self-criticism)."*

- Richard Paul

Rationale

Discussion promotes learning because students engage in dialogue that enhances thinking and understanding. Rather than being a recipient of information transmitted by the teacher, students actively engage in conversation to construct their own knowledge about the topic. When discussion is incorporated as a classroom strategy, the teacher becomes the "guide on the side" rather than the "sage on the stage."

Debate about a topic expands, clarifies, and focuses thoughts, promotes discussion, and creates a stimulating learning environment. Interactive discussions allow students to closely examine a topic by exchanging their understanding, ideas, and questions. When students exchange different perspectives and personal perceptions, issues become real and believable. Through discussion, students develop an awareness of their own beliefs and values and perceive ways that their thinking about a topic may differ from their classmates. A sense of creative freedom evolves which encourages ownership of ideas and helps to build independent thinkers.

Discussion strategies are designed so ALL students are active participants. All too often a conversation consists of a few bright, verbal students competing to exchange ideas with each other or with the teacher. The teacher and student's role must be clearly articulated. The teacher serves as a facilitator of the discussion and does not impose personal values, beliefs, or ideals. Students learn to be active participants, and establishing classroom norms will help create student-directed discussions.

Successful classroom discussion:
- Considers room arrangement with chairs in a circle
- Involves open-ended, higher level thinking questions
- Encourages student-to-student questions and/or sharing of information
- Provides wait time for student response
- Allows students to create their own questions about the topic
- Includes active listening skills and listening respectfully to each other
- Allows students occasionally to respond in pairs before the large group
- Provides methods to assess the effectiveness of group and individual participation

Discussion strategies included in this section.

	Page
• Community Circle	193
• Read and Reflect	194
• Creative Debate	195
• Discussion Web	197
• Scored Discussion	200

Assessing Effectiveness of Group Discussion Example

Group	**Rating** 5 high - 1 low	**Rationale**
We were clear about the goal of the discussion.	5 4 3 2 1	
Everyone was a participant.	5 4 3 2 1	
We supported each other's thinking.	5 4 3 2 1	
We stayed on task.	5 4 3 2 1	
We used active listening skills.	5 4 3 2 1	
We restated ideas and asked for clarification.	5 4 3 2 1	
We made group decisions.	5 4 3 2 1	
We conducted a productive discussion.	5 4 3 2 1	

Individual		
I contributed ideas.	5 4 3 2 1	
I was an active listener.	5 4 3 2 1	
I made eye contact with the person speaking.	5 4 3 2 1	
I encouraged thinking from other group members.	5 4 3 2 1	
I was open to new ideas.	5 4 3 2 1	
I feel good about my participation in the discussion.	5 4 3 2 1	

Community Circle

Community Circle is a form of discussion that emphasizes active listening and effective speaking skills. Each student responds to an open-ended statement posed by a group leader. Divergent thinking is encouraged. The Community Circle is a safe structure for introducing young children and/or English Language Learners to discussion.

How to Use the Strategy

1) Initiate conversation with the students about effective discussion skills. Emphasize the importance of active listening and effective speaking skills. Brainstorm and record active listening skills. Examples include:
   - Eyes on the speaker
   - Ears listening to the speaker
   - Mind thinking about what the speaker is saying
   - Eyes continuing to focus until the speaker is finished speaking
   - Brainstorm and record effective speaking skills
   - Use a loud, clear voice
   - Keep hands away from the face
   - Look at the audience

2) Explain the Community Circle form of discussion. All participants sit in a circle formation. Begin with one Community Circle. Once students learn the process, students can work in smaller groups if appropriate.

3) Pose an open-ended statement. The teacher models the leader position the first time. Examples:
   - When I grow up I want to . . .
   - One thing I would like to improve is . . .
   - The best thing about a zoo is . . .
   - The safest way to travel is . . . because . . .
   - Students should/should not be allowed to graduate from high school if they do not pass the state assessments because . . .

4) After ample wait-time, the leader completes the statement first, followed by the student to the right, until all students have had a chance to respond. Each student is encouraged to answer using a loud, clear voice. Students may say "Pass" if they cannot think of a response.

5) All students actively listen to each idea stated. Questions to clarify, elaborate, and/or extend thinking may be asked after an idea is communicated. The teacher models the questioning process.

6) After all students have participated in the Community Circle, the leader asks participants to reflect on their use of the active listening skills and effective speaking skills. Students can express through group discussion personal opinions about their effectiveness, reflect on a written rating scale, or use a hand signal with five fingers being very effective to zero fingers not effective.

Benefits of the Strategy

- Involves all students as active participants
- Teaches active listening skills
- Develops creative, divergent thinkers
- Emphasizes effective speaking skills
- Causes students to be critical listeners and thinkers
- Incorporates questioning of ideas expressed
- Encourages self-assessment of both active listening and speaking skills
- Promotes discussion for primary age children

Reference: Adapted from Lorna Curran, *Cooperative Learning Lessons for Little Ones*

Option

Quality discussion emphasizes effective communication skills. To teach and practice communication tools, have students work in pairs using the following Read and Reflect process.

Read and Reflect

- Select a partner and designate an "A" and a "B" person.

- Preview the selection to be read. Discuss prior knowledge related to the selected topic.

- Both partners read the first paragraph silently, highlighting key ideas.

- Process the paragraph in the following manner:
  "A" says, "A key idea for me . . . "
  "B" paraphrases and inquires
  (for example, "You like the author's choice of words. What seems unique about the author's way of telling the story?")

- Reverse roles and repeat the process with the first paragraph.

- Continue the reading process with the remaining paragraphs.

Creative Debate

The Creative Debate stimulates creative thinking as well as thinking from different perspectives. Students determine whether they are for or against an issue and select a character representative of their position. They debate the issue from that character's point of view. Creative Debates are suited for any course requiring more than one perspective such as science, economics, history, psychology, and literature selections.

How to Use the Strategy

1) The teacher selects a debate topic and asks students to determine their position on the issue. The topic is written on the board and students write their name on the side representative of their beliefs. Examples:

FOR---------criminal punishment---------AGAINST
Character = Local politician
FOR DEVELOPMENT----Transcontinental Railroad---AGAINST DEVELOPMENT
Character = Buffalo Bill
FOR-------Japanese killing whales for research purposes------AGAINST
Character = Japanese Prime Minister
FOR-----Honor Anne Frank's memory-------AGAINST
Character = Otto Frank, Anne's father
FOR------Bombing Hiroshima and Nagasaki-------AGAINST
Character = President Harry S. Truman
FOR------Treatment of siblings-------AGAINST
Character = Cinderella

2) Students select a character representative of their position and gather evidence to support their position. They may come dressed in appropriate costumes, use researched phrases, and gestures for their characters.

3) On the day of the debate divide the class into three groups: a group for the issue, a group against, and the third group observe the debate. The group for the topic turns their chairs to face the group against it. Class observers collect data for students involved in the debate. Students establish effective debate criteria (see Assessing Effectiveness of Group Discussion, p. 192) in advance.

4) As the debate begins have students introduce themselves as the character and their position to the rest of the class.

5) Students debate from their character's point of view for ten to fifteen minutes. They cite references from their research to backup their points. Observers may ask a question of either position or of a particular character.

6) Students switch positions so all observers are given a chance to debate the topic. Debate continues an appropriate amount of time with new observers collecting data.

7) Observers share the data collected with the class. If appropriate, data can be shared at the end of each fifteen minute debate.

8) Conclude the debate with small groups processing their involvement in the Creative Debate. Students make suggestions for future debates.

Variation: During the debate students may decide to change their position and move to a chair on the opposite team.

Variation: Creative Debate can be used as an impromptu activity with positions assigned the day of class debate. Students do not have to agree with the assigned position.

Benefits of the Strategy
- Stimulates lively discussions
- Encourages students to think from different perspectives
- Incorporates humor in a meaningful way
- Involves research skills
- Develops critical and creative thinkers
- Enhances persuasive thinking
- Unveils student's beliefs and values about an issue

The children of this nation are seeds of greatness for this country of ours. Some of them land in rocky soil, and others land, fortunately, in fertile soil. But to my mind, they all have potential. Our task is to help all of them grow so that wherever they land is a place that gives them challenging high standards and helps build standards of character. Here in this United States of America in 1995, there must be no weeds in the gardens of our schools.
- Richard Riley

Discussion Web

The Discussion Web (Alvermann, 1991) creates a framework for considering all sides of an issue being discussed. Students organize their thinking using a graphic web. A question about the topic is written in the center of the web and opposing viewpoints are organized on each side of the web. The Discussion Web encourages each student to think individually about the items they want to express in the discussion. The Discussion Web incorporates listening, speaking, reading, and writing in a meaningful way.

How to Use the Strategy

1) Determine the issue for discussion and assign students a selection(s) to read.
2) Generate a question about the selection that generates more than one point of view. "Should Goldilocks be punished?" "Was Charlotte's method of getting food cruel?" "Was the Vietnam War justified?" "Was Napoleon a great leader?" Using an overhead transparency of the graphic web, write the question in the center of it.
3) Have students work with a partner to generate pro and con responses to the question.
4) Encourage partners to list an equal number of pro and con responses.
5) Organize pairs into groups of four and have them evaluate the question and all pro and con ideas. Students can disagree or agree with ideas shared, add new ideas to their web, and then reach a conclusion to share with the class. Students clearly state their conclusion at the bottom of the web in the box labeled Conclusion. One group member is selected to report their conclusion to the class.
6) Engage in further discussion as an entire class about the pros and cons of the question. Dissenting opinions can be expressed during the large group discussion. A large group consensus can be reached.
7) The Discussion Web can be used as a pre-writing activity. Students follow the discussion by writing a persuasive essay outlining their opinions.

Benefits of the Strategy

- Incorporates a graphic web to organize thinking
- Encourages critical thinking skills
- Gives all students an opportunity to assume responsibility for a position
- Involves all students in sharing their own ideas
- Incorporates writing skills
- Develops research skills
- Causes students to consider different sides of an issue before drawing conclusions
- Allows students to experiment with ideas in the text, raise questions, and express opinions about the text
- Develops individual accountability

Discussion Web Example

Charlotte's Web: Chapters 5, 6

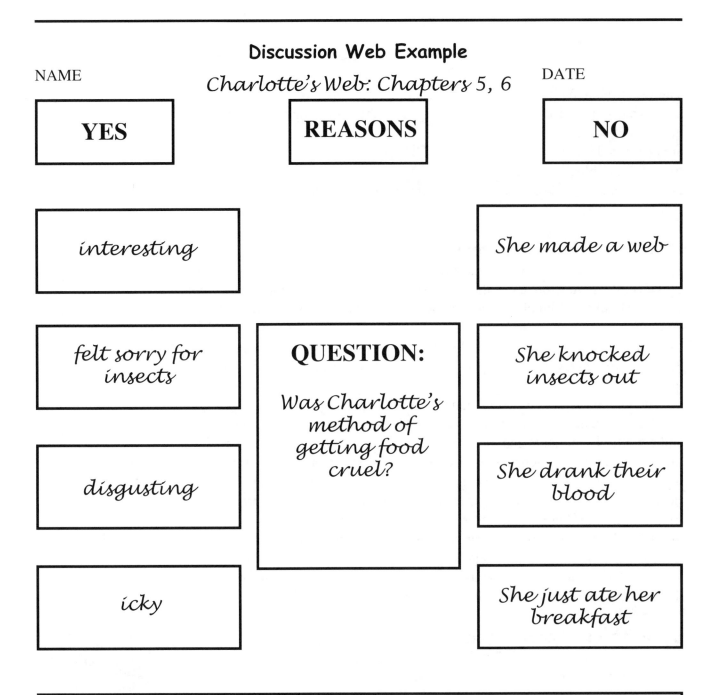

NAME   DATE

YES	REASONS	NO
interesting		She made a web
felt sorry for insects	**QUESTION:** Was Charlotte's method of getting food cruel?	She knocked insects out
disgusting		She drank their blood
icky		She just ate her breakfast

CONCLUSION: *What do you think?*

No, it was not cruel because that's the way insects survive.

 www.rachelbillmeyer.com • *Strategies to Engage the Mind of the Learner* • © 2006 Rachel Billmeyer

Discussion Web

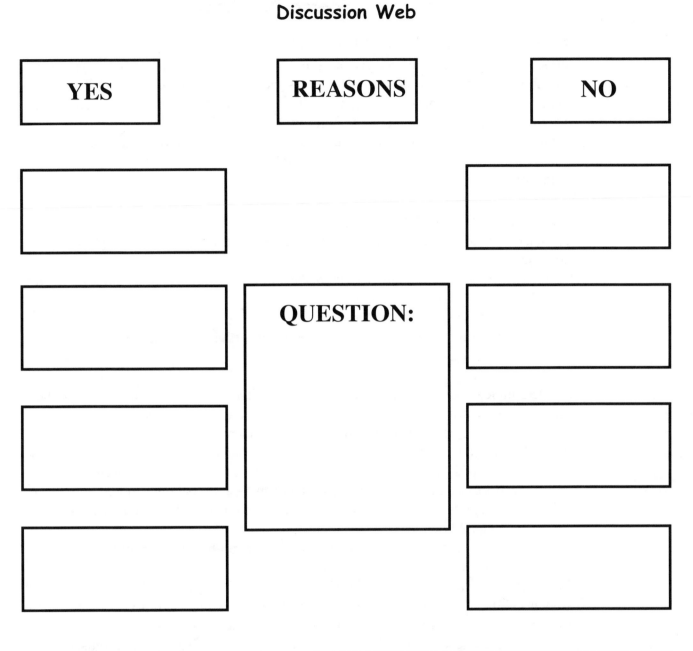

YES

REASONS

NO

QUESTION:

CONCLUSION:

Scored Discussion

Scored Discussion (Newmann, 1970) is a discussion strategy intended to assist students in expressing ideas clearly as a member of a social group. The strategy uses a fishbowl structure in which half of the class is seated in a small circle while the remaining class members form an outer circle. The inner group of students conducts a content-related discussion and the outer group observes and scores individual contributions to the discussion. In advance, the teacher and students determine criteria and/or indicators of a successful social dialogue. Students are awarded points or lose points based on how they participate.

How to Use the Strategy

1) Select a topic for discussion and assign readings. Example: providing for the homeless in our city

2) Instruct students to read the assigned selections and organize their thinking around the following discussion agenda:
   - Define the issue or problem
   - Determine what position the writer of the article takes on the issue
   - Determine own position
   - Decide how the author's position agrees or disagrees with own position

3) Determine the criteria and or/indicators of a successful discussion. Organize the criteria into a scoring format and distribute a copy to each observer.

4) Teach the Scored Discussion strategy to the students:
   - Explain the fishbowl structure of an inner and outer circle of students.
   - Review the criteria and/or indicators to be used by the outer circle for scoring the discussion. Each student can be assigned one student to observe or students can observe all members of the inner circle randomly collecting data based on the criteria.
   - Model for students how positive examples might sound about the issue they will be discussing.

5) Determine which students will be in the inner circle to discuss the issue and which students will be a member of the outer circle who score the discussion.

6) Conduct the discussion for fifteen to twenty minutes.

7) End with the teacher and observing students providing feedback to discussion members using the examples collected on the criteria sheets.

8) Conclude with a large group discussion about the benefits of a Scored Discussion.

Benefits of the Strategy
   - Develops comprehensive levels of understanding about content
   - Encourages the development of skills for controversial conversation
   - Promotes respectful listening of divergent points of view
   - Develops critical thinkers
   - Provides students an opportunity to share their knowledge with classmates
   - Serves as an assessment of students' knowledge about a topic
   - Builds individual accountability
   - Creates positive peer interdependence

Scored Discussion - An Assessment Strategy

Name _____ Topic _____

Pluses of the Scored Discussion	Wishes for Next Discussion	Personal Learnings

Scored Discussion Criteria

Name _____ Topic _____

Positive/Productive Behavior	Points		Non-productive Behavior	Points
(2) Taking a position on a question.	_____	(-2)	Not paying attention or distracting others	_____
(1) Making a relevant comment	_____	(-2)	Interrupting the speaker	_____
(2) Using evidence to support a position or presenting factual information	_____	(-1)	Making an irrelevant comment	_____
(1) Drawing another student into the discussion	_____	(-3)	Monopolizing discussion time	_____
(2) Recognizing contradictions in another person's statements	_____	(-3)	Personal attack of another person's comment	_____
(2) Using active listening skills	_____			
(2) Rephrasing or restating what another person says to show understanding	_____			
(2) Recognizing when another person makes an irrelevant comment	_____			
(2) Making an analogy	_____			
(1) Asking a clarifying question or moving the discussion forward	_____		Points Earned _____	

Section 8 - Grouping and Energizing Activities

Notes:

"Long after they forgot what we taught them,
they'll remember how we treated them."

Rationale

Grouping and energizing activities promote collaborative, fun-filled learning environments. Both kinds of activities provide opportunities for movement that brain research confirms increases performance. Movement enhances learning. When you change your physiology you change your internal state. Movement involves the thalamus which produces that "feel good" effect. Jensen (2000) states that when students move they learn more. Master presenter, Bob Garmston, has taught me first hand that energy is a critical ingredient for learning. If the students are "energyless," as Bob says (1997), the teacher needs to use grouping and energizing activities to build energy.

Students of all ages need many opportunities to share with each other throughout the day, semester, and school year. When students exchange ideas with a learning buddy it keeps them involved as active rather than passive participants. Everyone is given a chance to participate rather than those few who always raise their hands. Students can work with a learning buddy to:
- Discuss a book or part of a book just read
- Explain ideas heard in a lecture
- Share insights gained from reading their partner's journal entry
- Explain steps for solving a math problem or conducting a science experiment

The ideas for partner learning are endless (examples p. 204). Learning buddies can be assigned for an entire unit of study, for a quick, one time energizing interaction, or until all of the assigned partners on the Learning Buddy activity have participated.

Productive and effective learning buddies thrive in a comfortable, supportive environment. Students need to know that all ideas have merit, and they will not be laughed at when relating them. Teachers find grouping activities to be more successful when students are willing to share and work with all class members. Partner learning encourages students to be in charge of their own learning, ultimately creating independent learners.

Humor is also an important ingredient of a collaborative environment. National presenter and colleague, John Dyer, taught the importance of humor in any learning environment. John always looks for humor and believes that humor comes from interactions within an environment. In his book *Outrageous Pursuits* (2000), he writes about activities for using humor to energize as well as to create a positive learning environment. Humor, used appropriately, creates

camaraderie, relieves stress, and causes people to feel at home with each other. When students work together they enjoy relating humorous events. In creating a productive learning climate it is important that teachers model an acceptance of all responses, encourage students to elaborate on their ideas, and incorporate appropriate examples of humor.

Grouping and Energizing activities included in this section.

	Page
• Grouping Activities	204
• Songs for Groups	204
• "Boastful" Adjective Groups	205
• Line-up Ideas for Groups	205
• Songs to Energize	210
• Quick Group Energizers	210

Grouping Activities

Baseball Team Mates (p. 206)
Clock Learning Buddies (p. 207)
Worldly Learning Buddies (p. 208)
C.C. (Common Characteristics) Friends
   • Find someone who has the same color of eyes as yours. Do you think eye color affects personality? How or why not?
   • Find someone with something numerically in common. Seek unique ideas no one else will think of, like number of brothers and sisters, birth date, or number of letters in name.
Content Concepts (ideas to reinforce concepts learned within the content areas)
   • Math Partners or Trios - Find someone who has the same mathematical equation you do. Match 1/2 with 50% and/or .50 or match 20% with .20 and/or 1/5.
   • Science Partners - Find someone who has the same symbol for the periodic table as yours. Match the H card with the Hydrogen card or the Zn card with Zinc.
   • Social Study Partners - Find someone who has the matching capitol for your state card. Match California with Sacramento or Nebraska with Lincoln.
   • Seasonal Partners - Instruct students to fold a piece of paper into fourths, label each box with a season, and sketch what the season means to them. Students find four different partners for each season.
   • Color Wheel Partners - Find matching partners for the primary colors.

Songs for Groups

Create song cards, five or six cards for each song. Sort the song cards into the correct number needed to create new groups. Place the correct number of song cards on each table. Each participant takes a song card and sings or hums the song on the card to find other group members.

Songs to use: My Bonnie, Three Blind Mice, Twinkle Twinkle Little Star, ABC Song, Doe a Deer, The Farmer in the Dell, I'm a Little Teapot, Old Mac Donald, Mary Had a Little Lamb, Row, Row, Row Your Boat, Happy Birthday, and during the holidays try holiday songs, such as Frosty the Snowman.

"Boastful" Adjective Groups

Create a list of boastful adjectives about the group. Write one word per card creating sets of five or six cards for each word. Sort the cards creating the correct number per group. Place the correct number of adjective word cards on each table. Instruct the participants to take a word card and to find other group members described the same way. Once the group members are seated with their new group members, have them decide why they match the adjective describing them. Groups have fun boasting about their talents when sharing with the large group.   Leave the cards in the middle of the table and periodically refer to them by saying, "Let's hear an idea from a brilliant person in the room." This activity is a great efficacy builder.

Sample adjective words include: terrific, awesome, intelligent, wonderful, brilliant, superb, fantastic, smart, cool, dazzling, sensational, magnificent, outstanding, thoughtful, alert, energized, enthusiastic, intriguing, fascinating, curious, independent, motivated.

Line-up Ideas for Groups

Everyone in the room lines up single file according to the activity chosen. After everyone is in line facing the presenter, ask them to share the information used to line-up. Participants can then be grouped into pairs, threes, or fours for the next activity. Line-ups work well after lunch to bring energy to the room.

Line-up examples:
- Birthday line up - month and date; everyone shares their birth date.
- High school/distance line up - the high school from which you graduated and line up according to the number of miles, closest to furthermost away; everyone tells their high school, city, state, or country.
- Content knowledge line up - how much do you know about the content we are learning on a scale of 1 - 10 with 1 a little and 10 lots; share number and why.
- Rise and shine line up - time you like to get up in the morning and then the time you prefer going to bed; compare the results.
- ABC Line-up - group lines up alphabetically using initials for first, middle, and last name.

Baseball Learning Team Mates

Make an appointment with four different people. Both persons record their appointment on this diagram of an infield. Only make the appointment if the same position is open in both of your infields. "Play ball!"

_____

2nd

_____

3rd

_____

1st

_____

Home

Clock Partners

Make an appointment with 12 different people--one for each hour on the clock. Be sure you both record the appointment on your clocks. Only make the appointment if there is an open slot at that hour on both of your clocks.

Periodic Table Appointments Example

For each of the families, fill out the following information with your person who has signed up for that particular appointment time.

1:00: Alkali Metal _____
Family # _____
Number of valence e- _____
Common elements _____
_____
Characteristics
_____
_____
_____

2:00: Alkali Metal _____
Family # _____
Number of valence e- _____
Common elements _____
_____
Characteristics
_____
_____
_____

3:00: Alkali Metal _____
Family # _____
Number of valence e- _____
Common elements _____
_____
Characteristics
_____
_____
_____

4:00: Alkali Metal _____
Family # _____
Number of valence e- _____
Common elements _____
_____
Characteristics
_____
_____
_____

Worldly Learning Buddies

Find seven different learning buddies in the room, people you do not work with or rarely see. Write their name on one of the continents and have them write your name on the SAME continent.

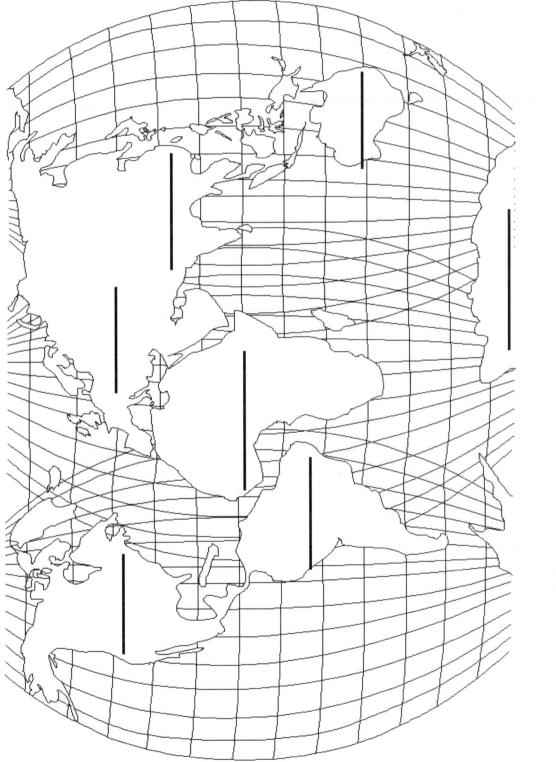

Do you know the seven continents? Label them.

Songs to Energize

• "My Bonnie Lies Over the Ocean" - students sing the song and shuttle between the standing and sitting position whenever they sing a word beginning with the "B" sound.

• "Oh Chester Have You Heard About Harry" - sung to the tune of "Yankee Doodle"

> CHESTer, have YOU HEARD about HARRY
>   (point to CHEST)   (point to SELF then EARS)   (point to HAIR)
>
> Just got BACK from the ARMY
> (point to BACK)   (point to ARM & SELF)
>
> He KNOWS he NEEDS to FACE deFEAT
> (point to NOSE) (point to KNEES) (point to FACE then FEET)
>
> HIP,   HIP,   HOORAY   for the ARMY
> (clap hands on hips twice, raise arms for cheer)(point to ARM & SELF)

• "Touch Red" - The teacher asks students to "touch red" which means move and touch something in the room that is red, emphasizing to touch in appropriate places. Change "touch red" to "touch a picture" or "touch the letter A." Many different examples can be used to reinforce different ideas or just to energize the group through movement.

Quick Group Energizers

• Power Clap
• Drum Roll
• Clam Clap (use fingers as clams)
• Round of Applause
• Give Yourself a Pat on the Back
• Give Yourself a Hug
• Thumbs Up
• High-Five
• Standing Ovation

Section 9 - Reflection Strategies   Notes:

"We learn by doing, if we reflect on what we have done."
                                                    - John Dewey

Rationale: The Power of Reflection
Students seldom question themselves about their learning experiences. They often just follow the instructions, wanting to get the assignment finished. When students reflect on what was learned and how it was learned they will begin to internalize their learning. Through reflection students become aware of and are able to control their cognitive processes. Working effectively at any challenging task requires significant amounts of reflection. Through reflective practice students develop skills that are transferable.

In order to create independent learners, students must be taught how to reflect on their strengths and weaknesses as learners. When students complete a project, take a written test, or use a reading strategy, ask them to reflect on themselves as a learner. Encourage students to journal about their strengths, their effectiveness as a learner, or what helps them learn. For example, with the K-W-L strategy (What I Know, What I Want to Know, and What I Learned) some teachers add a fourth column called How I Learned It. The fourth column asks the students to reflect on themselves as learners.

The classroom climate will affect students' willingness to reflect on their levels of reflective thinking. Honest evaluation of what you are doing or the completed project can only take place in a safe, risk-taking, collaborative environment. Students must feel that it is okay for them to share their learning, complete or incomplete. They need to be assured that they will not be scrutinized, but rather that they will be respected for their efforts and will be able to use their learning in future situations. Deep reflective practice helps all of us build new possibilities. Fran Prolman (1998) believes that a school culture based on reflection makes "thought muscles" stronger for students and teachers. The result is higher achievement.

Students can reflect orally and/or in writing. There are many strategies that provide opportunities for reflection. The selection of a strategy that is congruent with the overall learning goal is key. Variety is also important to challenge and encourage thinking. These strategies work for adult learners too.

Reflection strategies included in this section.

	Page
• Back-to-Back Thinking, Face-to-Face Conversing . .	212
• F.I.R.E.	214
• One Minute Assessment	216
• Partner Roundup	218
• Pinwheel Discovery	221
• Think, Ink, Pair, Share	224
• Three Minute Pause	226

BACK-to-BACK Thinking
FACE-to-FACE Conversing

How to Use the Strategy

1) Assign each person a partner. Participants designate roles with one person being an "O" and the other a "K" (seeking OK pairs).

2) Have pairs discuss the following question:
"What are reflective conversations and why are they valuable for enhancing thinking?"
Share ideas with the large group.

3) Develop and display thoughtful questions about the topic on a chart or overhead.

4) Show the first question on the chart to the group. Read it aloud. Ask pairs to stand "Back to Back to Think" about their own answer to the question. After they have each developed a response (approximately 30 seconds) they turn "Face to Face to Converse."

        O's = sharing their response to the question
        K's = listening, restating, and inquiring

Allow the O's to share for two - three minutes, signal, and ask the pairs to reverse roles with the K's sharing two - three minutes .

5) After each person has reflected on the first question ask each pair to discuss how the conversation pushed their thinking.

6) For best results, model this process with a participant before pairs begin to share. Ask one participant to be the "O" and share ideas to the first question with the teacher listening, restating, and inquiring. Invite the observers to jot down ideas, verbal and nonverbal, that push the thinking of "O" person. After a brief conversation, ask pairs to compare notes and then discuss their ideas with the large group.

7) Continue the process with each question listed.

8) Students can switch partners for each question shared.

9) End with a large group share about their learnings. Discuss benefits of the strategy.

Benefits of the Strategy

       • Involves all participants
       • Promotes critical thinking about the topic
       • Causes participants to be reflective
       • Promotes active listening
       • Focuses on the use of effective communication skills

BACK-to-BACK Thinking
FACE-to-FACE Conversing Examples

Cognitive Coaching - Questions to initiate thinking
- How would you define Cognitive Coaching to a friend?
- What Cognitive Coaching skills are you finding useful. Why are they useful?
- In what ways do the five States of Mind broaden your thinking?
- Compare your thinking when planning using the coaching planning map versus not using the map?

Reading in the Content Areas - Questions to initiate thinking
- What are you learning about yourself as a reader?
- What reading strategies are you finding beneficial? Why are they working?
- As a result of participating in the reading training, how do you view reading in your content areas?
- How do you explain the importance of reading in your content area to students and parents?

Novel Approach - Questions to initiate thinking
- What challenges do you think the main character faced?
- What did the character do to cope with those challenges?
- How did you think the character was affected by those challenges? What difference do you see?

Managing Your Resources - Questions to initiate thinking
- Why are goal setting, problem solving, and decision making important resources for living?
- How might you best put your personal resources to work?
- What types of community resources are available in your area?
- What helps you see challenges and problems as opportunities?
- What resources do you use to deal with challenges and problems?

The ultimate measure of a man is not where he stands in moments of comfort and convenience, but where he stands at times of challenge and controversy.
- Martin Luther King, Jr.

F.I.R.E. Strategy

"When you give away some of the light from a candle by lighting another person's flame, there isn't any less light because you've given some away, there's more. When everybody grows, there isn't less of anybody, there's more of and for everybody."

- Kaleel Jamison

The F.I.R.E. strategy is a reflective process based on questioning. It causes students to think critically about their learnings and themselves as learners. Webster uses the following words to define the noun and verb "question": to inquire, doubt, puzzle, and investigate. The brain is a curious sort of thing seeking to know answers to questions posed. For example, when someone asks you the title of a book and you know it but you cannot remember it at that moment, do you let it go and just forget about it? Probably not! You keep thinking about the title of the book until you remember it. We want students to be curious learners, eager and persistent in investigating topics being studied.

How to Use the Strategy

1) Discuss the importance of reflection with students.

2) Explain the strategy and what each letter in the word F.I.R.E. means.

"F" = Formulate a question that causes students to think critically about the topic studied or about themselves as learners.

"I" = Internalize the question by providing the necessary wait time needed to think about the question and formulate an answer.

"R" = Record your thinking; thoughts become more specific when they are written down.

"E" = Exchange ideas with another learner in order to compare and contrast thinking. Students expand their learning when they share their ideas with another, observing similarities and differences. Hearing your own ideas voiced aloud can be motivational as well.

3) Select reading material about the topic to be studied. Create several thought-provoking questions.

Example questions:
- Science - How does the process of photosynthesis impact your life?
- Social Studies - Did the Industrial Revolution help the working people? Support your answer with specific examples.
- Art - In what ways does art impact your life?
- Language Arts - How would you describe Brian's problem-solving strategies in the story *Hatchet*?

4) Assign students a passage to read. Develop an appropriate, thought-provoking question about the passage. This can be shared with students before they read.

5) Ask students to review the F.I.R.E. strategy. Work with students through each step of the strategy.

6) As a large group process learning about the topic, then discuss benefits of the strategy.

Benefits of the Strategy

- Facilitates learning in any unit of study
- Encourages students to develop thought-provoking questions
- Extends thinking when problem solving by having students reflect on their own behavior when solving the problem
- Causes students to think critically about their learnings and themselves as learners
- Reinforces the importance of wait-time when asking a question
- Encourages thoughtful thinking about questions
- Incorporates writing as a meaningful activity
- Incorporates a meaningful structure for conversation
- Creates a community of learners

Reference: Adapted from Harvey Silver

F	I	R	E
Formulate	Internalize	Record	Exchange

How to Use the Strategy

1) While teaching a concept, stop periodically and asks the students to reflect on their thinking/learning about the concept at that moment.

2) Students are provided an 8"x11" paper with "One Minute Assessment" written on the front. Students fold the paper over and record their one minute thinking on the inside of the folded paper. Students date each entry.

3) Sentence starters might be shared to start their thinking:

- I could learn better if we could . . .
- I am bored and don't learn as well when . . .
- I am challenged to learn best when . . .
- One thing in this class I would like to see changed so I can learn better is. . .
- I feel special when I am learning . . .
- I would like to have more choice in . . .
- I think I could learn better if . . .
- The class is fun and learning is easier when we . . .
- When we leave our class each day, I usually feel my learning is . . .
- Learning in our class would be better if . . .
- At the beginning of class I like to learn about . . .
- What I know about my learning is . . .

4) Students can be paired to talk about their assessments and compare how each is thinking. Students can be asked to help each other with confusing ideas.

5) To provide feedback, periodically read and respond to students' one minute assessments.

6) The activity can be used on an individual basis as well. When a student seems really engaged or disengaged with an activity or learning, the teacher asks the student at the completion of the learning activity, "What was it about this activity that had you so engaged or disengaged?" Ask the student to write a one minute assessment.

Benefits of the Strategy

- Provides diagnostic information for the teacher
- Causes learners to reflect on their own learning processes
- Provides an opportunity to diagnose learning of a student engaged or disengaged with an activity
- Helps teachers align teaching and learning activities with students' strengths
- Creates consciousness about the learner's thinking in the moment
- Incorporates journal keeping in a meaningful way

Reference: Sue Presler, Consultant, Omaha, NE & Guy Todnem, Consultant, Aurora, IL

One Minute Assessment

Name _____

Unit of Study _____

The Partner Roundup strategy encourages students to expand their thinking by applying what they are learning to their life. It causes them to be more directive and purposeful in their learning. Partner Roundup is a three part strategy and may take several days to complete.

How to Use the Strategy

1) Part I of the strategy provides students an opportunity to write about their learnings. To make connections between the topic being studied and their life, create a broad application question. Write it on chart paper or an overhead and give students three to five minutes to record their ideas.

Part I: Reflective Writing

Reflective writing is an important part of the Partner Roundup strategy. Students must be given time to formulate their own thoughts before sharing them. This part of the strategy could be incorporated on a day prior to Parts II and III. For example in science, students studying the changing of the seasons were asked to respond to this question:

> • "What are some things you are noticing outside that let you know winter is coming?" "How do you prepare for winter in your family?" In Language Arts, students read *James and the Giant Peach* and reflected on this question:
> • "If you were James struggling with malevolent aunts, how would you solve the problem?" "What would you do to foster a respectful relationship?"

In music, students studying famous composers, Mozart, Bach, Beethoven, reflected on this question:

> • "If you were an employer interviewing applicants for the position of composer, what qualifications would you incorporate into the interview?"

2) Students work with a learning buddy for Part II. Share with students that Part II incorporates reflective conversations. Explain that a reflective conversation is between two people in which one person is the speaker who shares ideas recorded in Part I and the other person is the listener who facilitates the conversation.

Model a reflective conversation with one student and ask the rest of the class to write down examples of verbal and nonverbal behaviors that cause reflection or thinking. Provide examples of verbal behaviors (questions, restates what is said) and nonverbal (listens without interrupting, maintains eye to eye contact, smiles). Model a reflective conversation three to four minutes. Students write down examples and then share examples with their partner. Next, have the large group share examples and record all ideas on chart paper. Ask the person who participated in the modeling to share examples of what the coach did to cause the person who shared to think deeper about the topic.

Next have the students conduct a reflective conversation with each other. Have students sit face to face and decide who is the "O" and who is the "K" (we want OK pairs). The "O" shares first and the "K" is the coach using some of the ideas listed on the chart. After three minutes stop the conversation and ask the OK pairs to process the conversation by discussing this question, "What did the coach do to cause the other person to reflect?" Allow partners a sixty second share and then ask for a couple of ideas to be shared with the large group.

Have the students switch chairs (signals to the brain - I have a new role) and conduct the second conversation following the same format. Another process question could be, "What are you learning about yourself as a coach, the one who listens, observes, and asks questions?"

Part II: Partners Explore Thinking
      O = share first
      K = listen, restate, inquire

3) The last part of Partners Roundup involves students learning ideas from each other. One pair joins with another pair. For five minutes they share ideas they gained from the reflective conversations. As they share ask them to listen to each other with a comparison frame of mind. How are their ideas similar and different? Tell them that they will need to share one or two learnings with the large group.

Part III: Partners Roundup to Compare Thinking
      Roundup your thinking and compare ideas. Sort for one or two
      ideas to share with large group.

4) Process the entire strategy with the students and ask them to share how the strategy assisted their learning about the topic.

Benefits of the Strategy
- Incorporates writing to learn through reflective writing
- Involves movement
- Allows students to learn from each other
- Develops reflective conversation skills, such as active listening, questioning, and restating ideas shared
- Causes students to reflect and elaborate on their learning
- Allows second language learners an opportunity to translate ideas, verbalize their interpretations, and increase understanding of the concept(s) presented
- Allows the teacher to be a facilitator of learning

Reflective Conversation
"Partner Roundup"

Part I: Reflective Writing
"What are you learning about yourself as a reader?"

Part II: Partners Explore Thinking
    O = share first
    K = listen, restate, inquire

Part III: Partners Roundup to
              Compare Thinking
Roundup your thinking and compare
    ideas. Sort for 1-2 ideas to share
    with large group.

Pinwheel Discovery

"Conversation does not have to reach conclusions in order to be of value."

- Parker Palmer

How to Use the Strategy

1) Explain to students that the Pinwheel Discovery is a reflection strategy consisting of three parts:
- Part I: Reflect in writing about a learning, experience, or application
- Part II: Observe a reflective conversation modeled by the teacher
- Part III: Conduct reflective conversations with different partners

2) Part I: Display the reflective writing statement on the overhead, chalkboard, or chart paper. Allow the students three to five minutes to record their thinking. Examples from various content areas:
- Physical Education - Being a "team player" means. . .
- Science - What did Neil Armstrong's quote, "One small step for man, one giant leap for mankind" say to us . . .
- Math - Complete each story problem and be ready to explain the rationale for your answer
- Social Studies - Write what you know about world hunger - who, what, where, why?
- Language Arts - How did Jack London portray that "only the strong will survive in the wild" in his novel, *The Call of the Wild*?

3) Part II: Explain to the students that part two models a reflective conversation. A reflective conversation is between two people in which one person, the speaker, explains ideas from the reflective writing in part one and the other person, a coach, listens, restates what is said, and asks inquiry questions. The role of the coach is to listen actively and expand the thinking of the speaker. Organize students into pairs. As they observe the model conversation ask them to record examples of verbal and nonverbal behaviors that cause the speaker to think and shows the coach is listening. Examples include: eye to eye contact, not interrupting the speaker, and asking the speaker to say more. Model the conversation for four to five minutes. At the completion of the modeling, ask the students to share recorded examples with their partners. As a large group, record student examples on a chart labeled "Characteristics of a Reflective Conversation."

4) Part III: Instruct students to create a pinwheel structure with partners facing each other. Chairs can be arranged in advance or students may stand. A pinwheel consists of four or five pairs facing each other, an inner circle of five students facing an outer circle of five students. Twenty students would require two pinwheels with five pairs each. The outer person is the speaker who shares and the inner person is the coach, the listener. The speaker shares for three minutes while the coach listens, asks questions, and restates ideas shared. At the end of the reflective conversation ask the pairs to discuss a process question such as, "What did the coach do to expand your thinking?" Process and elicit a couple of responses from the large group.

Next, each outer person, the speaker, stands and pinwheels clockwise to the next chair. All coaches on the inner chairs remain seated in the same chair. Ask the speakers to share another idea from their reflective writing. Again, all coaches listen actively for several minutes. End the round with another process question, "Coach, what are you learning about yourself as a listener?"

For round three, again the speaker pinwheels clockwise to the next chair for a new partner BUT this time exchanges chairs with the coach sitting on the inner chair. Students reverse roles! The coach now becomes the speaker and will share ideas from the reflective writing and the speaker becomes the coach. Review the role of the coach with the students on the inner chairs. Continue the Pinwheel Discovery strategy with two more reflective conversations, the speaker sharing for three minutes, the coach listening, and the conversation concluding with a process question. Example process questions:
- "What are we learning about reflective conversations?"
- "In what ways does the coach support your thinking?"
- "How would you explain the difference between the coach's chair and the speaker's chair?"
- "What are the benefits of each role, the coach and the speaker?"

5) Conclude with a large group discussion about content learnings and benefits of the strategy.

Benefits of the Strategy
- Encourages students to have conversations with many students
- Incorporates reflective journal writing
- Involves movement for maximum learning
- Allows students to learn from each other
- Develops reflective conversation skills such as active listening and questioning
- Incorporates process questions so students focus on the process as well as the content
- Allows second language learners an opportunity to translate ideas, verbalize their interpretations, and increase understanding of the concept(s) presented
- Allows the teacher to be a facilitator of learning

Pinwheel Discovery

Record three "discoveries" you have made as a result of reading *Catcher in the Rye* by J.D. Salinger. Explain why the discoveries are important to you.

- Discovery

- Importance

- Discovery

- Importance

- Discovery

- Importance

How to Use the Strategy

1) Instruct students about the type of critical thinking required during the Think, Ink, Pair, Share strategy (making predictions, problem solving, decision making, consensus building).

2) Structure the learning environment so that students can work comfortably with partners or on teams. If using a team format, assign teams before beginning the strategy.

3) Assign a passage for the students to read or chart a question for them to Think about regarding the topic read. Examples from various content areas include:

- Physical Education - Explain why positive sportsmanship is an important element of any athletic event.
- Social Studies - What impact did the Transcontinental Railroad have on ...?
- Science - Why is cell division an important science concept? Explain how the process works.
- Language Arts - What is the major theme embedded in George Orwell's book *Animal Farm*? How is that theme evident in society today?
- Health - What is a healthy diet? How might your diet differ from a friend's?
- Math - What are the essential characteristics of an equation? Provide an example.
- Music - How has jazz influenced society? What is the origin of jazz music?

4) Give the students time to think about the topic or question and to formulate their response.

5) Instruct the students that the next part of the strategy is for them to Ink their thinking. Option 1 - Partners: Ask students to individually Ink about their thinking in their journal or on a sheet of paper. Allow students ample time to record their ideas. Option 2 - Teams: Have students first discuss their responses with a partner and then Ink the response that will be shared with their team. Responses could be a sentence, web, picture, or in a form designed by the students.

6) Pair each student with a partner to Share written response. Have students decide who will share first. Review active listening skills. Model with a student how to listen actively, restate, and inquire of the person in order to push thinking. Another alternative for sharing to incorporate reading is to have one member of the pair read the other member's written response, restate, and inquire. If students are to read each other's Inked response instead of discussing them, announce this step to the students ahead of time to encourage legibility.

7) Switch roles after the first student shares for several minutes .

8) End the sharing portion with a process question which invites the pairs or teams to discuss how the conversations encouraged each other to think deeper about the topic.

9) End with a large group discussion about content and process learning.

Benefits of the Strategy

- Enables students to become reflective learners
- Encourages the students to formulate opinions about the topic
- Incorporates wait time to promote student thinking (Think then Ink)
- Provides students the opportunity to learn from each other
- Incorporates higher-order questions to develop critical thinkers
- Engages students in reflective conversations based on active listening, restating, and inquiring
- Provides an opportunity for students to stretch their thinking and to problem solve before making decisions
- Allows the teacher to be a facilitator of learning

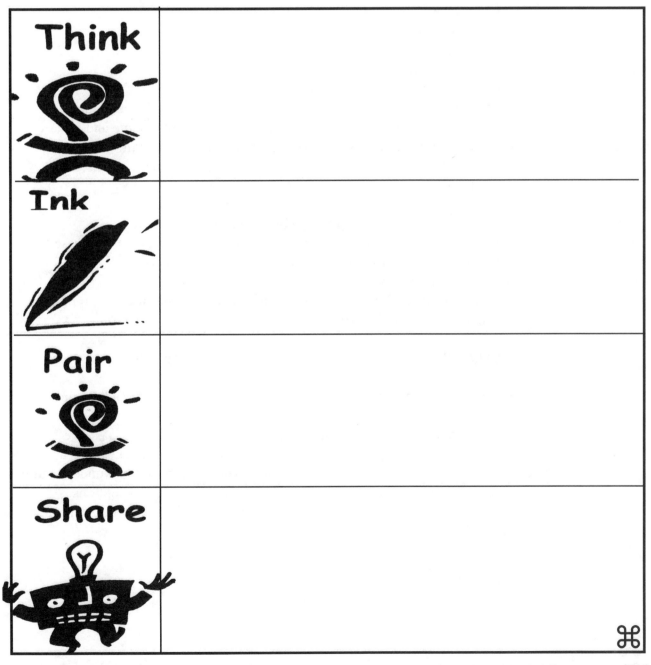

How to Use the Strategy

1) Organize the students into pairs or learning teams.

2) Instruct students to read the first page or two of a chapter or show them a ten to fifteen minute segment of a video. The length of listening time depends upon the age of the learner and listening time correlates with age. A ten year old can listen approximately ten minutes and then needs to stop and process the information shared. The more difficult the material, the greater the need for students to stop and process more frequently. For example, a 35 minute class for eleven year olds might follow this pattern:

- 11 minutes for input
- 3 minutes to pause and process
- 2 minutes for the teacher to redirect if necessary
- 11 minutes for input
- 3 minutes to pause and process
- 5 minutes for summary/conclusion/journal learnings/review notes

3) Pause after presenting information the appropriate length of time and ask students to spend three minutes processing. During the pause, pairs or learning teams discuss their notes, clarify difficult ideas, and fill the gaps in their notes. The following ideas might be displayed on an overhead:

Three Minute Pause

- Summarizing with partner or team the information that was discussed.
- Telling partner or team what was most interesting about the information shared.
- Identifying anything that is confusing and try to clear it up or prepare a question to ask the group.

4) Model how the conversation would sound when working with a partner or learning team members.

5) Remind students that during the pause they are not to ask the teacher questions

but to work with their partner or learning team members.

6) Provide students an opportunity after the pause portion to ask questions about unclear concepts, to add their own information that would strengthen understanding of important points or issues, and to seek clarity about any misconceptions.

7) Continue to provide information and pause for the students to process throughout the entire presentation.

Benefits of the Strategy

- Allows students time to process new information and concepts during large group instruction
- Provides students the opportunity to think about and relate to prior knowledge, or to clear up any misconceptions about the topic being studied
- Improves the students' retention rate, heightens an understanding of the subject matter, and helps to promote a positive feeling about what they are learning
- Moves new learning from short-term memory to long-term storage
- Creates independent and interdependent learners who develop problem solving and decision making skills
- Provides an opportunity for students to share ideas and opinions
- Allows second language learners an opportunity to translate ideas, verbalize their interpretations, and increase understanding of the concept(s) presented

Three Minute Pause

- Summarize with your partner the information that was discussed.

- Tell your partner what was most interesting about the information shared.

- Identify anything that is confusing and try to clear it up or prepare a question to ask the group.

Section 10 - Closing Strategies   Notes:

"People do not learn from the experience.
They learn from the processing of the experience."
- John Dewey

Rationale

Educational consultant and mentor Ernie Stachowski claims that closure is an essential element of the learning process. Closing strategies allow the student's mind to summarize the learning just experienced. He compares closure with a watercolor painting. After the color is painted on the paper, the painter waits for it to dry so the next color does not run into it. If all of the colors run together the clear picture would not be portrayed. Likewise, the human brain needs time to organize and commit to memory the information learned.

Closure is elicited by the teacher and performed by all students. Examples of quick closure activities frequently used by teachers are:
- In your learning journal summarize the theme from the story and your reaction to this idea.
- List the five rules we learned about playing tennis.
- Explain the thinking process you use when adding fractions, and have your partner explain the thinking process when subtracting fractions.
- Name one thing we learned about safety, and have your partner tell you another until all six ideas have been recalled.

Bob Garmston, trainer and friend, models the power of closings. He believes closing strategies produce at least five benefits for learners (1997). Closing strategies: 1) sort and store information into long term memory, 2) develop a community of learners, 3) invite reflection and inquiry, 4) promote personal growth, and 5) support commitment for futher learning. Closure assists learning at the end of class, before a planned break, and at the end of a chunk of incremental learning. Using a variety of closing strategies creates meaningful and interesting learning opportunities.

Closing strategies included in this section.

					Page
• 3-2-1 Send Off	.	.	.	.	230
• Four Square Summary	.	.	.	.	231
• Head, Heart, Sole	.	.	.	.	232
• Personal Action Plan	.	.	.	.	233
• Shaping Up a Review	.	.	.	.	234
• START - STOP - SAVE	.	.	.	.	235
• Three-Point Thinking	.	.	.	.	236

3-2-1 Send Off

3-2-1 Send Off provides structure to a journal or learning log entry. After previewing a video, listening to a guest speaker, reading an article, or at the end of class students record their impressions. This closing strategy causes students to focus on key ideas and record six summary statements.

3-2-1 Send Off examples include:

- 3 important facts
- 2 interesting ideas
- 1 insight about yourself as a learner

or

- 3 key words
- 2 ideas to try
- 1 thought to think about

or

- 3 words to summarize the concept
- 2 words to organize your thinking
- 1 word to share with friends

or

- 3 strategies you found helpful
- 2 important events from the story
- 1 thing you will do differently next time

After students have recorded their own responses, they can share their ideas with a partner. Partners join with another pair, organize all ideas, and share them with the large group. Ideas can be recorded into a class graphic organizer for future use.

Four Square Summary

Four Square Summary is a meaningful way to collect written data at the end of a unit of study or semester. The strategy causes students to reflect as well as provide diagnostic information for the teacher. Sentence stems are helpful for activating thinking. Four Square Summary can be used as a journal writing activity.

Four Square Summary

As a result of this unit of study, here are:

New ideas I've gained	Ways I contributed
Questions raised in my mind	Feelings I've experienced

Examples of sentence stems:
- Ideas I gained from audience participation
- Examples I synthesized from the survey
- Thoughts I have about how our team works
- Things I value about this course
- Ways I can improve my attitude
- Insights about myself as a group member

Head, Heart, Sole

Head, Heart, and Sole not only activates thinking about the topic studied but an emotional response as well. After participating in a musical event, a play, a debate, or a sport event, Head, Heart, Sole forces students to think about their performance from three different perspectives. The strategy causes students to examine the relationship between their emotions and their behaviors. The Sole - A STEP I WILL TAKE can be developed into a goal setting action plan.

 Head - AN IDEA I HAD

 Heart - A FEELING I EXPERIENCED

 Sole - A STEP I WILL TAKE

Personal Action Plan

A Personal Action Plan focuses on goal setting. Students examine a recent experience, such as a report card conference, behavior modification plan, or a performance in a play, and determine an area of growth. Students complete their Personal Action Plan and then discuss their plan with the teacher, their parents, or friends. Plans must be monitored and adjusted to be effective. Ongoing conversations with friends, parents, and/or teachers help students assess their progress. Implementing a Personal Action Plan requires effort and can be hard work. Periodically celebrating successes encourages students to continue. When students reach their goal or stop working toward it, examining the amount of effort put forth and implications for future goal setting opportunities is a beneficial practice.

Personal Action Plan

• What is an important learning, strategy, or idea you want to use? Be specific!!

• How and when will you use your learning, strategy, or idea? Be specific!!

• What support will you need from the teacher, your parents, or friends to help you apply your learning, strategy, or idea?

• What criteria will you use to help determine if the learning, strategy, or idea you are using is making a difference in your performance/behavior?

Shaping Up a Review helps the learner organize and summarize information learned. Students think analytically about the topic studied and synthesize learnings. The strategy reinforces reflection in a visual way. Students enjoy sharing their ideas with other students. Shaping Up a Review serves as a vehicle for small-group discussion.

On the SQUARE write down the ideas from this course that square with your own beliefs and values. **OR**
On the SQUARE record four things that square with your thinking about this topic.

On the TRIANGLE write down the three most important points you want to remember. **OR**
On the TRIANGLE record three ideas you plan to share or use.

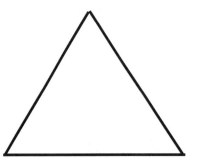

On the CIRCLE write down one question going around in your mind. **OR**
On the CIRCLE record some thoughts going around in your head.

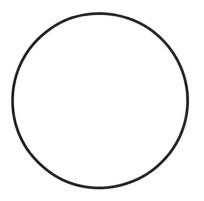

START-STOP-SAVE
GREEN-RED-YELLOW

START - STOP - SAVE provides an opportunity for students to focus on their performance or behavior. For example, after participating in a cooperative group lesson students analyze their behavior during group work. They determine what they will start to do, stop doing, and continue to do or save for the next time they work in a group. Another example, after students have given a speech and watched a video of their performance, they record learnings for the next time they give a speech. Students share their ideas with group members, the class, or their parents. START - STOP - SAVE is an excellent self-assessment strategy because it encourages students to analyze their behavior/performance in three different ways.

As I think about my performance, here is one thing I will...

START

STOP

SAVE

Three-Point Thinking

Directions: Reflect on a passage read, a topic discussed, or a concept learned. Record **Main Points** you want to remember in Section A, **Feelings** that surfaced or **Connections** made in **Section B**, and a **Summary** of learnings in Section C.

Option - To reinforce the reading classroom, have students read a passage and think from three different reading perspectives - **Text to Self**, **Text to Text**, and **Text to World**.

Option - Have participants personalize the information by thinking from three different perspectives: **Here's What** - a brief summary of the information read, **So What** - a statement expressing what the information means to you, **Now What** - this is what you will do with the information.

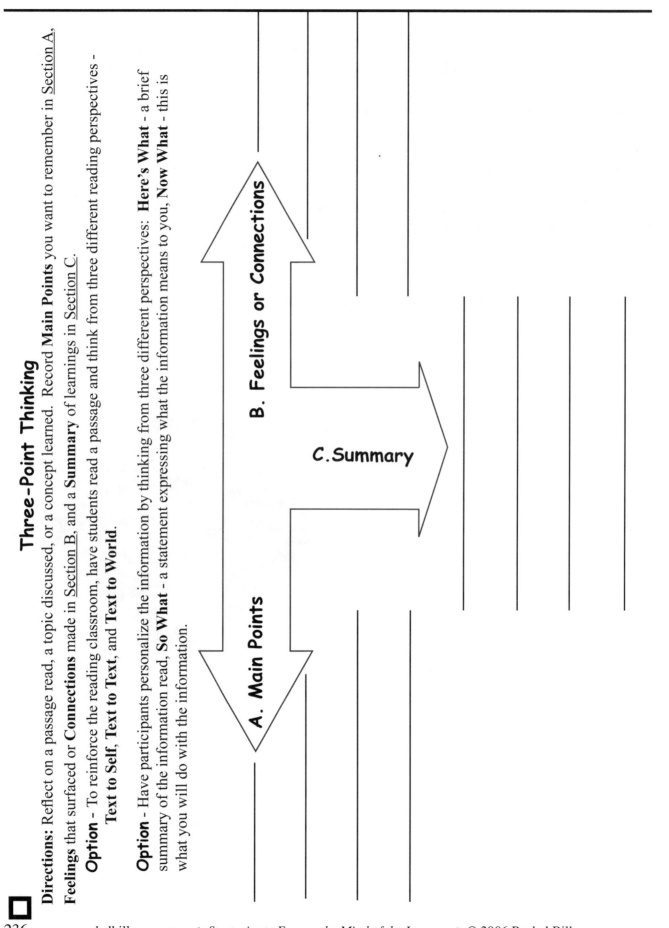

B. Feelings or Connections

A. Main Points

C. Summary

Chapter 4
Strategy Instruction

If you want kids to think differently, you have to teach differently.

Strategic learning is a direct result of strategic teaching; strategic teaching emphasizes purposeful and thoughtful planning based on students' knowledge and needs. Developing strategic learners requires a dual focus. First, determine the desired outcome and select strategies to build toward that result (See Criteria for Strategy Selection p. 4), differentiating instruction to address student differences and needs. Second, teach the strategy(ies) with clear examples to prepare learners to independently transfer the strategy(ies) to new encounters.

Using Strategies to Differentiate Instruction

Differentiating instruction may be done with the entire class, in small groups, or individually. Strategies particularly suited for differentiation include the use of various graphic organizers, learning logs, journals, questioning/ discussion activities, and frameworks for helping students build information. The random use of strategies is ineffective; students must not only know how the strategy works but when to use it. When instruction is differentiated on a regular basis, both teachers and students become adept with strategy use and are more likely to achieve designated learning goals.

This book offers a cache of options which teachers can use to help their students explore various content, processes, and products to demonstrate learning. The following chart shows how strategies might be matched to content, process, and product, as well as to students' readiness levels, interests, and learning profiles. While this is not exhaustive, it does provide a framework for thinking about methods to meet a variety of students' needs through strategic reading activities. By using the strategies in this book to differentiate, teachers can create powerful, relevant, and consequently motivating learning opportunities.

There is more to teaching with texts than assigning and telling. Assigning and telling are common but uninspired teaching practices that bog students down in the mire of passive learning. Assign and tell more often than not dampens active involvement in learning and denies students ownership and responsibility for the acquistion of content.
- Vacca & Vacca, 1993

Three-Tiered Planning for Differentiating Instruction

Differentiate ⟶ ↓ According to Students'	Content What Students Learn	Process How Students Make Sense of What They Are Learning	Product How Students Show What They Have Learned
Readiness	For example: • Use vocabulary strategies like Concept Definition Map and Frayer Model as a means of determining what your students already know (preassessment). • Provide texts at a variety of levels. • RAFT using more and less complex roles, audiences, and formats. • Thinking From Different Perspectives using more and less complex perspectives.	For example: • Group processing activities such as Reciprocal Teaching allow students to take on the "right" job for them. • Some students need pre-determined graphic organizers; some develop their own. • Some students need small group teaching, review, and "think alouds" about the use of strategies, some students can get right to it.	For example: • Team-based strategies such as Discussion Web or Literature Circles allow all students to share their personal learning. • Vocabulary strategies such as Act the Word, Mind Sketching, and Vocabulary Concept Chain allow students to demonstrate learning using different modalities.
Interests	For example: • Open-ended strategies such as Story Mapping, Directed-Reading Thinking Activity (DRTA), and PREP can be applied to student chosen texts.	For example: • Provide a menu of strategy choices and allow students to choose those most interesting or the best "fit" for them.	
Learning Profiles	• Use opening and reflective strategies such as Strength Bombardment, Pinwheel Summary, and Three Minute Pause to help students understand themselves as learners. • Encourage students to keep a strategy notebook or log that helps them focus on the things that help them the most. • Once students have learned a variety of strategies, allow them to choose those which best meet their styles (see Chapter 5 Reflecting on Strategy Use).		

(Developed by Chery Becker Dobbertin)

Nuts and Bolts of Teaching a Strategy

Strategies need to be taught in meaningful ways so students can apply them appropriately and independently. If the goal is to develop strategic learners who have a repertoire of strategies in their tool kit, time must be committed to strategy instruction. Simply introducing students to a strategy or having them use it one time will not cause them to be proficient at using the strategy on their own. Explicit strategy instruction is necessary and involves three phases (Silver, Strong, & Perini, 2000).
- Introduce and Model the Strategy
- Practice Using the Strategy
- Use the Strategy Independently

• Introduce and Model the Strategy

Strategy instruction begins by explaining what the strategy is and reasons for using it. Students must understand the steps involved in using the strategy. Strategies need to be explained explicitly and with clear examples.

Effective instruction involves modeling the strategy with explanations, analogies, metaphors, and examples. It is important that teachers share their own thinking while using the strategy (think-aloud) so that students understand the cognitive processes involved when using the strategy. Effective instruction focuses on process as well as content.

Explicit instruction provides a scaffold for students as they learn how to use the strategy. As students become more confident with strategy use, the scaffold is slowly removed with less feedback, direction, or support provided.

• Practice Using the Strategy

Knowing how a strategy should be used and being able to complete it effectively is the quantum leap in strategic learning. The springboard for that leap is developed by guided practice. For students to become proficient in using a strategy, they must understand the purpose and steps of the strategy and practice using it many times. During the practice phase, students need guidance and feedback about what is correct and what needs to be improved. Guidance from the teacher minimizes errors, and feedback improves performance.

Students also benefit from working with their peers during the practice phase. Strategies are not as easy to use effectively and productively as one might think. A comment frequently heard from participants when trying out strategies during training is, "I had no idea this strategy would be so hard to complete. I am glad we are working in groups." Students may need assistance in completing strategies as well as reassurance that they are using them productively. Once students are familiar and comfortable with the strategy, they can move from collaborative to independent work.

For implementation to be accurate and effective, students need criteria for using the strategy successfully. When students know what successful implementation looks like, they are able to reflect on their efforts. Reflection allows them to evaluate the effectiveness and outcome of the strategy. The practice phase is critical for developing strategic learners; during this phase students develop into confident, independent strategy users.

- **Independent Strategy Use**

Strategic learners know when and how to use strategies on their own. For this to occur, students need to generate examples of when and how strategies might be used to learn in other areas. Teacher guidance as well as opportunities to select and use strategies with material of their choosing is important. As students use a strategy they must be encouraged to adapt it to their own needs. For example, a student using Concept Definition Mapping (p. 28), a strategy for vocabulary development, may begin to illustrate what the word means instead of writing "what the word is like."

During the independent phase, it is crucial that students reflect upon their decisions regarding strategy selection, adaptation, and results attributing successful learning to appropriate use of strategies. Reflection while using the strategy promotes self-regulated learning. Independent, reflective thinkers are strategic learners!

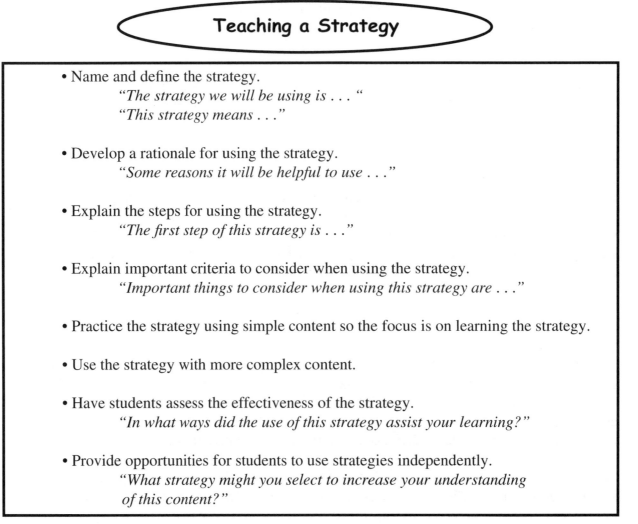

Teaching a Strategy

- Name and define the strategy.
    "The strategy we will be using is . . . "
    "This strategy means . . ."

- Develop a rationale for using the strategy.
    "Some reasons it will be helpful to use . . ."

- Explain the steps for using the strategy.
    "The first step of this strategy is . . ."

- Explain important criteria to consider when using the strategy.
    "Important things to consider when using this strategy are . . ."

- Practice the strategy using simple content so the focus is on learning the strategy.

- Use the strategy with more complex content.

- Have students assess the effectiveness of the strategy.
    "In what ways did the use of this strategy assist your learning?"

- Provide opportunities for students to use strategies independently.
    "What strategy might you select to increase your understanding of this content?"

Chapter 5
Reflecting on Strategy Use

"Life can only be understood backwards, but it must be lived forwards."
- Soren Kierkegaard

In a strategic learning classroom there is a distinct metacognitive component of self-assessment. Teachers and students alike reflect on the effects of using strategies (Weir, 1998). Art Costa and Bena Kallick (2000) state, "To be reflective means to mentally wander through where you have been and to try to make some sense of it" (p. 61). Teachers and students use reflection as an opportunity to construct meaning from their work. Both are reflective learners who think about their thinking before, during, and after learning.

Students must be given a chance to reflect on what they did to complete the strategy and how the use of the strategy enhanced their learning. As teachers incorporate strategies it is important they help students understand why the strategy is important and how the strategy works. When students know the why and how of strategy application, they are able to adapt the use of the strategy if they are dissatisfied with their first efforts. Strategy use goes beyond knowing the steps of a strategy; it must include internalizing why the strategy works in specific situations (Cook, 1989).

Teachers create reflective classrooms when they establish learning environments that allow students to take risks, to experiment with new ways of using strategies, and to ask probing questions. Students know they are in a reflective environment when teachers are as interested in questions students pose about the content and strategy application as they are in the formulated answers students are to provide. There are no failures in reflective classrooms, only learning as experience to produce personal insights. Verbal or written feedback from students helps teachers evaluate the classroom climate. Reflection is supported by a climate of trust.

Reflection does not seem to be an inherent part of most learning environments. If we want students to become reflective learners, they need to see reflection as an integral part of an adult's working day. Teachers need to model habits of continual learning through reflection, providing students with images to mirror. Time (our most precious gift) must be dedicated for reflection on a regular basis; at the beginning of the day or the lesson, before or after lunch, at the end of the day or lesson or any other time that is beneficial. For reflection to make a difference in learning it must be an established priority.

Strategies for Reflection

"What is a classroom? A place for students and teachers.
Students struggle, succeed, fail, give up, try again. Teachers struggle,
succeed, fail, give up, try again."
- Esther Wright

Developing reflective learners is a life-long process and requires the use of different strategies. Consistent use of strategies causes reflection to become a natural, automatic part of the learning process. When students take the initiative to reflect upon their own learning, they are indeed strategic learners.

K-W-L-H Reflection

The K-W-L strategy (p. 73) can be extended to include a self-assessment column. The fourth column is titled "How did you learn it?" Students reflect on what they learned during the unit of study and analyze how activities helped them learn about the topic. For example, one student studying the pros and cons of a democratic government wrote the following comments in the fourth column:

- Participating in the debate was beneficial because our values were expressed and everyone really wanted to argue for their belief.
- Using the Internet to read different editorial columns about democratic rule gave me many new insights.
- Working with other classmates was helpful because we shared different ideas we found interesting and beneficial.

K-W-L-H CHART

What We Know	What We Want to Find Out	What We Learned	How We Learned It - Reflection
Dinosaurs are large.	How long ago did they live?	An archeologist has an exciting life.	Research from Internet, current information.
Dinosaurs are dead.	Why did they die?	Dinosaurs eat plants.	Field trips helped us understand.
They lived many many years ago.	How do we know what they looked like?	Some dinosaurs were gigantic, but had small brains.	Archeological digs, actually doing one.
	Who are the people who study dinosaurs?	Fossils uncover dinosaur traits.	Internet search with Joe was the most helpful.

Journal Learnings

> *"Keep a journal. Pay so much honor to visit the truths of your mind*
> *as to record them."*
>
> - Ralph Waldo Emerson

Reflective journal writing enriches the learning process for students and teachers. Journal keeping offers the learner an opportunity to reflect backward and inward instead of forward and outward. When thinking is recorded students gain a historical perspective of their work. They can measure their progress, compare their thinking from one situation to another, plot next steps, or analyze performance at the beginning, middle, and end of a project. Writing in a journal helps students process their experiences.

One teacher asked her students to list in their journals all the strategies they used to help them understand the science experiment. Student responses ranged from, "You are trying to get us to ask questions while we work," or "If I summarize the main points as I work, it is easier in the end," or "You want us to notice what confuses us so we figure it out." After students shared their journal entries in class, the teacher concluded that students were developing metacognitive awareness of the strategies they were using (Weir, 1998).

Some students find journal writing difficult and need to be jump started. Providing sentence stems can stimulate thinking and cause thoughtful reflections.

Sentence Stems
- What I learned about myself as I used this strategy . . .
- This strategy caused me to . . .
- When I use this I feel . . . because . . .
- I know how to adapt strategies when . . .
- This is similar to what I know in that . . .
- What really surprised me about this strategy was . . .
- I selected this strategy because . . .
- When I compare this journal entry with past entries, I notice . . .
- What puzzles me is . . .
- One thing I might do to understand this more clearly . . .
- What new ideas have we acquired?
- What ideas are we sure about, curious about, or need to pursue?
- What new resources have we discovered?
- What are we learning about working with each other?
- What are our next steps as a team?

Team Reflections

Reflection can be done individually or with a team. Guidelines for a team reflection are:

- pause to reflect on each question before responding,
- incorporate active listening skills, and
- seek to understand each team member's response.

Questions for a team reflection are:

- What new ideas have we acquired?
- What ideas are we sure about, curious about, or need to pursue?
- What are we learning about working with each other?
- What are our next steps as a team?

Rating Scales

A rating scale allows students the opportunity to rate the effectiveness of the strategy using a 1 (least effective) to 10 (highly effective) continuum. Students mark the correct number on the scale and write their rationale for scoring the strategy as they did.

Example:

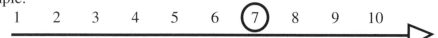

1   2   3   4   5   6   ⑦   8   9   10

"I rated the strategy a 7 because it made the learning more fun. The Opinion Guide really got me thinking about energy in different ways. I have studied energy in science before but I usually just memorized the facts. With this I had to give rationale for my opinions. I think I learned more because of this strategy."

Feedback Reflection

Responding to the following questions causes students to analyze themselves as learners and also provides valuable feedback for the teacher.

- Rate yourself as a learner today. 1 = low, 10 = High
- What did you do to assist your learning?
- What (if anything) got in the way of your learning?
- What did the teacher do to assist your learning?
- What questions and/or concerns do you have?

Rating Scale Example

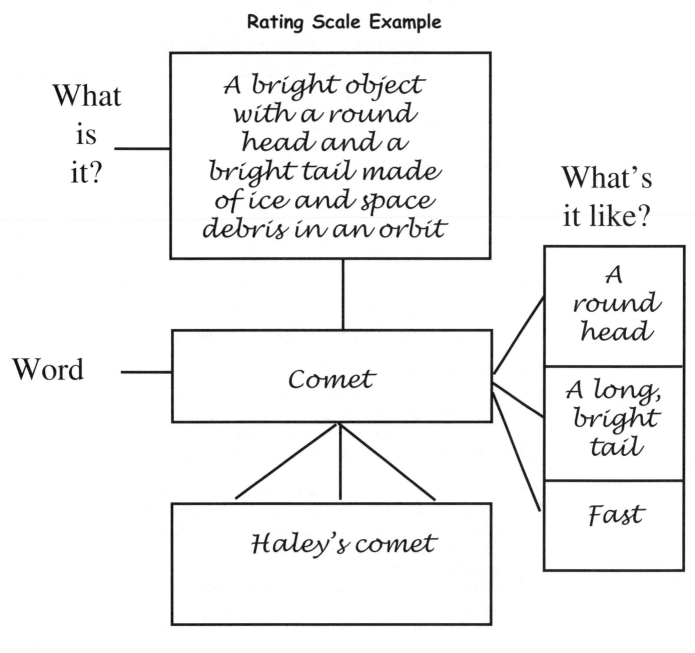

What
is
it?

A bright object
with a round
head and a
bright tail made
of ice and space
debris in an orbit

What's
it like?

Word

Comet

A round head

A long, bright tail

Fast

Haley's comet

Examples

Reflecting on the strategy.
*"I'd rate it an 8 - fun activity, but a lot of steps
to do, it caused me to think in different ways."*

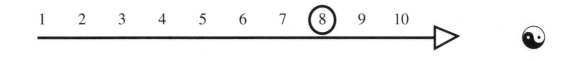

1   2   3   4   5   6   7   ⑧   9   10

Benefits of Student Reflection

- Creates awareness of what students are learning, as well as how they are learning it
- Engages the student actively in the learning
- Causes students to analyze their beliefs and purposes for learning
- Incorporates writing in a meaningful way
- Develops metacognitive awareness of strategies by causing students to "think about their own thinking"
- Allows for the transfer of strategies to other situations
- Provides opportunities to connect, synthesize, and revise learnings

Benefits of Teacher Reflection

- Encourages teachers to analyze teaching as a decision-making process
- Creates opportunities to diagnose and document student learning
- Provides interaction with peers to share knowledge and learning
- Allows application of meaning beyond the situation in which it was learned
- Causes teachers to examine which strategies are being taught and if students are being introduced to a variety of useful strategies
- Encourages analysis of strategy effectiveness to determine if it caused students to think about the content in a manner congruent with the objective(s) of the lesson
- Assists in evaluation of the classroom climate for aspects that cause students to be reflective
- Develops efficacious teachers who believe "we do make a difference!"

I skate to where the puck is going to be, not to where it has been.
- Wayne Gretzky

References

Alvermann, D.E. (1991). The discussion web: A graphic aid for learning across the curriculum. *The Reading Teacher*, 45 (2), 92-99.

Anderson, R.C., and Biddle, W.B. (1975). On asking people about what they do when they are reading. In G. Bower (Ed.), *Psychology of learning and motivation.* New York: Academic Press.

Anderson, R. C., & Faust, G. W. (1973). *Educational psychology: The science of instruction and learning.* New York: Harper & Row Publishers.

Anthony, R.J., Johnson, T.D., Mickelson, M.I., & Preece, A. (1991). *Evaluating literacy: A perspective for change.* Portsmouth, NH: Heinemann.

Aulls, Mark W. (1982). *Developing readers in today's elementary school.* Toronto: Allyn and Bacon, Inc.

Beck, I. L., McKeown, M. G., Hamilton, R. L, & Kucan, L. (1997). *Questioning the author: An approach for enhancing student engagement with text.* Newark, DE: International Reading Association.

Billmeyer, R. (2001). *Capturing all of the reader through the reading assessment system.* Omaha, NE: Rachel & Associates, Inc.

Billmeyer, R. (2004). *Strategic reading in the content areas.* Omaha, NE: Rachel & Associates, Inc.

Braselton, S. and Decker, B. (1994). Using graphic organizers to improve the reading of mathematics. *The Reading Teacher*, 48 (3), 276-281.

Brown, A.L., Day, J.D., & Jones, R. (1983). The development of plans for summarizing texts. *Child Development*, 54, 968-979.

Brown, J.E., Phillips, L.B., & Stephens, E.C. (1993). *Toward literacy: Theory and applications for teaching writing in the content areas.* Belmont, CA: Wadsworth.

Buehl, Doug. (2001). *Strategies for interactive learning.* Newark, DE: International Reading Association.

Chapman, C. (1993). *If the shoe fits.* Palatine, IL: IRI/Skylight Publishing, Inc.

Cook, D. (1989). *Strategic learning in the content areas.* Wisconsin Department of Public Instruction, Madison, WI.

Costa, A. & Kallick, B. (2000). *Discovering & exploring habits of mind. A developmental series.* Alexandria, VA: Association for Supervision and Curriculum Development.

Costa, A. and Kallick, B. (2000). Getting into the habit of reflection. *Educational Leadership*, 57 (7), 60-62.

Cummings, C. (1990). *Teaching makes a difference.* Edmonds, WA: Teaching, Inc.

Cutts, Ken. (2002). *Teaching Reading in the Content Areas.* Presentation at Area Education Agency, Cedar Falls, IA.

Davey, B. (1983). Think aloud: Modeling the cognitive processes of reading comprehension. *Journal of Reading*, 27 (1), 44-47.

Dyer, J. (2000). *Outrageous pursuits: 40, 50, 100 many, many outrageous activities to enhance a positive learning environment.* Calgary, Alberta: HeadSmart Inc.

Eisner, Elliot. (2002). The kind of schools we need. *Phi Delta Kappan*, 83 (8), 576-583.

Fleischman, P. (1997). *Seedfolks.* NY: Harper Trophy, a division of Harper Collins Publishers.

Frayer, D.A., Frederick, W.C., & Klausmeier, H.J. (1969). *A schema for testing the level of concept mastery* (Technical Report No. 16). Madison, WI: University of Wisconsin Research and Development Center for Cognitive Learning.

Friend, R. (2001). Teaching summarization as a content area reading strategy. *Journal of Adolescent & Adult Literacy*, 44 (4), 320-329.

Gardner, H. (1982). *Art, mind and brain.* New York: Basic Books.

Garmston, R. (1997). *The presenter's fieldbook: A practical guide.* Norwood, MA: Christopher-Gordon Publishers, Inc.

Garmston, R. and Wellman, B. (2002). *The adaptive school: Developing collaborative groups* (syllabus). Norwood, MA: Christopher-Gordon Publishers, Inc.

Graves, M. (1986). Costs and benefits of different methods of vocabulary instruction. *Journal of Reading*, 29 (6), 596-602.

Goodlad, J. (1983). Improving schooling in the 1980's: Toward the non-replication of non-events. *Educational Leadership*, 40 (7), 4-7.

Halloway, John. (2000). How does the brain learn science?. *Educational Leadership*, 58 (3), 85-86.

Herber, H. (1978). *Teaching reading in content areas.* (2nd ed.). Englewood Cliffs, NJ: Prentice-Hall.

Herman, J.L., Aschbacher, P.R., & Winters, L. (1992). *A practical guide to alternative assessment.* Alexandria, VA: Association for Supervision and Curriculum Development.

Ivey, G. and Fisher, D. (2006). When thinking skills trump reading skills. *Educational Leadership*, 64, (2), 16-21.

Jacobs, H. H. (2006). *Active literacy k-12: Cross-disciplinary reading, writing, speaking, listening in every classroom.* Larchmont, NY: Eye on Education.

Jensen, E. (2000). Moving with the brain in mind. *Educational Leadership*, 58 (3), 34-37.

Johnson, E.B. (1992). Concept question chain: A framework for thinking and learning about text. *Reading Horizons*, 32 (4), 263-278.

Johnson, D.D., & Pearson, P.D. (1984). T*eaching reading vocabulary*. (2nd ed.). New York: Holt, Rinehart and Winston.

Juntune, J. (1983). *Working with the gifted.* Presentation at NE State Gifted Conference, Omaha, NE.

Kagan, S. (1992). *Cooperative learning.* Capistrano, CA: Resources for Teachers, Inc.

Kagan, S. (1990). *Cooperative learning*: *Resources for teachers*. Capistrano, CA: Resources for Teachers, Inc.

Langer, L.A. (1981, November). From theory to practice: A prereading plan. *Journal of Reading*, 25, 152-156.

Lipton, L., & Wellman, B. (1999). *Pathways to understanding*. (2nd ed.). Guilford, VT: Guilford Publishing.

Marzano, R. J. (2004). *Building background knowledge for academic achievement*. Alexandria, VA: Association for Supervision and Curriculum Development.

Marzano, R., Pickering, D., and Pollock, J. (2001). *Classroom instruction that works*. Alexandria, VA: Association for Supervision and Curriculum Development.

McNeil, J.D. (1984). *Reading comprehension: New directions for classroom practice*. Glenview, IL: Scott, Foresman, and Company.

Moore, D.W., Readance, J.E., & Rickelman, R.J. (1982). *Prereading activities for content area reading and learning*. Newark, DE: International Reading Association.

Newmann, F.M. and Oliver, D.W. (1970). Clarifying public controversy: An approach to teaching social studies. Boston, MA: Little, Brown.

Ogle, D. M. (1989). The know, want to know, learning strategy. In K. D. Muth (Ed.), *Children's comprehension of text* (pp. 205-223). Newark, DE: International Reading Association.

Opitz, M., & Rasinski, T. (1998). *Good-bye round robin.* Portsmouth, NH: Heinemann.

Palinscar, A.S., & Brown, A.L. (1986). Interactive teaching to promote independent learning from text. *The Reading Teacher*, 39 (8), 771-777.

Palinscar, A.S., & Brown, A.L. (1984). Reciprocal teaching of comprehension-fostering and comprehension-monitoring activities. *Cognition and Instruction*, 1 (5), 117-175.

Paulsen, Gary. (1989). *The winter room.* NY: Bantam Books, a division of Bantam Doubleday Dell Publishing Group.

Perkins, D. (1993, October). Teaching & learning for understanding. *NJEA Review*, 10-17.

Prolman, Fran. (1998). Purposeful reflection. *Education Update*, 40 (8), Alexandria, VA: Association for Supervision and Curriculum Development, p. 7.

Raphael, T.E. (1986). Teaching question-answer relationships, revisited. *The Reading Teacher*, 39, 516-522.

Rasinski, T., & Padak, N. (2000). *Effective reading strategies.* (2nd ed.). Columbus, OH: Merrill, an imprint of Prentice-Hall.

Resnick, L.B. (1987). *Education and learning to think.* Washinton, DC: National Academy Press.

Robinson, F. (1961). *Effective study.* New York: Harper and Row.

Routman, R. (1991). *Invitations: Changing as teachers and learners K-12.* Portsmouth, NH: Heinemann.

Santa, C.M. (1988). *Content reading including study systems.* Dubuque, IA: Kendall Hunt.

Schwartz, R., & Raphael, T. (1985, November). Concept definition: A key to improving students' vocabulary. *The Reading Teacher*, 39 (2), 676-682.

Shor, I. (1992). *Empowering education: Critical teaching for social change.* Chicago, IL: The University of Chicago Press.

Silver, H., Strong, R., & Perini, M. (2000). *Discovering nonfiction.* Santa Monica, CA: Canter & Associates, Inc.

Silver, H., Strong, R., and Perini, M. (2000). *Reading for Meaning.* Woodbridge, NJ: The Thoughtful Education Press.

Schmoker, M. (2006). Results now. Alexandria, VA: Association for Supervision and Curriculum Development.

Strong, R.W., Silver, H.F., Perini, M.J., & Tuculescu, G.M. (2002). *Reading for Academic Success*. Thousand Oaks, CA: Corwin Press, Inc.

Sylwester, R. (1995). *A celebration of neurons: An educator's guide to the human brain*. Alexandria, VA: Association for Supervision and Curriculum Development.

Tomlinson, C. A. (2001). *How to differentiate instruction in mixed-ability classrooms*. (2nd ed.). Alexandria, VA: Association for Supervision and Curriculum Development.

Thurber, Lynn. (1999). *SAW: Student action words*. Millard Public School, Omaha, NE.

Vaughn, J., & Estes, T. (1986). *Reading and reasoning beyond the primary grades*. Boston, MA: Allyn and Bacon.

Vygotsky, L.S. (1978). *Mind and society: The development of higher mental processes*. Cambridge, MA: Harvard University Press.

Weir, Carol. (1998). Using embedded questions to jump-start metacognition in middle school remedial readers. *Journal of Adolescent & Adult Literacy*, 41 (6), 458-467.

Wolfe, Patricia. (2001). *Brain matters*. Alexandria, VA: Association for Supervision and Curriculum Development.

Wolfe, P. & Nevills, P. (2004). *Building the reading brain, PreK-3*. Thousand Oaks, CA: Corwin Press.

Wood, K. (1988). Guiding students through informational text. *The Reading Teacher*, 41 (9), 912-920.

Excellence is an art won by training and habituation. We do not act rightly because we have virtue or excellence, but we rather have those because we have acted rightly. We are what we repeatedly do. Excellence, then, is not an act but a habit.

- Aristotle

APPENDIX
Strategies to Engage the Mind of the Learner
Strategies Chart

A strategic learner engages in three phases of thinking: before, during, and after learning. Strategies can be organized into the three phases and should be selected to emphasize certain phases of thinking (See Principles of Learning p. 11).

Strategies		Three Phases of Thinking to Engage the Mind		
Section 1 – Opening Strategies	**Page#**	**Before**	**During**	**After**
Facts and Fibs	15	•		
Group Activator	16	•		
MVP – Most Valuable Point	17	•	•	•
People Search	18	•		
Strength Bombardment	20	•		
Team Interview	21	•		
Team Resume	22	•		
Thats Me	23	•		
Section 2 – Vocabulary Development				
Act the Word	26		•	•
Concept Definition Map	28	•	•	•
Forecast	33	•		
Frayer Model	34	•	•	•
Mind Sketching	39		•	•
Prevoke/Vocabogram	40	•		
Semantic Feature Analysis	42			•
Stephens Vocabulary Elaboration	46	•	•	•
SAW – Student Action Words	50		•	•
Super Word Web	54		•	•
Vocabulary Concept Chain	55			•
Word Sorts	57	•	•	•
Section 3 – Narrative and Informative Text				
Anticipation/Prediction Guide	61	•		•
Character Map	64			•
Cloze Method	65		•	•
Cooperative Retelling	67			•
DRTA – Directed Reading/Thinking Activity	69	•	•	
Group Summarizing	71			•
K-W-L	73	•		•
Learning Log Format	76	•	•	•
Look for the Signals	80		•	
Pairs Read	81		•	•
PREP- Preview, Read, Examine, Prompt	83	•	•	•

Strategies		Three Phases of Thinking to Engage the Mind		
Section 3 – Narrative/Informative	Page#	Before	During	After
Probable Passage	86	•		
Problem Solving Plan	88			•
Proposition/Support Outlines	91		•	
Raft – Role, Audience, Format, Topic	95			•
Reciprocal Teaching	97	•	•	•
Save the Last Word for Me	103		•	•
Story Mapping – Circular Pictures	106			•
SQ3R – Survey, Question, Read, Recite, Review	108	•	•	•
Summary Wheel	111			•
Text Previewing	115	•		
Text Tagging	118		•	•
Think-Aloud	120	•	•	•
Thinking from Different Perspectives	122		•	•
Window Pane Summary	126		•	•
Write to Learn	129	•	•	•
Section 4 – Questioning Strategies				
Chat and Go Questions	133	•	•	•
Concept Question Chain	136		•	
Enlighten Your Thinking Questions	138	•	•	•
Question-Answer Relationships (QAR)	141		•	•
Unwrap Your Thinking Questions	145	•	•	
Questioning the Author	147			•
Section 5 – Graphic Organizers				
Semantic Mapping	151			•
Story Mapping for Narrative Text	153		•	•
Thinking/Writing Organizational Patterns	159	•	•	•
Section 6 – Information-Building				
Carousel Brainstorming	174	•	•	•
FIRST-MIDDLE-LAST Word	175	•	•	•
Four Corner Challenge	176	•	•	•
Give 1 to Get 1	177	•	•	•
Idea Exchange	180	•	•	•
L.E.T.S. Connect	181		•	
Numbered Heads Together	183		•	•
Paired Verbal Fluency	184	•	•	•
Stir-the-Class	185			•
Synectics Search	186	•		•
Teammates Consult	187		•	
Walk About Survey	188	•		•

Strategies		Three Phases of Thinking to Engage the Mind		
Section 7 – Discussion Strategies	**Page#**	**Before**	**During**	**After**
Community Circle	193			•
Read and Reflect	194			•
Creative Debate	195			•
Discussion Web	197			•
Scored Discussion	200			•
Section 8 – Grouping & Energizing Activities				
Grouping Activities	204	•	•	•
Songs for Groups	204	•	•	•
"Boastful" Adjective Groups	205	•	•	•
Line-up Ideas for Groups	205	•	•	•
Songs to Energize	210	•	•	•
Quick Group Energizers	210	•	•	•
Section 9 – Reflection Strategies				
Back-to-Back Thinking	212		•	•
F.I.R.E.	214		•	•
One Minute Assessment	216	•	•	•
Partner Roundup	218			•
Pinwheel Discovery	221			•
Think, Ink, Pair, Share	224	•	•	•
Three Minute Pause	226		•	•
Section 10 – Closing Activities				
3-2-1 Send Off	230			•
Four Square Summary	231			•
Head, Heart, Sole	232			•
Personal Action Plan	233			•
Shaping Up a Review	234			•
START-STOP-SAVE	235			•
Three-Point Thinking	236			•

Crosswalk Between
Strategies to Engage the Mind of the Learner
and Classroom Instruction That Works

Research clearly indicates that the individual classroom teacher has a profound effect on student achievement. *Classroom Instruction That Works* (Marzano, 2001) identifies nine broad categories of instructional strategies that affect student achievement. The following chart provides a crosswalk between strategies highlighted in *Strategies to Engage the Mind of the Learner* and the nine strategies outlined in *Classroom Instruction That Works*. When planning instructional units teachers can systematically use strategies in this book to support the implementation of Marzano's nine instructional strategies. The chart is not an exhaustive list but is intended to initiate thinking about the relationship between the two resources.

Nine Instructional Strategies from Classroom Instruction That Works	Strategies from Strategies to Engage the Mind of the Learner	Page #
Identifying Similarities and Differences	Semantic Feature Analysis	42
	Chat and Go Questions	133
	Enlighten your Thinking	138
	Synectics Search	186
Summarizing and Note Taking	Concept Definition Map	28
	Frayer Model	34
	Stephens Vocabulary Elaboration	46
	SAW - Student Action Words	50
	Super Word Web	54
	Vocabulary Concept Chain	55
	Character Map	64
	DRTA	69
	Group Summarizing	71
	K-W-L	73
	Learning Log Format	76
	Pairs Read	81
	PREP	83
	Problem-Solving Plan	88
	Proposition-Support Outline	91
	RAFT	95
	Reciprocal Teaching	97
	Summary Wheel	111
	Window Pane Summary	126
	Write to Learn	129
	First, Middle, Last Word	175
	3 Minute Pause	226
Homework and Practice	Learning Log Format	76
	Look for the Signals	80

Nine Instructional Strategies from Classroom Instruction That Works	Strategies from Strategies to Engage the Mind of the Learner	Page #
Nonlinguistic Representations	Act the Word	26
	Concept Definition Map	28
	Frayer Model	34
	Mind Sketching	39
	Stephens Vocabulary Elaboration	46
	SAW - Student Action Words	50
	Probable Passage	86
	Story Mapping Through Circular Pictures	106
	Text Tagging	118
	Graphic Organizers	149
	Semantic Mapping	151
Reinforcing Effort and Providing Recognition	Facts and Fibs	15
	People Search	18
	Strength Bombardment	20
	Team Resume	22
	That's Me	23
	PREP	83
Questions, Cues, & Advanced Organizers	Group Activator	16
	M-V-P	17
	Team Interview	21
	Forecast	33
	Prevoke/Vocabogram	40
	Word Sorts	57
	Anticipation Guide	61
	DRTA	69
	K-W-L	73
	Look for the Signals	80
	PREP	83
	Probable Passage	86
	SQ3R	108
	Text Previewing	115
	Chat and Go Questions	133
	Concept Question Chain	136
	Enlighten Your Thinking Questions	138
	Question-Answer Relationships (QAR)	141
	Unwrap Your Thinking Questions	145
	Questioning the Author	147
	Story Mapping for Narrative Text	153
	Thinking/Writing Patterns and Organizational Patterns	159

Nine Instructional Strategies from Classroom Instruction That Works	Strategies from Strategies to Engage the Mind of the Learner	Page #
Setting Goals and Providing Feedback	DRTA	69
	K-W-L	73
	SQ3R	108
	Think Aloud	120
	One Minute Assessment	216
	Personal Action Plan	233
Generating and Testing Hypotheses	Cloze Method	65
	Proposition/Support Outlines	91
	Thinking from Different Perspectives	122
Cooperative Learning	Collaborative Retelling	67
	Group Summarizing	71
	Pairs Read	81
	Reciprocal Teaching	97
	Save the Last Word for Me	103
	Carousel Brainstorm	174
	First-Middle-Last Word	175
	Four Corner Challenge	176
	Give 1 to Get 1	177
	Idea Exchange	180
	L.E.T.S. Connect	181
	Numbered Heads Together	183
	Paired Verbal Fluency	184
	Stir-the-Class	185
	Teammates Consult	187
	Walk About Survey	188
	Community Circle	193
	Read and Reflect	194
	Creative Debate	195
	Discussion Web	197
	Scored Discussion	200
	Baseball Learning Team Mates	206
	Clock Learning Partners	207
	Back-to-Back Thinking	212
	F.I.R.E,	214
	Partner Roundup	218
	Pinwheel Discovery	221
	Think, Ink, Pair, Share	224

(Developed by Sue Presler)

About the Author

Internationally known educational consultant Rachel Ann Billmeyer has extensive experience putting educational theory into practice. Rachel has taught elementary, secondary, and university level classes, and has worked with renowned educational researchers. She has served in leadership positions, including Director of Professional Development and Instruction for a nationally recognized school district, member of the Nebraska Association of Supervision and Curriculum Development (ASCD) Board, and Program Chair for the Midwest ASCD Regional Conference.

Rachel is a dynamic presenter. She conducts workshops, seminars, and training sessions in the following areas:
- Teaching Reading in the Content Areas
- Strategies to Engage the Mind of the Learner
- The Reading Assessment System.

To learn more about her workshops, seminars, and training sessions, contact Dr. Billmeyer at—

Dr. Rachel Billmeyer
17445 Riviera Drive
Omaha, NE 68136
phone: (402)932-1417
e-mail: rachelb2@cox.net
website: www.rachelbillmeyer.com

Literacy and Learning: A Trilogy By Rachel Billmeyer

	ITEM	ITEM DESCRIPTION	PRICE
Literacy and Learning: A Trilogy 3 Book Set	TRG	Contains all three volumes of the Literacy and Learning Set: **Vol. I -** *Strategic Reading in the Content Areas* **Vol. II -** *Strategies to Engage the Mind of the Learner, Building Strategic Learners* **Vol. III -** *Capturing All of the Reader Through the Reading Assessment System* **++(VOLUME DISCOUNTS DO NOT APPLY TO THE TRILOGY SET)**	$85.00++ ($94.85 Value)
Vol. I - *Strategic Reading in the Content Areas* *Practical Applications for Creating A Thinking Environment*	1BK	**Vol. I -** *Strategic Reading in the Content Areas* *Practical Applications for Creating A Thinking Environment* Volume 1 Foreword by Arthur L. Costa, 259 pages examining the current information about the role of metacognition; the interactive reading ingredients (context, reader, text) and current research on vocabulary development. Book features guidelines and strategies for teaching reading in all content areas, children's bibliography for all content areas and grade levels, and resources for special education, English Language Learners, and the young child.	$29.95
	1WP	**Text Structure Wall Chart** Chart is 20" x 24" and contains the Narrative Text Story Elements and Informative Text Organizational Patterns. Poster is ready to be laminated.	$5.00
	1SR	**Summarizing Rules Wall Chart** Chart is 20" x 24" and is ready to be laminated.	$5.00
	1BCD	**Strategic Reading Blackline Masters CD** 30 Blackline Masters to make overheads or student copies.	$15.00
	1RP	**Strategic Reader Wall Chart** Single wall chart with definition of a strategic reader.	$5.00
	1FH	**Facilitator Handbook for Strategic Reading Learning Team Study**	$8.00
Vol. II - *Strategies to Engage the Mind of the Learner* *Building Strategic Learners* *Second Edition*	2BK	**Vol. II -** *Strategies to Engage the Mind of the Learner* *Building Strategic Learners - Second Edition* Volume 2 Foreword by Robert J. Garmston, 258 pages containing 92 strategies for all grade levels and all content areas. Strategies focus on vocabulary development, narrative and informative text, questioning, graphic organizers, discussion, energizing and grouping activities, information building, and reflection.	$29.95
	2QCD	**Questioning Activities From *Strategies to Engage The Mind of the Learner* - CD*** CD contains all premade questions for the three questioning activities explained in Section 4: Chat & Go, Enlighten Your Thinking & Unwrap Your Thinking • **Chat and Go - (Questions that Promote Conversation)** *31 Questions for narrative and informative each in a text box* • **Enlighten Your Thinking - (Habits of Mind strategy)** *50 Questions on lightbulbs* • **Unwrap Your Thinking (SAR Strategy)** *40 Questions on candy wrappers*	$15.00
	2QP	***Print each set of questions and then copy on colored paper, laminate, and cut.*** **Questioning Activities From *Strategies to Engage The Mind of the Learner* - Complete Set** 3 sets of premade questions assembled on rings for each questioning activity explained in Section 4:	$15.00
	2CG	• **Chat and Go - (Questions that Promote Conversation)** *31 Questions for narrative and informative each in a text box (Approx. 8" x 1")*	$3.00
	2ET	• **Enlighten Your Thinking - (Habits of Mind strategy)** *50 Questions on lightbulbs (Approx. 4.25" x 5.5")*	$7.00
	2UT	• **Unwrap Your Thinking (QAR Strategy)** *40 Questions on candy wrappers (Approx. 8.5" x 3.5")*	$5.00
	2BM	**Focused Reading Bookmarks** Each bookmark has icons to focus the reader's thinking when reading	$1 for 10
	2BCD	**Strategies Blackline Masters CD** 72 Blackline Masters to make overheads or student copies.	$15
	2RT	**Reciprocal Teaching Tents** 8 Sets of Reciprocal Teaching Tents (4 Tents Per Set - 32 Tents Total)	$15
	2RBM	**Reciprocal Teaching Bookmarks - Two-Sided Bookmarks** Each bookmark contains key verbs and questions to stimulate thinking when reading.	$3 for 20
	2RTP	**Reciprocal Teaching Wall Chart** Contains key verbs and questions to stimulate thinking when reading. (5 wall charts in set)	$20
	2QAP	**Question-Answer Relationships Wall Chart** Contains cue words and question starters. (2 wall charts in set)	$10
	2T&RBM	**Think and Read Bookmark** Bookmarks contain icons and ideas to assist comprehension	$3 for 20
	2MBM	**Reading to Solve Story Problems - Two-Sided Bookmark** Bookmarks contains icons, ideas, and key questions to support problem solving	$4 for 20
	2RRBM	**Reading Rocks Bookmark - Two-Sided Bookmark** (Elementary Students) Folded bookmark containing questions to support comprehension Before-During-After Reading and a reading "Place Marker"	$5 for 20
	2SRBM	**Be a Strategic Reader Bookmark - Two-Sided Bookmark** (Secondary Students) Folded bookmark containing ideas to support comprehension Before-During-After Reading and a reading "Place Marker"	$5 for 20

ITEM #	ITEM DESCRIPTION	PRICE
3BK	**Vol. III - *Capturing All of the Reader Through the Reading Assessment System*** ***Practical Applications for Guiding Strategic Readers - Second Edition*** Volume 3 Foreword by Richard J. Stiggins, 255 pages explaining the 4 traits and attributes of a strategic reader, scoring guides for each trait in narrative and informative text, strategies, graphic organizers, checklist, and 17 assessment tasks.	**$34.95**
3MM	**Strategic Reader Memory Mats** Laminated memory mats serve as a "desk mat" for quick reference to the 4 traits and attributes of a strategic reader or the scoring guides to accompany the traits and attributes.	**4 Sets $30** 8 mats, 16 sides total
3MM1	Set 1 - Outlines the 4 traits of a Strategic Reader and the narrative and informative attributes associated with each trait. (Red)	**1 Set $8** 2 mat, 4 sides total
3MM2	Set 2 - Outlines the 4 traits with 4 Reading Continuums of attributes for grades K-3 (Yellow)	
3MM3	Set 3 - Outlines the 4 traits with 4 Narrative Scoring Guides of attributes for grades 3 - 12 (Orange)	
3MM4	Set 4 - Outlines the 4 traits with 4 Informative Scoring Guides of attributes for grades 3 - 12 (Blue)	
3MRY	Sets 1 & 2, Traits and Attributes (Red) & K-3 Continuums (Yellow)	**2 Sets $15** 4 mats, 8 sides total
3MRO	Sets 1 & 3, Traits and Attributes (Red) & 3-12 Narrative Scoring Guides (Orange)	
3MRB	Sets 1 & 4, Traits and Attributes (Red) & 3-12 Informative Scoring Guides (Blue)	
3MOB	Sets 3 & 4, 3-12 Narrative Scoring Guides (Orange) & 3-12 Informative Scoring Guides (Blue)	
3MOY	Sets 2 & 3, K-3 Continuums (Yellow) & 3-12 Narrative Scoring Guides (Orange)	
3MBY	Sets 2 & 4, K-3 Continuums (Yellow) & 3-12 Informative Scoring Guides (Blue)	
	* PLEASE INDICATE SET NUMBERS WHEN ORDERING MEMORY MATS	
3WC	**4 Traits of a Strategic Reader Wall Charts** Sets contain 5 charts total: • 1 chart is 10" x 24" titled Traits of a Strategic Reader • 4 charts are 20" x 24" each containing one trait with complete description Each set contains 5 posters ready to be laminated and hung in the classroom.	**$20.00**
3BCD	**Capturing Reading Blackline Masters CD** 79 Blackline Masters to make overheads or student copies.	**$15.00**

Vol. III - *Capturing All of the Reader Through the Reading Assessment System*

Practical Applications for Guiding Strategic Readers

Second Edition

BILL TO:

Name _____

Institution _____

Address _____

City _____ State _____ Zip _____

Daytime Phone _____

SHIP TO: (if different from bill to)

Name _____

Institution _____

Address _____

City _____ State _____ Zip _____

Daytime Phone _____

METHOD OF PAYMENT:

<u>Individuals</u>: Check ❏ Money Order ❏ VISA ❏ MASTERCARD ❏ DISCOVER ❏ **Make Checks & Money Orders Payable to: Rachel & Associates**

<u>Schools and Institutions</u>: Check ❏ Money Order ❏ VISA ❏ MASTERCARD ❏ DISCOVER ❏ Signed P.O. ❏

Card # _____ Expiration Date _____ Please bill. (Attach signed P.O.) P.O. # _____

ITEM #	QTY	PRICE	TOTAL	ITEM #	QTY	PRICE	TOTAL

* **SALES TAX** (except for not-for-profit institutions) • Nebraska residents pay 7% sales tax

**SHIPPING AND HANDLING COSTS:
Continental United States Orders: <u>Standard Shipping</u> - 10% of purchase price before discount, $5 minimum. (Shipping is 5-10 business day delivery) <u>Priority Shipping</u> - 20% of purchase price before discount, $15 minimum. (Shipping is 2-3 business day delivery). Shipping and handling for the Trilogy Set is $9.50 per set.

Alaska, Hawaii, U.S. Territories & International Orders: Orders will ship via UPS and will incur additional shipping charges which will be added to your order. To request a quote, please contact the distributor at 402-593-1080 prior to ordering.

***PLEASE ORDER CAREFULLY. We do not accept returns of books or merchandise. If your order is incorrect or damaged, please contact Kelly at Printco Graphics 402-593-1080.

25-49 Books/Products	10% Discount
50+ Books/Products	15% Discount

Quantity discounts on single title volume purchases only

Subtotal	
* Sales Tax	
** Shipping	
Total Due	

Mail or fax your order to the distributor:
14112 Industrial Road Omaha, NE 68144
Phone: 402-593-1080 or 1-888-593-1080
Fax: 402-593-1077

Order form 7/08

Prices subject to change.